The Gnosis And Christianity

he Gnosis And Christianity

(Formerly published under the title THE GNOSIS OR
ANCIENT WISDOM IN THE CHRISTIAN SCRIPTURES)

by William Kingsland

*God's wisdom in a mystery, even
the wisdom that hath been
hidden*

I COR. II. 7

*O Gnosis of Light passing all
knowledge, I praise thee*

THE GNOSIS OF THE LIGHT
(CODEX BRUCIANUS)

A QUEST BOOK

Published under a grant from the Kern Foundation

THE THEOSOPHICAL PUBLISHING HOUSE
Wheaton, Ill., U.S.A.
Madras, India / London, England

FIRST PUBLISHED IN 1937
SECOND IMPRESSION 1954
THIRD IMPRESSION 1956
FOURTH IMPRESSION 1958
FIFTH IMPRESSION 1962

Second Quest Book printing 1975
Published by The Theosophical Publishing House, Wheaton, Illinois, a department of The Theosophical Society in America, by special arrangement with George Allen & Unwin Ltd., London

ISBN: 8356-0013-0
Library of Congress Catalog Card Number 71-98268

Manufactured in the United States of America

EDITOR'S PREFACE TO FIRST EDITION

THIS book is the last work of the late William Kingsland and is published under the auspices of "The Kingsland Literary Trust." This Trust was inaugurated by the author shortly before his death, and is by his wish composed of the Council of the Blavatsky Association, who are thereby empowered to publish his MSS. at their discretion.

The "Gnosis" had occupied much of Kingsland's time and thought during the last two years of his life, and was not completed until shortly before his death; he had, indeed, hoped to make a few alterations to the manuscript but did not live to do so, and except for the correction of some typist's errors it is published as it left the author's hand.

In this work Kingsland shows how the fundamental teachings given to the world at the beginning of the Christian era were derived from the Gnosis or Ancient Wisdom, but in time have become so perverted that the modern interpretation of Christianity represents merely their debased survival.

It should be mentioned that the author's title for this work was *The Gnosis in the Christian Scriptures*, which the Trust altered to its present form.

The cost of the publication* has been met by many friends whom William Kingsland had helped to a truer concept of the realities of life through his deep understanding of the Ancient Wisdom. The contributors have been glad to assist in the production of this work as a memorial to one whom they regard with enduring gratitude and affection.

THE KINGSLAND LITERARY TRUST

26 BEDFORD GARDENS, LONDON, W.8

November 1936

*First edition 1937

CONTENTS

CHAPTER   PAGE

Editor's Preface   7

Introduction   11

I.   RELIGION AND RELIGIONS   49

II.   THE BIBLE   73

III.   THE ANCIENT WISDOM OR GNOSIS   93

IV.   THE GENESIS NARRATIVE   111

V.   THE NEW TESTAMENT SCRIPTURES   141
       I. THE GOSPELS

VI.   THE NEW TESTAMENT SCRIPTURES   172
       II. PAUL'S EPISTLES

VII.   PRACTICAL RELIGION   190

Bibliography   219

Index   223

THE GNOSIS OR ANCIENT WISDOM IN THE CHRISTIAN SCRIPTURES

INTRODUCTION

This work is written mainly for a class of readers and students who find themselves altogether out of touch with " Christianity " in any of its current doctrinal or sacerdotal forms, but who, notwithstanding this, have some more or less clear apprehension that behind those forms, and in the Christian Scriptures themselves, there lies a deèp spiritual truth, a real *Gnosis* (Gr. *knowledge*) of Man's origin, nature, and destiny which has simply been *materialized* by the Church in the traditional interpretation of those Scriptures based upon their literal acceptation.

Not that one does not recognize that even in its most irrational and unacceptable dogmas, so-called " Christianity " makes an appeal to a certain class of minds; and, indeed, is perhaps the only form of " religion " which could make any appeal to that particular class.

However irrational Christian dogmas may be in the light of our modern knowledge—and still more so in the light of the deeper knowledge of the *Gnosis*—they do, if genuinely believed in, serve to keep the average individual more or less on a straight path of moral rectitude, and they afford him a certain amount of comforting assurance that he is not " a lost sinner "; whilst in some cases they are undoubtedly the inspiring beliefs giving rise to noble and self-sacrificing lives. Precisely the same may be said, however, of other religions which differ radically from Christianity in their formulated beliefs. In short, the evidence of the life of an individual is no proof of the truth of his creed. It is sufficient that he believes in it; the rest is mere psychology. The *One Spirit* overshadows and works in all, but the *form* in which that working is presented through the mind or intellect is a matter of the psychological make-up of the individual, the lower personal self with its heredity, conventions, and environment. Thus Krishna, speaking on the Supreme Spirit in *Bhagavad Gītā*, says:

> "In whatever form a devotee desires with faith to worship, it is I alone who inspire him with constancy therein, and depending on that faith he seeks the propitiation of that God, obtaining the object of his wishes as is ordained by me alone."[1]

A general recognition of this principle would put an end to all religious intolerance.

It is no part of my task in this work to set forth the numerous reasons which can be given for the rejection of the traditional beliefs which have hitherto constituted what is generally known as "Christianity." That rejection is becoming more and more in evidence as knowledge increases, whilst in the Church itself—using the term Church to cover all and every Christian community—we have the greatest possible differences of opinion regarding the *truth* of both "facts" and doctrines which for centuries have been regarded as the very foundations of the "Faith": e.g. miracles, the virgin birth, original sin, the atonement, the resurrection, the ascension, the second coming, the nature of the eucharist, and the clauses of the Athanasian and other Creeds. Concerning each and all of these, leading authorities in the Church itself are to-day hopelessly at variance,[2] whilst very few professing lay Christians are aware to what an extent the commonly received conceptions as to the origin of Christianity, based on the supposed historical veracity of the Gospel narratives, are in question to-day by those scholars who have made the closest study of the actual historical evidences.

But although I am not dealing directly with these controversies, one cannot ignore them altogether, and some references must necessarily be made to them. Moreover, the correspondence of the Bible allegories with those of the earlier Mystery Cults, such for example as those of Orpheus and of Mithra, as also those of more ancient Egyptian and Aryan sources, implies some historical connection in origins; and although this is exceedingly obscure owing to the destruction

---

[1] Chapter vii.

[2] Those who wish to consult actual statements may read with profit *The Churches and Modern Thought*, by Vivian Phelips (see Bibliography, p. 221).

by the early Church creed-makers of every particle of evidence of this connection which they could lay their hands on, many clues still remain to which some allusion must be made.

This present work, therefore, is not written for controversial purposes, or for the purpose of upsetting the " faith " of anyone, whatsoever that " faith " may be. I am not concerned to convince or convert anyone to the views herein expressed. In matters of fact I stand open to correction where I may possibly be in error. But those who have come to some apprehension of the fact that Christianity in its traditional form is not merely open to many objections on rational grounds, but also that it is only one of a number of formulated religions which are just as efficacious as itself for the " salvation " of the individual, cannot adopt the proselytizing spirit which is such a marked feature of " Christianity." In so far as " Christianity " is exclusive, dogmatic, proselytizing, I am its, perhaps somewhat bitter, opponent. When it dares to say that the individual can be " saved " only by believing in what it teaches about a certain historical character, I say that the good Jew, or Buddhist, or Moslem, or Parsi has just as good a chance—nay, in many cases a better chance—of being " saved " than thousands of professing Christians.

What I do offer here is something much more universal than that of any exclusive religion, i.e. certain principles which have been given out by various great teachers from time to time in a *form* appropriate to the age and people to whom they were addressed. These, however, have subsequently been largely overlaid and obscured by the feeble understanding and individual interests of partisans. As I shall presently show, there is no greater example of this than in so-called " Christianity."

While, therefore, I have no desire to turn anyone aside from their present " faith ": recognizing as I do that that " faith " must necessarily suffice to meet the present needs of the individual: it is possible that those who have encased themselves in a hardened shell of what they call " truth," based on supposed historical facts as given in the literal word of Scripture, may hereby get some glimpse of the inadequacy of their hitherto cherished beliefs, and of a deeper knowledge which has always been available; aye, even to that supreme knowledge which confers god-like powers on its possessor. It is useless to offer this deeper knowledge to those who have not perceived the limitations of what they already possess. That may and does suffice for their present needs; but sooner or later they must come up against facts and experiences which will shake them out of their present contentment, and make them realize that for all their assurance of " salvation " they are still very far indeed from the ultimate goal of spiritual knowledge and freedom. It is only the man who knows how little he knows, and the *necessity* of knowing more if he would escape from the present deplorable condition of mankind, and recover his divine birthright as a " Son of God," who can, or will, reach out for that supreme knowledge, that " pearl of great price " which can be obtained only when he has " sold all that he had."[1] Of this more hereafter; but I may remark here that this and other similar parables clearly show Jesus to have been an Initiate in the Ancient Wisdom or Gnosis.

It is my endeavour now to show how that supreme knowledge which I am here referring to as the *Ancient Wisdom* or *Gnosis* is embodied in the Christian Scriptures, albeit sadly overlaid with " the precepts and doctrines of men."

I am not using the term *Gnosis* as applying merely to the tenets of certain Gnostic sects which were more or less in evidence in the early centuries of the Christian era, but I am using it in connection with a definite *super-knowledge* which can be traced back to the remotest ages and the oldest Scriptures of which we have any literary records, and which was taught by Initiates, Adepts, and Masters of the Ancient Wisdom in the inner circles of those *Mysteries* and Mystery Cults which are known to have existed in Egypt and elsewhere, even in remotest times. That is the sense in which the term was originally understood. It is the mystic knowledge which effects regeneration, rebirth into the full consciousness of one's divine nature and powers as a " Son of God."

The Gnostic Sects of the early Christian centuries who were

---

[1] *Matt.* xiii. 46.

so virulently attacked by some of the dogma-making Church " Fathers," derived their teachings from these Mystery Cults, but at the same time many of them claimed the Christian Scriptures—though not the afterwards recognized canonical Books only—as an authority for their teachings.

" However much the Gnostics may have been indebted to heathen thought, they still wished and meant to be Christians, and indeed set up a claim to possess a deeper knowledge of Christian truth than the Psychici of the Church. Like their opponents they also appealed to Scripture in proof of their peculiar doctrines. Nay, it would even seem that the Gnostics were the first to make for that purpose a profitable appeal to the Scriptures of the New Testament. And besides this, they also boasted to be in possession of genuine apostolical traditions, deriving their doctrines, some from Paul, others from St. Peter, and others again from Judas, Thomas, Philip, and Matthew. In addition, moreover, to the secret doctrine which they professed to have received by oral tradition, they appealed also to alleged writings of the apostles themselves or their disciples."[1]

" We have no reason to think that the earliest Gnostics intended to found sects separated from the Church and called after their own names. Their disciples were to be Christians, only elevated above the rest as acquainted with deeper mysteries, and called γνωστικόι because possessed of a Gnosis superior to the simple faith of the multitude."[2]

" Gnosticism desired only to add to the confession of Faith for the ψυχικόι a secret doctrine for the πνευματικόι."[3]

Gradually, however, as " Christian " doctrine became hardened and more and more dogmatic, and the government of the Church fell into the hands of prelates ambitious for worldly power, and quarrelling among themselves for precedence, this higher knowledge became a heresy, and what records are left of it are mainly the misrepresentations of its bitter opponents among the Church " Fathers."

The Essenes, to which community Jesus probably belonged,[4] were certainly Gnostics in the sense in which I am here using the term. Also the writings of Philo show clearly that he was acquainted with this Gnosis, although it does not appear that any of the communities of his time had yet begun to

---

[1] Smith and Wace, *Dictionary of Christian Biography*, art. " Irenaeus," vol. iii, p. 269.

[2] Ibid., art. " Gnosticism," vol. ii, p. 679.

[3] Ibid., art. " Manicheans," vol. iii, p. 797. [4] See p. 150 *infra*.

be called Gnostics. He was contemporary with Jesus, yet never mentions him, although he teaches the doctrine of the *Logos* as the " Son of God."

" Wherever we meet with the word Logos, we know that we have to deal with a word of Greek extraction. When Philo adopted that word, it could have meant for him substantially neither more nor less than what it had meant before in the schools of Greek philosophy. Thus, when the ideal creation or the Logos had been called by Philo the only begotten or unique son (υἱὸς μονογενής), the Son of God (υἱὸς θεοῦ), and when that name was afterwards transferred by the author of the Fourth Gospel to Christ, what was predicated of him can only have been in substance what was contained before in these technical terms, as used at first at Athens and afterwards at Alexandria.[1] (See p. 177 *infra*.)

It would appear that among some of the sections of the early Christian Church—and it must not be supposed that even the earliest " Church " was one and undivided as a community or in doctrine—the practice common to all the genuine Gnostic cults was followed in having at least three degrees of membership or initiation. It was only in the highest degree that the deepest " mysteries " were *orally* communicated; and even so it was never the case that the Initiate, the Adept, the Master could be *made* by any communicated instruction. He is not *made*, he *becomes*. He must know of the truth of the communicated teaching from his own actual experience. What was committed to writing was never more than *exoteric*. It is just as great a mistake to harden the symbolism of the Gnostic Scriptures into a definite theogony or cosmogony as it is to construct an anthropomorphic theology from the narratives of the Old or New Testaments. The real Gnosis, therefore, is a mystical knowledge and *experience* transcending that *appearance* of things which the ordinary individual accepts as the only " reality."

It is my contention in this work not merely that this ancient Gnosis did and does exist, and was represented to some extent in the teachings of these Christian Gnostic sects, but also that their claim " To possess a deeper knowledge of Christian truth than the Psychici of the Church " is one which must be sustained. In fact, that the traditional dogmas of the Church which have come down to us through the centuries are gross

[1] Max Müller, *Theosophy or Psychological Religion*, p. 403.

materializations of the real teaching as to the spiritual nature and origin of Man as contained in the Gnosis. These dogmas are the result of the literal historicizing of narratives—in some cases, however, having a semi-historical basis—which were originally intended as allegories covering deep spiritual truths.

The real fact, therefore, is not that Gnosticism was a " heresy," a departure from the true " Christianity," but precisely the opposite, i.e. that Christianity in its dogmatic and ecclesiastical development was a travesty of the original Gnostic teachings.[1]

Dean Inge comes fairly near to this view in his work on *Christian Mysticism*, Appendix B, " The Greek Mysteries and Christian Mysticism." Thus he says (p. 350):

" A doctrine is not necessarily un-Christian because it is ' Greek ' or ' Pagan.' I know of no stranger perversity than for men who rest the whole weight of their religion upon ' history ' to suppose that our Lord meant to raise an universal religion on a purely Jewish basis."

How much Christianity really owes to " Pagan " sources he says is difficult to ascertain by reason of " the loss of documents, and by the extreme difficulty of tracing the pedigree of religious ideas and customs." Nevertheless this indebtedness is gradually being brought to light, and is gradually destroying the idea of the uniqueness of Christianity.

" Dionysius uses the mystery words frequently, and gives to the orders of the Christian ministry the names which distinguish the officiating priests at the Mysteries. The aim of these writers (Clement and others) was to prove that the Church offers a mysteriosophy which includes all the good elements of the old Mysteries without their corruptions. The alliance between a Mystery-religion and speculative Mysticism within the Church was at this time as close as that between Neoplatonic philosophy and the revived pagan Mystery-cults."[2]

" Christianity conquered Hellenism by borrowing from it all its best elements; and I do not see that a Christian need feel any reluctance to make this admission."[3]

" For over half a millennium the approach to religion for thoughtful minds was by the *Gnostic* path. Such facts—since no religion persists by its falsehood, but by its truth—entitle the ancient Mysteries to due consideration. As an important background to early Christianity, and as the chief medium of sacramentarianism to the West they cannot be neglected; for to fail to recognize the moral and spiritual values of

[1] See p. 23 *infra*. [2] W. R. Inge, *Christian Mysticism*, p. 350.
[3] Ibid., p. 355.

Hellenistic-Oriental paganism is to misunderstand the early Christian centuries and to do injustice to the victory of Christianity."[1]

The *early* Christian centuries certainly, until the Gnosis became finally extinguished as a heresy. But the " victory " of so-called " Christianity " as recorded in the history of the dark ages of the Western world cannot possibly be attributed to its moral and spiritual values. And where is that " victory " to-day in the general state of the world? The moral and spiritual values are undoubtedly there, but the Church must get back to the Gnosis, and thus bring its fundamental teachings into line with our modern knowledge before it can re-conquer the modern world.

This ancient Gnosis, as I shall presently show, is indeed being re-stated to-day in many directions outside of the Church; and sooner or later the Church must come into line with it—or gradually become an extinct community.

This ancient Gnosis we may define as that knowledge of the nature of Man and of his place in the Universe which transcends the mere *appearance* of things as presented to the senses and the intellect, and which contacts *Reality* in a region of pure Truth. The beginning of this knowledge, therefore, is the realization that *things are not what they seem*; and no one who is a crude realist—as are all orthodox Christians, both in respect of the physical world and of their own Scriptures—can make any approach to this super-knowledge.

Of course all philosophy is an effort to apprehend *Reality*; but it is an effort of the intellect merely, and as such it is, and must always be, a fruitless effort. It is one of the fundamental teachings of the Ancient Wisdom that the intellect must be transcended before *Reality* can be contacted, for intellect can only deal with *Appearances*.

Some of our modern philosophers are beginning to apprehend this fact: notably Henri Bergson, who speaks of a higher faculty which he calls *intuition*, and which he says must replace intellect if we would contact Reality. F. H. Bradley's great work *Appearance and Reality* also throws a strong light on this fundamental principle.

[1] S. Angus, *The Mystery-Religions and Christianity*, p. vii.

William James also tells us that :

" For my own part I have finally found myself compelled to *give up the logic*, fairly, squarely, and irrevocably. It has an imperishable use in human life, but that use is not to make us theoretically acquainted with the essential nature of reality."[1]

This inability of the intellect to transcend its own categories of time, space, and causation—which is also the main thesis of Kant's philosophy—rules out the validity of all theological speculation and assertion, whether " progressive " or otherwise. " God " as the Absolute must ever be beyond all assertion of this or that. But this was clearly perceived ages before Kant or Christianity.

"Who asks doth err, Who answers errs. Say nought!"[2]

> " Not by speech, not by mind,
> Not by sight can He be apprehended.
> How can He be comprehended
> Otherwise than by one saying ' He is '? "[3]

This is precisely the equivalent of the " I AM THAT I AM " of *Exodus* iii. 14.

" The fountain-head of Christian mysticism is Dionysius the Areopagite. He describes the absolute truth by negatives exclusively."[4]

It is a simple proposition that that which is ALL cannot " create " anything outside of itself. In 1 *Corinthians* xv. 28, Paul tells us that when all things have been subjected to the " Son " (or Logos), " then shall the Son himself be subjected to him that did subject all things unto him, that God may be all in all."

What! Is not then God all in all *now*?

To this we should reply: Yes, as including both *Reality* and *Appearance*; but No when we speak, as Paul is here doing, from the point of view of *Appearance* merely.

But what is this distinction between Reality and Appearance save a mere concession to the *duality* of the intellect? The ancient Aryan philosophers, perceiving this well, considered the world of Appearances to be *Māyā*, an illusion. And in

---

[1] *A Pluralistic Universe*, p. 212. [2] *The Light of Asia.*
[3] *Katha Upanishad*, 6, 12.
[4] Wm. James, *The Varieties of Religious Experience*, p. 416.

truth Paul here only repeats a fundamental principle of the Ancient Wisdom, i.e. that there is a gradual withdrawal of the manifested or *appearance* universe into the ONE from which it originally proceeded. In Eastern philosophy this outgoing and return is postulated as an eternal periodical process: the outgoing being called a " Day " of Brahma (the Logos or Demiurge), and the complete withdrawal—which lasts as long as the outgoing, an incalculable period—a " Night " of Brahma. Man, being the mirror or reflection of the *cosmic* process, has the same outgoing and return—as I shall show more explicitly, as taught in the Christian Scriptures, in subsequent chapters of this work.

We may note here that in this saying of Paul we have one more instance and evidence of his knowledge and teaching of the ancient Gnosis.

To satisfy the intellect of man in its present development, a *creative* God has to be postulated: whether called the Logos, or the Demiurgos, or by some specific name such as Jehovah or Brahma. From this necessity of the intellect arise theogonies and theologies, varieties of Trinities, anthropomorphic gods, etc. The simplest concept in terms of *human* nature is the Trinity of Father-Mother-Son. But this will not always be so. Intellect, as Man evolves, will assume other aspects, and will certainly transcend its present limitations. Do not therefore accept the limitations of its present formulations as " Gospel Truth." They have their use it is true; but let the seeker after truth thoroughly understand their nature and limitations, and put them in their proper place.

Robert Browning in his poem *Paracelsus* puts the following words into the mouth of that great Adept.

> " There is an inmost centre in us all,
>   Where truth abides in fulness; and around,
>   Wall upon wall, the gross flesh hems it in,
>   This perfect, clear perception—which is truth.
>   A baffling and perverting carnal mesh
>   Binds it, and makes all error; and to KNOW
>   Rather consists in opening out a way
>   Whence the imprisoned splendour may escape,
>   Than in effecting entry for a light
>   Supposed to be without."

Now that " inmost centre " is, in the teaching of the ancient Gnosis, the real SELF; the eternal, immortal, divine SELF which is *one* with the universal SELF, commonly called *God*. Thus the root teaching of this Ancient Wisdom at all times has been *the divine nature of Man*; and what was taught in the inner schools of the *Mysteries*—a teaching which can still be obtained—was the method of achieving this supreme knowledge in a practical manner; that is to say the attainment of god-like character and powers. Every man is potentially *a* god, however feeble may be his powers at the present time. At root he *is* God.

Knowledge is power. The supreme knowledge confers on its possessor powers the possibility of which is not even dreamed of by the ordinary individual—or the ordinary Christian for that matter, notwithstanding the repeated assertions of that possibility in the Christian Scriptures. Yet there have been some mystics in the Christian Church even in modern times who have recognized this fundamental fact of man's nature. Thus Archdeacon Wilberforce writes in *Mystic Immanence* (p. 89):

" Meanwhile remember ' the Kingdom of Heaven is within you,' all the power you can possibly need is at your disposal, you need no helper to give it you, it is yours now."

Perhaps I may be allowed to quote here from a work of my own, *Scientific Idealism*, published in 1909 (p. xiv):

" All the Cosmic Powers of the Universe are Man's, did he but know how to utilize them. They are more than *his*, they are *Himself*."

But this supreme knowledge can never be attained by those who are content to rest in a " faith " which leaves them powerless to conquer even the commonest disabilities of this physical world, let alone those higher planes of consciousness which lie immediately above—or rather *within*—and which are infinitely more *real* than this so apparently real physical world.

This potential divinity of every man in the power of the *indwelling* Christ or *Christos* principle runs all through the teaching of Jesus and Paul—as I shall presently show. It is the teaching which the Church *ought* always to have presented, and which *was* presented in the early Christian Gnostic sects until these were suppressed by the ignorant materializers and carnalizers of teachings they could not understand. It is the teaching which, if the Church were to present it to-day, would be the salvation both of itself and of the world. Fortunately thousands have come to an understanding of it from other sources.

The individual must have *knowledge* (*Gnosis*) as well as *faith* (*Pistis*). He must have the knowledge that *conquers* each and all of the disabilities under which he, and Humanity as a whole, at present suffer, apparently in helpless ignorance. For it is simply *ignorance* that is the cause of " humanity's great pain." But that ignorance is not a necessity to which man must submit without a remedy—a remedy *here and now*. Six hundred years B.C.—not to go any further back—the Buddha taught that:

> " Ho! ye who suffer! know
> Ye suffer from yourselves. None else compels.
> Higher than Indra's ye may lift your lot,
> And sink it lower than the worm or gnat.
> Within yourselves deliverance must be sought;
> Each man his prison makes."[1]

These words apply to the individual; yet what is the whole vast struggle of Humanity but simply the effort to rise from ignorance to knowledge—and who shall say what is the limit of that knowledge?

It is here that the Ancient Wisdom or Gnosis proclaims its message. *There is no limit.* Moreover there have always been, and there are to-day, Initiates, Adepts, Mahātmās (*lit.* Great Souls) who have achieved that knowledge; aye, even to its most glorious heights.

Thus the individual may step out in front of the Race. He may achieve this knowledge because there are Masters of the Wisdom waiting to instruct him so soon as he has shown himself ready and fit to receive the instruction. But these Masters will not, any more than the Master whose words are partially recorded in the New Testament documents, " cast their pearls before swine." They will not, any more than he did, disclose

---

[1] *The Light of Asia.*

the treasures of their knowledge to the world otherwise than in allegory and symbol.

When may the individual be said to be ready? When at last, through the strife and stress and sorrows and failures of repeated incarnations, he has learnt that there is no rest, no satisfaction in "the things of this world" after which he has hitherto been striving, and after which the great majority of the Race still strive. When he has not merely purified himself of all worldly lusts and desires, but also from any pride of intellect which may claim to be a knower of the truth in this, that, or the other *form*. When with an open mind he is prepared to go deeper than mind (intellect) and the man-made doctrines of men, into a region where truth is formless and immediate. When he has accomplished this—with which I shall deal more fully later on—then, and not till then, he is ready to knock at the Portal of the Temple of Initiation into that higher knowledge to which I have referred, and which I shall endeavour to elucidate to some extent in its Christian form—or rather I should say in the form in which it is presented *in the Christian Scriptures*: for what is known traditionally and historically as " Christianity " consists of man-made dogmas based on a literal interpretation of those Scriptures, and not on their allegorical, mystical, and gnostic nature.

It cannot be emphasized too strongly that religion is not a matter of *escape*, of getting safely into " heaven." It is a matter of *conquest*. " Christianity," so-called, lulls its devotees into a false sense of security, or " salvation "; whereas the whole history of humanity, and of religion itself, shows us that:

> " The path by which to Deity we climb
> Is arduous, rough, ineffable, sublime."[1]

Yet the great attraction which the Christian " faith " has offered has been that it is so *easy*: a mere matter of belief in certain dogmas of the Church; at most one short lifetime, with possibly in some cases the sharp death of a martyr, and then an eternity of bliss. Wherein is that any different or better than the belief of the fanatical Moslem who rushes to death against the bayonets and bullets of the " infidel," believing

[1] See p. 44 *infra*.

that thereby he is assured of all the sensual joys of the Paradise described in the Koran?

It has hitherto been the contention of Christian doctrinaires that the historical Jesus Christ by his coming and work " abolished death, and brought life and incorruption to light "[1] in a hitherto dark and ignorant world. Nothing could be further from the truth as concerns the world at large. It was not even true of that little Jewish world to which the supposed Gospel was first preached. The Essenes, the ultra strict Jewish sect, believed firmly in immortality, and in a future state of rewards and punishments. Death was regarded as a great gain for the righteous, but they did not believe in the resurrection of the body.

As for the world at large, and taking one example only: nothing was deeper ingrained in the religion of the Egyptians than the belief in immortality.

" Indefinite time, without beginning and without end, hath been given to me; I inherit eternity, and everlastingness hath been bestowed upon me."[2]

Yet when we have apprehended what is really meant by the *Christ* (*Christos*) as distinguished from any personal historical " man called Jesus," the verse from *Timothy* which I have just quoted is seen to be profoundly true, as I shall hereafter show.

Now the Christian has unfortunately always been taught that he will leave all the disabilities and sin and sorrow of this present world behind him when he dies, and that his " faith " will ensure him an eternity of bliss " for ever and ever "; that he will have finished with this world for good and all, and will have naught more to do with its strife and conflict. This is a soul-killing doctrine: as indeed we see in such a multitude of professing Christians. They " have a name that they live, but are (spiritually) dead."

But that Gnosis with which I am now dealing has always taught that the individual cannot thus sever himself from the great stream of human evolution. He belongs to the Race from beginning to end of the great Cycle. The progress of

---

[1] 2 *Tim.* i. 10.   [2] *Book of the Dead*, chapter lxii.

the Race is accomplished only by the progress of the individuals composing it, and this is accomplished by repeated incarnations. It is true that after physical death the individual who has any spiritual nature left in him may enjoy a supreme bliss for a season, in freedom from physical conditions and limitations. The " sleep " of death is simply the equivalent between incarnations of the sleep of the body between one day and another. But again and again the individual must come back, be reincarnated; not merely to play his part in the progress of the Race; not merely to gain further knowledge himself, but also to reap what he has sown in his past incarnations, to work out his *Karma*.

> " He cometh reaper of the things he sowed,
>   Sesamun, corn, so much cast in past birth;
> And so much weed and poison stuff, which mar
>   Him and the aching earth."[1]

This is an age-long teaching. It was also taught, as I shall presently show, in the early Christian Church.

What a vast difference it would make to this world of ours if each individual realized that he must play his part therein and contribute to the progrèss or retardation of the Race from beginning to end of the Cycle; that he *cannot* take any short cut to eternal bliss; that he *must* work out, not merely his own salvation, but also that of the Race. The Christian Scriptures *when esoterically interpreted* tell us how this must be done; and thereby they come into line with that which had always been taught in the inner Shrines of the Temples of Initiation.

Why in the inner Shrines? Why not openly and publicly? Do we need to ask that question when the great teacher whose words we are supposed to have in the Canonical Gospels " taught only in parables," and is reported to have said to his Disciples: " Unto you it is given to know the mysteries of the kingdom of heaven, but to them it is not given "?[2] This fact is in itself a proof that the teachings in the Gospels are derived from and belong to that ancient Gnosis of which I am speaking. Nevertheless these " Mysteries " are not recorded as having been

---

[1] *The Light of Asia*, Book the Eighth.　　　　　　[2] *Matt.* xiii. 11.

given to the disciples in any of the Canonical Gospels. We have to go to the " apocryphal "[1] writings, such as the *Pistis Sophia*, to obtain them. Indeed Jesus is reported to have said to his Disciples:

> " I have yet many things to say unto you, but ye cannot bear them now. . . . These things have I spoken unto you in proverbs (or parables): the hour cometh, when I shall no more speak unto you in proverbs, but shall tell you plainly of the Father " (*John* xvi. 12 and 25).

Note that this appears in *John*, the *Gnostic* Gospel, while its fulfilment appears more particularly in the *Pistis Sophia*, which purports to be those further teachings of the *Mysteries* given by Jesus to his Disciples eleven years after his resurrection.

There always has been and there always must be an *exoteric* doctrine for the masses, and *esoteric* teaching for those who—as Plotinus says[2]—" are fortunately able to perceive it."

But in fact these " mysteries " cannot be stated in any language but that of allegory and symbolism. How can that which lies altogether beyond our common consciousness of time and space and the crude realism of the common conception of this world of physical matter: how can such things be expressed otherwise than by physical *analogies* (allegories) and in a physical language which can only be symbolical, never literal? But the mischief lies in this, that the allegory is taken by the uninstructed for literal history and the symbol for reality. Is it not so even to-day with thousands of sincere Christians? Is not the Garden of Eden allegory still taken as literal history, let alone the allegories of the New Testament? If our modern physicists now find that *matter*, that apparently " solid, massy, hard, impenetrable " substance, is in reality the veriest wraith, with spaces between the atoms comparable to inter-planetary spaces, and whose essential nature can only be approximately expressed in a mathematical symbolism which it requires a highly trained mind to understand: think you that the nature of the *soul* can be demonstrated to the common people—or even to the most intellectual for that matter—as easily as the *exoteric* nature of water as a simple H_2O: the combination of two atoms of hydrogen with one of

---

[1] Apocryphal—hidden.   See p. 73 *infra*.   [2] See p. 74 *infra*.

oxygen, without any enquiry as to what the "atom" really is? That was simple enough so long as the atom was thought of only as some sort of indestructible particle; and indeed it was dogmatically declared by the materialistic scientists of last century that the atom *could not* be resolved into anything else. Thus Professor Clerk-Maxwell, at the meeting of the British Association in 1873, said that:

"Though in the course of ages catastrophes have occurred and may yet occur in the heavens, though ancient systems may be dissolved and new systems evolved out of their ruins, the molecules out of which these systems are built—the foundation-stones of the material universe—remain unbroken and unworn. They continue this day as they were created—perfect in number and measure and weight."

Note the idea of "creation" entering in here. But how stands it to-day? The atom has turned out not merely to be destructible, resolvable into protons, electrons, neutrons, and even possibly into a mere wave form: but it is seen that in reality there is no such thing as physical matter *per se*; it must be accounted for in terms of something much more *cosmic*, even possibly in terms of "mind-stuff."[1]

Thus it is now apprehended that there is mystery within mystery in matter itself. It can no longer be regarded as a "created" thing. Crude realism has here had to give way to a deeper knowledge, though that knowledge has as yet only penetrated a little more than skin deep.

It is hardly necessary to point out that this modern discovery that physical matter is not a thing *per se*, that it is not *sui generis*, or a "created" thing, goes a long way towards the negation of the crude orthodox theology which has always thus regarded it; and with that a good deal more in that theology also goes overboard. Little as our discoveries have penetrated into the nature of that *Root Substance* from which physical matter is derived, they go a long way towards confirming

[1] "To put the conclusion crudely—the stuff of the world is mind-stuff. . . . The mind-stuff is the aggregation of relations and relata which form the building material for the physical world." (Professor Eddington, *The Nature of the Physical World*, pp. 276, 278.)

"The theory of wave mechanics reduces the last building stones of the universe to something like a spiritual throb that comes as near as possible to our concept of pure thought." (James Murphy in his biographical Introduction to Erwin Schrödinger's *Science and the Human Temperament*.)

the teachings of the Gnosis as to the nature of *Hyle*. What modern science has now discovered experimentally has always been known and taught by the Adepts and Initiates, not to mention the Alchemists.

Think you, then, that the nature of the soul is any simpler than that of matter? Think you that it is adequately explained in the crude realism of the Christian Creed; or that it is sufficient to say that the soul was " created " by God? Are the assertions of our dogmatic theologians to be accepted with any greater confidence than those of our dogmatic scientists of last century? There is not one of them who really *knows* anything about the " God " they speak of so freely as acting in this, that, or the other manner. Nor do they know what the human soul is in its essential nature. They know less of that than our physicists now know of the nature of matter. Yet the knowledge is available, has always been available for those who knock aright at the door of the Temple of Initiation. Those who think that they can rest in a mere *belief* in this, that, or the other Creed, are simply delaying their own evolution and that of the Race. Religion is not belief, it is practical knowledge of the way to regain one's birthright as a " Son of God "; which knowledge brings with it the power to conquer and command the *natural* forces of the Universe both visible and invisible, both material and immaterial.

What other than this conquest is it that is assured to us in the Christian Scriptures, in the teachings of Jesus and of Paul? Is it not there explicitely stated that we are to become " Sons of God "? What does that mean if it does not mean the acquisition of god-like powers.

" How slowly we learn that God and man are one. Do away with your limitations. Stand out free in the strong life of God. You are like children with your walls and partitions, your churches and chapels."[1]

These words from " the other side " are merely an echo of what has always been taught in the ancient Gnosis, and which are also the explicit—or perhaps we should rather say *implicit*— teaching of the Christian Scriptures. Yet there are some passages which are explicit enough. For example:

[1] *Christ in You.* See Bibliography.

" For as many as are led by the Spirit of God, these are sons of God " (*Rom.* viii. 14).

" For ye are all sons of God, through faith, in Christ Jesus " (*Gal.* iii. 26).

In several places in the revised version of the Testament the Greek word *tekna* is translated children where formerly it was translated *sons.* For example:

" But as many as received him, to them gave he the right to become children (tekna) of God " (*John* i. 12).

So also in *Philippians* ii. 15; and in 1 *John* iii. 1. But this does not alter the meaning. In the seventeenth verse of the eighth chapter of *Romans*—following the fourteenth which I have quoted above—Paul used the word children: evidently referring to what he has just said.

" We are children of God: and if children, then heirs; heirs of God and joint-heirs with Christ."

Why does not the Christian Church teach this oneness of man and God? Why do not Christians " stand out free in the strong life of God "? Why do they not claim their birthright as " sons of God," with all the *powers* that that confers on them? The answer is simply because all this has been obscured by the man-made dogmas of a priestly hierarchy striving for *worldly* power and dominance.

This oneness of God and man (not the theological God however) is no new teaching. It was a teaching given in the Mystery Schools long, long before the Christian Scriptures put it into a new *form.* The whole motif of the Egyptian *Book of the Dead* is this conquest of the lower self, and the achievement of union with the divine Self. It was called *Osirification,* or identification with the supreme God Osiris. What matters whether that Supreme ONE is called Brahma, or Osiris, or Jehovah, or by any other name? It is the *fact* that matters, not the form in which that fact is stated.

" I am the Ibis which cometh forth from Het-Ptah-ka.[1] Heaven is opened to me, and the earth is opened unto me. I have obtained the mastery over my heart. I have obtained the mastery over my members.

[1] The House of the *Ka* (astral body or double) or Ptah. Exoterically and geographically, Memphis.

I have obtained the mastery over my mind. . . . O Ra, I am thy son. O Thoth, I am thy eyes, O Osiris, I am thy Power."[1]

Also as the keynote of the ancient Upanishads we have that fundamental teaching expressed in the aphorism " *That art Thou.*"

The question as to the character and personality of the central figure of the New Testament documents naturally enters largely into the subject with which we are now dealing. There are three views advocated by various writers, (*a*) the extreme view that there never was a historical Jesus; (*b*) the view that he was simply an exceptional man; and (*c*) the further view that he was " very God of very God." This, however, is not a mere problem of modern scholarship, it pertained to the first and second centuries, and is even evidenced in St. Paul's Epistles. Those who have made a study of the Ancient Wisdom or Gnosis are, however, for the most part quite indifferent to these controversies. They recognize in the Christian Scriptures—albeit in a very distorted and garbled manner in our English version—the same essential teaching as to Man's origin, nature, and destiny which they have learnt from other sources. In these Scriptures it is dressed up in a certain allegorical form to suit the nation and people to whom it was addressed. What is rejected is not these Scriptures but the interpretation which has been put upon them by the literalists, and the man-made dogmas, based on the literal interpretation, which have prevailed for so many ages in the West, but which are now happily being widely repudiated by the more intelligent knowledge of our age. In short, we have to-day a totally different outlook on the universe than that which was possessed by these early dogmatists; and it is not possible for us to think either of its " Creator," or of Man, or of historical " facts " in the same terms. Hence on the one hand the widespread indifference to or total rejection of " Christianity "; and on the other hand the effort of " Modernism " to bring it within the lines of modern thought. Our modern knowledge of cosmology, of anthropology, and of the real facts of history, forbids us to think that the world was " created " in the manner so long current in Christian

[1] *Book of the Dead*, Budge's edition, pp. 690, 691.

doctrine; nor is it governed by such a deity as is therein conceived.

Ages before " Christianity " made its appearance, man had discovered " the way to God "; and Initiates and Seers and divine Avatāras had declared it for those who had ears to hear. This is the one great fact that our modern knowledge of ancient literature—practically unknown during the first half of last century—has brought to light. The Christian Scriptures can no longer claim to be unique; can no longer claim to be the only and sole guide for distracted humanity in its effort to discover the whence, why, and whither. Doubtless it can claim to be the sole guide for those who know of no other— and how many professing Christians do know of the literature of which I have spoken; or, knowing of it, simply reject it as " heathen "? How many professing Christians know of their own *mystical* literature? That literature touches in many of its aspects the teaching of the Ancient Wisdom. How many, even among theological students, are acquainted with or can recognize the profound teaching of that great Christian mystic and seer, Jacob Boehme, for example? I shall have occasion to quote from him, and to show that he—although uninstructed and uninitiated in any of the Mystery Schools—*saw*, by his own natural faculty, those same deep truths which are taught in those Schools.

Anyone who has taken the trouble to wade through even a small portion of the enormous mass of polemical writings or of Biblical exegesis which belong to modern scholarship, must very quickly come to the conclusion that there is no hope of arriving at the real truth in that direction. The most profound scholarship and the keenest critical faculty have been brought to bear upon the documents in our possession, with the result that hardly any two critics are in complete agreement, whilst many are diametrically opposed in their view. The general impression left upon us by these works is simply that nothing is known for certain, not even the existence of a historical man Jesus. It is all conjecture, conjecture, and again conjecture. The real question is not what these Apostles and Disciples and Church Fathers believed to be " history " or " truth "; the real question is as to what we, with our modern knowledge, can believe. Scholarship takes us nowhere—or rather into a morass from which we are glad to escape to the firmer ground of present facts.

Its most positive results are destructive rather than constructive. It has destroyed once and for all the possibility of the old belief—and of a good deal of modern belief also—that the Bible is the veritable and infallible " Word of God "; at least it has destroyed that for those who have any knowledge of Biblical criticism. Unfortunately most Christians are either too indolent or too much afraid of having their " faith " upset to enquire into the rational grounds of their beliefs; and what Bishop, or Priest, or Pastor, or Parson will instruct his flock here—if indeed he has any knowledge of the matter himself?

Yet Tennyson struck the right note when he wrote:

> " He fought his doubts and gather'd strength,
>   He would not make his judgments blind,
>   He faced the spectres of the mind
> And laid them: thus he came at length

> " To find a stronger faith his own;
>   And Power was with him in the night,
>   Which makes the darkness and the light,
> And dwells not in the light alone."

As an example of the uncertainty of scholarship read the work by C. Clemen, *Primitive Christianity and its Non-Jewish Sources.*

Every page is crammed with references to this, that, or the other scholar who either supports or contradicts some particular theory, or who either is or is not in agreement with Mr. Clemen's own theory. There is a formidable index of references to 348 of these modern authors. Yet when all is said and done Mr. Clemen himself acknowledges that his own conclusions are mostly hypothetical.

" If, then, we leave such external matters definitely on one side, the New Testament *ideas* that are *perhaps* derived from non-Jewish sources —for we may emphasize once more the hypothetical nature of most of our results—lie mainly on the fringe of Christianity, and do not touch its vital essence."[1]

[1] Pages 371-2. The italics are the author's.

Well, what is that "vital essence"? Surely not, as Mr. Clemen would have us believe, in the main those dogmas which are associated with the traditional interpretation of the Scriptures. He apparently fails to see that although the innumerable parallels in other Scriptures and teachings to the "history" and sayings contained in the Gospels and Epistles may not have any direct derivative connection, they undoubtedly point, in many cases, to a common tradition, in others to similarities of belief and teaching. In short, the "vital essence" —I will not say of Christianity in its traditional form, but—of the Christian Scriptures, was known and taught by Sages and Initiates ages before the Initiate Jesus or Jehoshua came on the scene, and endeavoured to present the old old Wisdom Teachings in a form appropriate to his time and his hearers.

It is the history of all such efforts that sooner or later—nay, even within a few generations—the teachings become perverted and overlaid with the conceptions of lesser minds, unable to grasp their "vital essence"—as Paul himself very quickly discovered. Was it not the conception of an almost immediate "Second Coming" that enthused the early disciples, and can that in any sense be called the "vital essence" of the teachings of Jesus and of Paul? Nay, did they teach it at all? Has it not been incorporated into their supposed sayings by subsequent writers of the Gospels and Epistles: writers who did not even hesitate to attach Paul's name to Epistles which he never wrote?

One of the latest efforts of scholarship to discover what is history and what is invention or myth in the Gospel narratives is the work of Dr. Martin Dibelius, *Die Formgeschichte des Evangeliums*, translated by Dr. Bertram Lee Woolf under the title *From Tradition to Gospel*. But although the employment in this work of the method of literary criticism which has become known as *Formgeschichte* serves in many instances to clear the ground of traditional accretions, it does not in reality carry us any nearer to historical certainty on the most vital matters; save perhaps we might say as to the actual existence of a historical man Jesus. It is full of such conjectural phrases as "if so," "if we suppose," "if in some such way the probability is established," "we may assume," "it seems to me highly probable," and so on.   In summing up results in the chapter on the Passion Story, the author says (p. 216):

" Thus historical and critical considerations may enable us to produce events in the Passion Story, which might always claim some probability, both in the positive and in the negative sense.   But such judgments can only be pronounced after the meaning of the Marcan presentation has been made clear, and this without regard to the question of historicity.   Only then do the Form-constructing forces come to light, which effected the formulation of pieces of tradition.   Thereby, in spite of superficial unity in the character of the Passion story, widely varied interests come into question.   But nowhere else must we be more aware of subjectivism than in examining the Passion story."

Outside of the Gospel narrative there is practically no contemporary evidence of the existence of the historical Jesus, much less any details of his life or mission.   Subsequent references by Josephus, Tacitus, and others, have every evidence of being later interpolations in the works of those writers.[1]

In his work on *The Messiah Jesus and John the Baptist,* Dr. Eisler writes as follows (p. 49):

" There remains at the end but the single hypothesis, confirmed by patristic evidence, that Josephus was not spared the indignities which Christian copyists did not hesitate to inflict upon the Christian fathers— nay, even upon the very Gospels themselves.   They falsified what he had written, suppressing things which he wished to say, and making him say things which he would never have dreamt of saying, they being altogether foreign to his own mode of thinking."

On the general question of the existence of documentary evidence he says:[2]

" There once existed a rich fund of historical tradition about the Messiah Jesus both among the Jews and the non-Christian Greeks and Romans.
" This precious material was deliberately destroyed or falsified, by a system of rigid censorship officially authorized ever since the time of Constantine I, and reinstituted in the reigns of Theodosius II and Valentinian III " (A.D. 477).

Why were these documents destroyed or falsified, as for example in the interpolations in Josephus and in Tacitus? Simply in the interests of those rigid and crude creeds and

---

[1] Cf. Dr. W. B. Smith's *Ecce Deus* for evidence of this.
[2] Ibid., author's Preface.

dogmas which have been the " orthodoxy " of the Church ever since those times, but which are now so largely in question, and in fact were largely in question by certain communities even in those early days. One of the most important of these protestators was the community known as the Pauliciani, who arose in the seventh century. They rejected altogether the traditional beliefs of the Greek and Latin Churches, but had a special reverence for the teachings of St. Paul. They were in fact more or less Gnostics, and as such they recognized the Gnostic element in St. Paul's teaching. They rejected the Old Testament Scriptures as having no connection with the later Christian Scriptures. Their central teaching appears to have been the inherent divine nature of the soul, its loss of the knowledge of this nature through its bodily thraldom in this world, or the kingdom of the Demiurge, and its possible redemption through the mystic Christ principle. They appear also to have taught reincarnation. In spite of severe persecution by the " orthodox " Christians they held their own for about three centuries, from about 668 to 976, and they played an important part in the history of that period, almost every historian of the Romans of the East giving some attention to them. Their teaching was in fact what we might perhaps designate as the earliest form of Protestantism.

" They were a steady protest in favour of the right of the laity to the possession and use of the Holy Scriptures. They were, in this respect, under the Byzantine despotism, what the Donatists, Lollards, Waldenses, and Puritans have been in other times and places."[1]

How is it that round the supposed history and personality of this mysterious character, Jesus of Nazareth, of whom we have practically no record whatsoever outside of the Gospel narratives, such a mass of contentious matter should have arisen, should have given rise to such varied and opposite opinions and doctrines, and—what is perhaps even more remarkable—to the vilest exhibition of human passions of hatred and cruelty that the world has ever seen? Is there some occult law in the spiritual world analogous to that in the physical world, namely, that action and reaction are equal

[1] Smith and Wace, *Dictionary of Christian Biography*, vol. iv, p. 220.

and opposite? Do we need to invent gods and demons of a *personal* nature to account for the good and evil which is so prominent in this world of ours? Is there anything which is to us " evil " for any other reason than that we have not control of some *natural* force? It can hardly be denied that there are beings in the invisible world who can use *natural* forces to work evil for mankind just as there are embodied souls who are incarnate devils in character; but these have no power to harm the MASTER, the man who has realized his divine nature and powers; and indeed such a one will deliberately *use* such intelligent or semi-intelligent beings for purposes of " good." Is not even the Devil of the Christian Scriptures supposed to be *used* by the God of the same Scriptures on certain occasions? I would only hint here, therefore, that there may be a natural law that the introduction or liberation, so to speak, of a certain amount of spiritual force in the world in any one direction, brings about automatically a corresponding liberation or opposition in the contrary direction. Do we not in fact find this law operating in our own individual nature? Does not any increase in our effort to spiritualize our nature call up from the depths of the subconscious a corresponding opposition, bringing to the surface slumbering and unsuspected atavisms of our lower animal nature and attachments? This is a well-known law in Occultism, and surely applies to the Race as well as to the individual. Thus in this view we might possibly regard the work centred in Jesus of Nazareth—and possibly not in him only at that time—as some outpouring of spiritual energy upon the world, and judge of the greatness of that by its opposite effect.

If we study carefully the history of the early Christian Church as exhibited in the reckless and acrimonious controversies which raged both before and after the various Councils had finally hardened the Creeds into their traditional orthodox form, we can only come to the conclusion that it was the human and not the divine element which finally gained the ascendancy. The documents of the Bible itself, very far from being the inspired word of " God," are exceedingly human documents; and—as Dr. Eisler says in the quotation I have just given from his work—even the Gospels themselves were falsified in order to bring them into line with " Orthodoxy." They are full of errors, contradictions unbelievable statements, and are replete with " the precepts and doctrines of men "; not to mention errors of translation and re-translation.

In particular, as regards the central figure of the Gospels—the supposed history of a man called Jesus Christ in those Gospels—they do not exhibit that history in any biographical sense, but simply a mass of legend and tradition passed from mouth to mouth during the first century and the first half of the second, and inevitably gathering, not truth but fable and miraculous elements on the way: just as was done for example with the " history " of Apollonius of Tyana, who was credited with so many miracles altogether on a par with those of Jesus, and was considered by many to have been a god. Dr. Dibelius in his work *Die Formgeschichte des Evangeliums* says:

" In the earliest period there was no connected narrative of the life, or at least of the work of Jesus, i.e. a narrative comparable to a literary biography or the legendary life of a saint. The stories contained in the synoptic Gospels, whose essential categories I have attempted to describe, were at first handed down in isolation as independent stories. Folk tradition as contained in the Gospels could pass on Paradigms, Tales, and Legends, but not a comprehensive description of Jesus' work."[1]

The so-called *Acts of the Apostles* suffers in the same manner, and is now very generally discredited by scholars. Thus, for example, M. Loisy,[2] in his *Les Acts des Apôtres* (p. 105), says:

" The editor of the *Acts* is a forger, and not unconscious of what was reprehensible in his work from the point of view of sincerity."

C. Clayton Dove, in his work *Paul of Tarsus* (p. 19), says:

" Acts contradicts Paul's Epistles with regard to events of great moment. This contradiction is of such a character that if Paul and the author of *Acts* were intimately acquainted either the one or the other must have been telling falsehoods."[3]

---

[1] Second edition translated by Dr. Bertram Lee Woolf under the title *From Tradition to Gospel*, p. 178.

[2] " One of the most significant figures in the religious history of our times." (Professor Jacks in *The Hibbert Journal*, April 1934.)

[3] Readers may be referred to this work for the contradictions in Paul's teachings as they stand in the Authorized Version, and if taken literally. The antitheses in the writings attributed to him are also freely acknowledged in the recent work by James S. Stewart, *A Man in Christ*.

Now Luke is supposed to have been the author of *Acts*, and Harnack, in his work *Luke the Physician* (p. 112), says:

" St. Luke is an author whose writings read smoothly; but one has only to look somewhat more closely to discover that there is scarcely another writer in the New Testament who is so careless an historian as he. Like a true Greek, he has paid careful attention to style and to all the formalities of literature; but in regard to his subject matter, in chapter after chapter he affords gross instances of carelessness, and often of complete confusion in the narrative. This is true both of the Gospel and the Acts."

It is likely, however, that many of the contradictions here referred to, as well as those in the Epistles themselves, are due to subsequent editing to make them appear to conform to the *orthodoxy* which already, in the second and third centuries, was hardening the original spiritual doctrine into a carnalized and intolerant dogmatism.

The Apocryphal *Acts of the Apostles* mentioned above makes instructive reading as to the methods of making " history " prevalent in those times. In an article on this work in Smith and Wace's *Dictionary* we read as follows:

" The real history of the lives and deaths of most of the Apostles being shrouded in obscurity, a pious imagination was very early busily employed in filling up the large lacunæ left in the historical reminiscences of the Church. Not a few of such narratives owe their origin simply to an endeavour to satisfy the pious curiosity or taste for the marvellous in members of the primitive Church; while others subserved the local interests of particular towns or districts which claimed to have derived their Christianity from the missionary activity of one of the Apostles, or their line of bishops from one immediately ordained by him. It likewise not infrequently happened that party spirit, theological or ecclesiastical, would take advantage of a pious credulity to further its own ends by manipulating the older, or inventing others entirely new, after a carefully preconceived form and pattern. And so almost every fresh editor of such narratives, using the freedom which all antiquity was wont to allow itself in dealing with literary monuments, would recast the materials which lay before him, excluding whatever might not suit his theological point of view."[1]

That the later Church Fathers adopted the same methods can hardly be disputed. Gibbon, in his *Decline and Fall*, says

[1] Vol. i, p. 18. In another place (vol. i, p. 137) they speak of "the great prevalence of forged letters and treatises in the first centuries after Christ." The Gospels and Epistles have very evidently not escaped this practice.

that " Eusebius himself indirectly confesses that he has related
whatever might redound to the glory, and that he has suppressed all that could tend to the disgrace, of religion " (vol. i,
chap. xvi). In a footnote he adds: " Such is the *fair* deduction
from two remarkable passages in Eusebius, L. viii. C.2, and
de Martyr, Palestin. C.12." Smith and Wace, however, in their
Dictionary, art. " Eusebius," contend against this interpretation.
It would appear, however, that we can hardly exonerate
Eusebius from gross exaggeration in many matters, more
particularly when he expatiates on the numbers and sufferings
of the martyrs. But possibly his greatest dishonesty is to
be found in his deliberate falsification of dates, more especially
Egyptian, to make the history of nations in general fit in with
the supposed Biblical chronology. Thus Bunsen in his
voluminous work *Egypt's Place in Universal History*, vol. i,
p. 206, says:

" He had undertaken a comprehensive scheme of adjustment between
the Scripture dates and those of all the other ancient nations. He is,
therefore, the originator of that systematic theory of synchronisms
which has so often subsequently maimed and mutilated history in its
Procrustean bed. There can be no doubt, as we have already remarked
in treating of Manetho, that Eusebius entered upon this undertaking in
a very unscrupulous and arbitrary spirit."

The reference which he here gives to his previous remarks is
as follows (vol. i, p. 83):

" Syncellus has done Eusebius no injustice in stigmatizing him not
only as superficial, but as having intentionally falsefied the Lists (of
Manetho) in order to force them into harmony with his own synchronistic
system. . . . We are bound, therefore, to regard his labours with the
greatest mistrust, and to pronounce it a most uncritical course to quote
him, as is the custom of many, as a competent authority in spite of this
delinquency, whenever it suits their purpose."

To what extent the Gospel narratives as we have them in
the Canonical Scriptures were made in this ancient manner of
making " history " has yet to be discovered: perhaps never
will be discovered by scholarship; yet it is already clearly seen
that there is much to be rejected in the light of our modern
knowledge.

It appears to the present writer that the strongest evidence
for the actual existence of a great teacher—whether called

Jesus, or Jehoshua, or by any other name—lies in the *Sayings* (*Logia*), and not at all in those portions of the Gospels which purport to give incidents in his life. Most critics are agreed that the origin of the Gospels—at all events the Synoptics— lies in the first instance in some such collection of *Sayings* which they call " Q " (German *Quella*—Source). Dr. Dibelius in his work already referred to says of this " Q " source:

" We know nothing certain about the extent of the source ' Q,' for we can only deduce ' Q ' in the places where the two parallels, Matthew and Luke, give the text in a somewhat similar fashion. We are not able to say how much of material special to each writer comes from ' Q ' (p. 234). . . . The present position of research into the source ' Q ' warrants our speaking rather of a stratum than of a document. We already recognize the effort of the Churches to gather together words of Jesus in the manner of ' Q,' but we do not know whether the result of these efforts was one or more books or indeed any books at all " (p. 235).

In an article in *The Hibbert Journal* for January 1936, on the apocryphal Gospel of Marcion, M. Paul-Louis Couchond contends that this Gospel was the original from which Luke drew his narrative; and moreover that:

" It is impossible to find in the source ' Q ' that homogeneity which would justify a belief in its existence, and the originality to which it lays claim ought to be divided in unequal proportions between Marcion and Matthew."

But as regards the Birth Stories, and the Crucifixion and Resurrection, these are palpably derived from earlier allegories. The early Christians endeavoured to destroy all traces of this derivation which appeared on the Egyptian and other monuments and in every Gnostic document they could lay their hands upon. That in itself is sufficient evidence of the pre-Christian origin of these allegories—which in fact conceal a knowledge of some of the deepest Cosmic facts, an approach to which is now being made by modern science.

Our present English Bible is not merely a translation and re-translation, but at some time, probably during the second century, the Canonical books were selected, and were edited, re-edited and over-written to conform to an already hardening theology, which subsequently became embodied in the traditional Creeds.

" The Gospel of Mark is no exception to the rule that church-writings of this type inevitably undergo recasting and supplementation until the advancing process of canonization at last fixes their text with unalterable rigidity."[1]

And the Creeds themselves: what of them? Read the history of the controversies of the third, fourth, and fifth centuries—not to go any further—controversies which raged round not merely questions of doctrine, but also as to the precedence in authority in the Church of this, that, or the other Patriarchate —more particularly as between Rome and Constantinople— and see if you can form any other opinion than that so-called " Christianity " in its doctrinal and sacerdotal form is a flat contradiction of all that is contained in the reputed Sayings of Jesus, whose mission, more clearly than anything else stated in the Gospels, was to abolish the priestly hierarchy and the formal worship of Temple or Sanctuary "built with hands " —as witness the discourse with the woman of Samaria (*John* iv. 7–15).

Gibbon, in his *Decline and Fall*, gives the following quotation from a work by Hilary, Bishop of Poitiers, died A.D. 368:[2]

" It is a thing equally deplorable and dangerous, that there are as many creeds as opinions among men, as many doctrines as inclinations, and as many sources of blasphemy as there are faults among us; because we make creeds arbitrarily, and explain them as arbitrarily. The *Homoousion*[3] is rejected, and received, and explained away by successive synods. The partial or total resemblance of the Father and of the Son, is a subject of dispute for these unhappy times. Every year, nay, every moon, we make new creeds to describe invisible mysteries. We repent of what we have done, we defend those who repent, we anathematize those whom we defended. We condemn either the doctrine of others in ourselves, or our own in that of others; and reciprocally tearing one another to pieces, we have been the cause of each other's ruin."

These were the men who determined what for so many centuries has been known as " Christianity."

Well then, what shall we say of this traditional " Christianity" which is being both widely advocated and widely repudiated

---

[1] B. W. Bacon, D.D., *The Making of the New Testament*, p. 170.

[2] Vol. i, chapter xxi.

[3] The doctrine of the common essence or substance of the Father and the Son.

to-day? We can only say one thing. It arose, and it is in vogue to-day, because it makes an appeal *to a certain class of mind.* Human nature is not so very different to-day from what it was twenty centuries ago. On all sides we contact credulity, superstition, acknowledgment of authority—more particularly sacerdotal authority—in place of reason. Of course the great mass of the community have neither the time nor the capacity to think out these complex questions for themselves. They accept without question—in any attention they may give to religion at all—the teachings of the religious community to which they may happen to have been brought up. Can we blame them? Barely ten per cent of our population make any profession of any kind of religion. Look also at the variety of Creeds and Sects—all supposed to take their authority from the same Scriptures. How shall the rational man choose? Yet, strange to say, what we see to-day is not merely the more or less unintelligent members of the community conforming without thought—or perhaps with what they do *think* is sufficient reason—to an inherited religion or a traditional authority, but we also see the most intelligent men, who profess to examine all sides of the question, joining this, that, or the other community, and in some cases renouncing previous convictions with which they have been associated from their birth upwards. A recent case was that of a Wesleyan minister who has gone over to the Roman Catholic Church. What might be called the modern classical example is that of Cardinal Newman. After a visit to Rome, in 1832, he wrote condemning the Roman Catholic Church in no measured terms; yet in 1845 he entered that Church. And did not Paul, after persecuting the Christians, ultimately become an ultra-Christian? We shall account for this, however, later on.

In all such cases there is something deeper than *intellect* which governs the choice. Indeed, we might say that the *function* of the intellect is to find " reasons " for these deeper motives, which lie hidden even from the individual himself. He *thinks* that he has ample reason for his choice. But if Truth is one and indisputable, how can valid " reasons " be found for such diverse and opposite doctrines?

But—I can hear my critics say—do not the same considerations apply to what you may put forward in this volume? Let me say at once, then, that most certainly they do. That is why I have said at the commencement of this *Introduction* that I am writing only for a certain class of students—or, if you like, for a certain class of minds. What I have here to say *will* appeal to these as truth, while for others it may be the deadliest error, even as Gnosticism was for those early Church Fathers who endeavoured to destroy all the Gnostic traces of the origin of their " Christianity."

But yet there is a difference: *must* be a difference between those who are seeking to choose between the conflicting opinions and creeds of so-called Christianity and those who have found a much deeper and more universal basis for their faith, and are thereby independent of all these sectarian and doctrinal controversies.

All truth is relative. It is the *how* of our perceptions. It is the perception of the relation and proportion of things; but there is a narrow and a wider perception of this relativity, this *appearance*. The Sun *appears* to move over the heavens from east to west, and primitive man considers this to be the *reality*. A deeper knowledge discloses other relations between the Sun and the Earth, and we pass from the crude realism of the primitive man to our modern astronomical knowledge. Yet there is certainly a still wider or deeper apprehension to be obtained of the relations and proportions of our Solar System—not to go any further into space-time—and this knowledge would certainly make our present conceptions appear as crudely realistic as those of primitive man compared with our modern knowledge.

Absolute truth, or fundamental Reality, would be the perception of a thing in *all* its relations and proportions; which perception, paradoxically, would take it out of all relation and proportion. In other words it would become the Absolute. But that perception, as already explained, is beyond the reach of the human mind or intellect.

And so in relation to questions of religion, which cannot be separated from those of cosmology and anthropology. We have to-day a much wider and deeper perception of the relation and proportion of things than that of the crude flat-earth creed-makers and dogmatists who, as late as the 16th century, burnt Bruno at the stake for opinions which are now common-place in our modern thought.

So also is it with our literary knowledge. We are in a vastly different position to-day with a knowledge of other ancient Scriptures than the Bible; in which Scriptures indeed we can trace precisely the same fundamental teachings concerning Man and his relation to Deity as we find in the Christian Scriptures when *esoterically interpreted*. It is therefore the *universality* of these teachings which gives us the assurance of their truth; which makes us independent of all the strifes of sects, creeds, and dogmas, and which enables us to value the Jewish and Christian Scriptures, not as unique documents, but simply as taking their place with the other great Scriptures as a certain *form* of the ancient Gnosis; a form moulded by and appropriate to the people and times in which they came into existence.

Thus the students who have the wider knowledge of these other Scriptures—and, we might add, the ancient philosophies also—are in quite a different position to appreciate *Truth* than is the man with only one Scripture and one religion. Such a man, it is true, may have consolation and peace and happiness in his religion; and it is just because he has these that he holds his religious beliefs to be true, however much opposed they may be to other beliefs. And of course they are true for him; but that is no proof of their *essential* truth. This " faith," or belief in certain formulated creeds, does not belong specially to any one religion, it is common to all. But some of us do not want consolation, we want Truth. Do we not see, indeed, that in the Christian religion as presented to us in our Churches and Chapels that very *consolation* which is offered is a bar to any further progress in real knowledge; that knowledge which we are told in the Christian Scriptures will finally conquer death itself? As the Christian only believes in one physical death, he interprets that conquest as meaning his safe entry into heaven, and an escape from " the second death " at the Judgment Day. Yet here again it was taught, long before it was re-presented in the Christian Scriptures, that the Master of the Hidden Knowledge achieves an actual conquest over the necessity for reincarnation, or physical birth and death.

Here is this teaching as given by the Buddha, and put into the beautiful language of Sir Edwin Arnold's *Light of Asia.*

> " Then he arose—radiant, rejoicing, strong—
> Beneath the Tree, and lifting high his voice
> Spake this, in hearing of all Times and Worlds:—
>
> " Many a House of Life
> Hath held me—seeking ever him who wrought
> These prisons of the senses, sorrow-fraught;
> Sore was my ceaseless strife!
>
> " But now,
> Thou Builder of this Tabernacle—Thou!
> I know Thee! Never shalt Thou build again
> These walls of pain,
> Nor raise the roof-tree of deceits, nor lay
> Fresh rafters on the clay;
> Broken Thy house is, and the ridge-pole split!
> Delusion fashioned it!
> Safe pass I thence—deliverance to obtain."

Perhaps we might say that it is only those who have reached the high status of a Buddha or a Christ who have really *attained.* Paul himself disclaims attainment " unto the resurrection from the dead."

" Not that I have already obtained (that resurrection), or am already made perfect; but I press on, if so be that I may apprehend that for which I also was apprehended by Christ Jesus. Brethren, I count not myself to have apprehended; but one thing I do, forgetting the things which are behind, and stretching forward to the things which are before, I press on towards the goal unto the prize of the high calling of God in Christ Jesus " (*Phil.* iii. 12–13).

The reference to " the resurrection from the dead " in the previous verse eleven, shows clearly that Paul meant by that something quite different from the physical resurrection at the " last trump " which he is represented as teaching in 1 *Corinthians* xv. 51. For if anyone could be said to be certain of such a resurrection at the " last day " in the orthodox sense, it was surely the Apostle Paul. We say that Paul's teaching of the resurrection was that of a resurrection from the spiritual deadness of our present natures; and that the final conquest for those who have attained " unto a full-grown man, unto the measure of the stature of the fulness of Christ," is the conquest of the necessity for further reincarnations and consequent deaths. That was the attainment of Gautama Buddha, and of many Buddhas before him. We say that the Christian Scriptures when *esoterically* interpreted teach the same doctrine of attainment. But the teaching is not merely veiled, it has been deliberately over-written and perverted in the documents as we have them, and the evidences of the derivation of those documents from earlier and Gnostic sources have been destroyed.

Irenaeus tells us that:

> " The Ophites, like other Gnostics, rejected the Old Testament altogether as a work of a subordinate divinity, and containing nothing of the revelations of their *Sophia*, or Divine Wisdom; whilst they held that the New, although originally of higher authority, had been so corrupted by the interpolations of the Apostles as to have lost all value as a revelation of Divine Truth. They drew the chief supports of their tenets out of the various ' Testaments ' and similar books then current, and ascribed to the Patriarchs and the most ancient Prophets, for example, the book of Enoch."[1]

The great fault that the student of world religions and world history has to find with " Christianity " in its traditional and dogmatic form is its insularity. Essentially Jewish, not merely in its geographical and historical setting, but also in its adoption of the Jewish Scriptures—and that in their literal interpretation —and the anthropomorphic concepts of the Jewish god Jehovah: it takes no account of the vast population of the world in other countries, and the uncounted millenniums of human history prior to a supposed date about 4000 B.C. and a supposed promise of the Jewish deity to Abraham—which has certainly never been fulfilled, and never can be fulfilled. What is missionary work to-day but an exhibition of this same insularity, and what of the exclusive claims of the Roman Catholic Church? All who are not " Christians " are " heathen " who must needs be saved by accepting—not the real Gospel of Christ, which is and can be universal, but—those dogmas of the Church

[1] Quoted from King's *Gnostics and their Remains*, second edition, p. 96.

into which ignorant men corrupted that Gospel, and which never were and never can be universal.

Jew and Gentile, Christian and Heathen—what are these distinctions in relation to that ONE LIFE which lives and moves in ALL: mineral, vegetable, animal, human, and beyond in unthinkable grades of existence from Man to Celestial Hierarchies and Dyhān Chohāns, and from them to the absolute ONE?

The real Gospel of the Christ is and can become universal because it is the ancient *Gnosis*; and *that*, as St. Augustine tells us, " existed among the ancients, and never did not exist."[1]

Let the Christian Church get back to that, and it may conquer the world; for all our advance in Knowledge will be found to be in conformity with it. But what hope is there that the ecclesiastical edifice will yield itself to such a reconstruction?

To sum up: the more one becomes acquainted with the available documents of the first four centuries of the Christian Era and the researches of scholars therein, the more one realizes that the historical facts as to the personality round which the traditional dogmas centre have yet to be discovered, as well as the earliest beginnings of that hierarchical cult which subsequently became known as the Christian Church. Yet there is one feature that stands out with the utmost clearness, at least for those who know that the deeper initiation knowledge has always existed, and indeed is evidenced in the writings of some of the Church Fathers themselves, not to mention the explicit statements of both Jesus and Paul. That feature is the gradual hardening and materialization of teachings which originally belonged to the Mystery Cults.

The dogmas and creeds with which the term " Christianity " became finally associated in its ecclesiastical hierarchical form were the result of an intense struggle between an original mystical and *esoteric* Christology, known to and taught by men who were more or less familiar with the Ancient Wisdom, and another set of men who were crude realists, literalists, and historicizers of the mystical allegories—commencing with the first chapter of *Genesis*. If the Garden of Eden story could be taken by these as literal history, can we be

[1] See p. 163 *infra*.

surprised at the dogmas which they subsequently based thereon? This literalizing of *Genesis* is a sample of all the rest.   And if the Church " Fathers " could so materialize the *spiritual* resurrection of the Race taught by Jesus and Paul as to make the resurrection that of the *physical* body at the " last day," can we be surprised at the ignorance and superstition which so quickly became associated with the hierarchical establishment and its mass of slavish adherents?   Nay, if we have seen this prevailing through so many centuries, and in existence even to-day, we can hardly be surprised at what happened in a community two thousand years ago in the entire absence of our modern knowledge of cosmology and anthrolopogy.

Even as early as St. Paul's time these strifes and divisions are in evidence in his Epistles; and he himself found himself compelled to teach mainly an *exoteric* doctrine.   Like Jesus he has " many things to say " which the communities to whom he addressed himself " were not able to bear."   How much of the real *esoteric* doctrine he did disclose " among the full-grown " —i.e. those who were prepared to receive it—we do not know; but knowing ourselves what that esoteric doctrine was—and always has been—we have no difficulty in recognizing his knowledge of it in many of the statements in his Epistles.

Later on, when the episcopate became established, the conflict raged in a still more fierce manner between those Church Fathers, such as Origen and Clement of Alexandria, who understood the esoteric teachings and the allegorical nature of the Bible narratives, and those " Fathers " who, as I have said, were crude realists, literalizers, and historicizers, and who were quite incapable of understanding the dynamic and flexible teachings of the Gnosis, their whole endeavour being to establish a rigid and dogmatic theology, and a priestly hierarchy holding sway over both the bodies and souls of men. How well they succeeded in doing this, and in suppressing not merely the Gnosis but all other learning besides, is written in letters of blood and fire and persecution in the subsequent dark ages of the Western nations.

CHAPTER I

RELIGION AND RELIGIONS

BEFORE dealing more specifically with the Christian Scriptures and the religion based thereon, it will be useful to survey to some extent the field of Religion in general; and it is fundamental to our subject to draw a very broad distinction between Religion and religions.

Religions are the *product* of Religion, but they are not Religion itself.

Religion itself is neither a belief, nor ritual, nor worship. These are the expression of the religious *instinct* in man, but they are not Religion itself; and when Religion itself has been found, they are transcended.

What then is Religion in its essential nature, and apart from any of the special forms or religions which are an endeavour to give it expression?

Religion is a *life*: the inherent life of the Spirit; but beliefs, ritual and worship pertain to the intellect. They express ideas *about* the things of the Spirit. They necessarily have a spiritual background, and they may even be said in a certain sense to minister to the life of the Spirit, just as clothes may be said to minister to the life of the body. They are in fact the clothes in which the intellect dresses up the *instinct* in man that he possesses a spiritual nature.

Beliefs are many, varied, and often in deadly conflict. Ritual is a form of ceremonial magic. Worship is mostly rooted in superstition and fear; in the idea that the deity requires to be propitiated and praised like an earthly king.

No one religion can claim to be unique, or to be the one and only guide for the individual in his effort to place himself *en rapport* with the spiritual world, or with any Being or Beings therein. We know of course that the claim to uniqueness is commonly made by the devotees of most religions, who look askance at, or consider to be "infidels," those who do not accept their own particular tenets. This has been particularly in evidence in two religions, Mahomedanism and Christianity, and it is at the root of all the religious hatreds, disputes, persecutions, and bloodshed with which the world has been so terribly afflicted, and which is still very widely in evidence. Happily there is to-day in a large section of the community a much wider tolerance; and there is also a very large body of intelligent people who refuse to attach themselves to any one sectarian religion, yet who are by no means irreligious, and might perhaps be called rather seekers after Truth than religious people. I speak of these now as being principally among our Western peoples. They are students of religion rather than being " religious " in the common acceptation of the term, and they can and do regard each and every religion from an outside point of view. They are mostly those who have rejected Christianity in its ecclesiastical or creedal form, but yet are by no means anti-Christian so far as the life and example of the central figure of the New Testament is concerned. It might perhaps be said of them that they accept Christ but reject Christianity in its traditional or dogmatic form. I shall have more to say of this, however, later on.

I think that it is coming to be more and more clearly recognized by impartial and unsectarian students of religions, that what is commonly called *religion* is more or less what we might call an *accident* of Religion in its real essential nature. These various religions of the world, so disputable in themselves, and so much at war with each other, are merely the outer expressions of a deep spiritual *instinct* in man, and they are necessarily based on and limited by the knowledge and experience of the individual or the community in which they arise or persist. Primitive times and primitive people give rise to primitive conceptions of man's relation to the world in which he lives; but more particularly to the unseen world with which he instinctively feels that he has some deeply rooted connection.

But there is a two-fold mischief here. In the first place these primitive conceptions are apt to survive and be carried on beyond their legitimate age, and into communities which have largely arrived at a wider and deeper knowledge; in which case these earlier concepts come into conflict with the more enlightened ones. In the second place, this survival is fostered by a hierarchy of religious officials whose very existence depends upon the survival of the old concepts, and who therefore discourage enquiry and research, and even foster ignorance and superstition in order to retain their authority and power.

This is seen very plainly to-day in the struggle of the old Christian theology with what is termed *Modernism*; and the trouble is that so many people here in the West, who have only had religion presented to them in a form which is for them utterly irrational, abandon religion altogether—as has been done in Russia on a wholesale scale—and thus starve the spiritual side of their nature. Where religion is only presented as something which an enlightened intellect must regard as superstition, the result can only be agnosticism, scepticism, or materialism. So far as the intellect is concerned, the remedy lies largely in a comparative study of religions; and this ought to lead—though it does not necessarily do so—to a deeper apprehension of what Religion itself is in its essential nature. It does not necessarily do so because the essence of Religion belongs to a region which transcends intellect; and a merely intellectual study of religions will never yield that which must be grasped by a faculty higher than intellect, and which— following Bergson—we may call by the not altogether satisfactory term intuition.

Intellect is more apt to belittle and materialize Religion than to expound it; as indeed is plainly to be seen in those formulated religious systems which have derived from some of the greatest religious teachers of the world, and which, in their creedal form, are so much in question to-day. Intellect can only invent creeds and dogmas within its own limitations; and these presently become overpassed, outworn, and obsolete: let alone the bitterness and dissensions to which they give rise among themselves.

The dogmas of the Christian Church have little in common with the teachings of Jesus. They were formulated by men who had the most primitive ideas of the nature of the Cosmos: ideas which are utterly childish in the light of our modern knowledge of cosmology and anthropology. Yet they still survive, for the reasons I have just given.

I might quote many writers who have recognized this

necessary distinction between Religion and religions. In *The Journal of Transactions of the Society for Promoting the Study of Religions*,[1] No. ix, June 1934, p. iii, we have the following:

" Religion is a mysterious power in human life which, in the course of historical civilizations, has thrown to the surface a thousand diverse religions. In a word: Religion produces religions."

H. Fielding, in his suggestive book *The Hearts of Men*, writes as follows:

" What you call religion I call only a reasoning about religion. The dogmas and creeds are not religion. They are summaries of the reasons that men give to explain those facts of life which are religion, just as philosophies are summaries of the theories men make to explain other facts of life. Both creeds and philosophies come from the reason. They are speculations, not facts. They are pessimistic terms of the brain. Religion is a different matter. It is a series of facts."

Instead of saying that " religion is a series of facts," I would rather say that it is the recognition of one supreme fact: the fact of *the inherent spiritual nature of man.*

We say that because man is a thinking animal he possesses *Mind.* But man is not merely a thinking animal: he is even more fundamentally and essentially a religious animal. The religious instinct lies much deeper in his nature than his mental acquirements; and therefore we say that because he is a religious animal he possesses *Spirit*: for Religion is concerned with the things of the Spirit—using that term for the ultimate *Principle* which must necessarily be the root and cause of all that exists in man or in the Cosmos, whatever name you may give to that *Ultimate*, or however you may conceive of it.

> " Some few, whose lamps shone brighter, have been led
> From cause to cause to nature's secret head,
> And found that one first Principle must be."

And here I would note that nothing can exist in man, or in any individual thing, be it an atom or a god, that is not in the first instance *cosmic* in its nature. If man has a physical body, it is because there is Cosmic Matter. If he has mind, it is because there is a Cosmic Mind. And if he has spirit—

---

[1] Address, 17 Bedford Square, London, W.C.1.

or rather, I would say, if he *is* Spirit in his essential nature—it is because there is a Cosmic Spirit. And it is this fact—on which I will presently enlarge—that lies at the root of his religious *instinct*, and that gives rise to religion in all its varied forms. Religion, therefore, I define as: *The instinctive recognition by man that he possesses a spiritual nature, and the effort which he makes to realize that nature.*

All history shows that man is essentially and instinctively a religious animal. What has not man done and suffered, what will he not do and suffer, for what he calls his religion? This is not a matter of one age or of one form of religion; it is evidenced in all ages and all religions. Asceticism and martyrdom have never been confined to any one religion.

It is not necessary that the individual should be conscious of his supra-conscious spiritual nature in order that it may exercise his influence. Modern psychology shows us the enormous influence of the sub-conscious, of which influence the individual is just as unconscious as he is in the vast majority of cases of the influence of the supra-conscious, or what we are here calling the higher Self, the spiritual Ego. Unconsciously feeling that influence, he makes his religion according to his intellectual capacity, and maintains that he has sound *reasons* for his formulated beliefs; for it is precisely the function of the intellect to supply those " reasons."

We may distinguish three grades or phases of religion as a recognition of a super-mundane or spiritual order in the universe.[1] The first of these grades is that of primitive Man, who deifies natural forces: more particularly those which he considers must be propitiated in order that he may not suffer injury from them. This phase we might distinguish broadly as the religion of *fear*.

The second grade introduces human conceptions of a *moral* nature, and endows its deities—or in monotheistic forms, its deity—with moral qualities which are a reflection of those which a more or less advanced civilization recognizes as necessary for the well-being of the community: such as justice, equity,

---

[1] The classification which I am here giving is substantially the same as that given by Einstein in his work *The World as I See It* (p. 23 ff.), to which I am indebted.

truth, honesty, non-injury; but also along with these the conception of the anger of the deity against transgressors, and arbitrary punishments for evil-doers. The deity is in fact still a purely anthropomorphic one, though conceived as embodying high human qualities, not excluding that of love. This phase we might distinguish broadly as the religion of *morality.*

The third grade rises above all anthropomorphic concepts, and recognizes a supreme, impersonal UNITARY PRINCIPLE, or ONE LIFE, as being not merely the *Source* of all that exists both in the seen and the unseen, but as being *all inclusive*; as being both the manifested and the unmanifested; as being, in fact, the Universe in its *totality,* and therefore not capable of being distinguished as this, that, or the other, either in existence or in quality; for to distinguish it thus would be to exclude the opposite, and would therefore nullify the primary postulate that IT IS ALL. This phase we might designate as *cosmic* religion. It is the religion of the philosopher, the mystic, and the initiate; and perhaps also of the scientist who has found himself compelled to abandon materialism. In it the individual recognizes his own oneness with the Cosmos. All that he is or can be exists as cosmic principles, and, *qua* individual, he is merely a particular and limited example of those principles. He asserts, therefore, that in his inmost deepest nature he is *one* with that UNITARY PRINCIPLE which IS the Universe, and his religious effort is to realize that to the fullest extent in consciousness.

This is the religion of the Ancient Wisdom, of the Gnosis. In its application to the individual it finds its highest expression in the aphorism " That art thou " of the *Upanishads*; and later —and in what I am more particularly trying to elucidate in this work—in the " I and the Father are one " of Jesus, and the " Christ in you " of St. Paul.

What can be more *cosmic* than Paul's magnificent address to the men of Athens? (*Acts* xvii. 24–8.)

" The God that made the world and all things therein, he, being Lord of heaven and earth, dwelleth not in temples made with hands; neither is he served by men's hands, as though he needed anything, seeing he himself giveth to all life, and breath, and all things; and he made of one every nation of men for to dwell on all the face of the earth, having determined their appointed seasons, and the bounds of their habitation; that they should seek God, if haply they might feel after him, and find him, though he is not far from each one of us; for in him we live, and move, and have our being; as certain even of your own poets have said. For we are also his offspring."

Cosmic Religion, the Ancient Wisdom or Gnosis, requires no "temples made with hands," for it teaches that "the kingdom of God is within you." It is dependent neither on tradition, nor book, nor priest. It is purely a matter between the individual and his own soul in the oneness of that soul with the ONE LIFE—commonly called "God"—*in* which "we live, and move, and have our being." Cosmic Religion is the effort of the individual to realize that oneness in ever increasing measure; whereas religions of ritual and ceremony and petitions addressed to an *external* God must ever keep the individual from that realization, until happily he has discovered their ineffectiveness.

These three phases or grades of religion naturally shade off, as it were, into one another. We may find elements of the one mixed with those of the next higher. This is specially the case with the first two grades, which we might describe as *communal* religions, they require a priestly caste, whilst as regards the third and highest grade, it is purely an individual matter: that is to say as between the individual and his own soul; and having no priestly hierarchy to dictate to it, or to come into conflict with *orthodoxy* in all its varied and disputable forms, it is free from the admixtures referred to, though it may have, and indeed has, many different methods of actual practice in the endeavour of the individual to attain to a full realization of the supreme unity.

There is no such thing, and there never can be any such thing, as a universal religion so long as humanity is what it is, at vastly different mental levels. The three grades of religion just enumerated correspond broadly to the grades of human intelligence. Christianity in its ecclesiastical form can never become a world-religion, for it is only one species of the numerous religions belonging to the second grade; and it is largely mixed also with elements of the first grade. But

Christianity as the religion of Jesus and of Paul belongs to the third grade, to *cosmic* religion, and ecclesiastical religion has little in common with it.

Go into a Roman Catholic Cathedral and witness the elaborate celebration of High Mass, with its pomp and circumstance, its ritual and vestments and incense and worship of the High Altar: and then ask yourself what connection there is between that and the religion of the teacher who said:

" But thou, when thou prayest, enter into thine inner chamber, and having shut thy door, pray to thy Father which is in secret " (*Matt.* vi. 6).

Even if we accept these words literally, and imagine that the " inner chamber " means an actual room in a house: what connection is there between such an *individual* religion, with no priestly intervention between the soul and God, and the *heathen* ritual of a priestly hierarchy as practised in the " Christian " Church? Every symbol and vestment and practice in this ritual is simply a survival of *pagan* ceremonies which have entirely lost their original *mystical* signification. The eucharist, for example, was originally a Mithraic rite, whilst sacramental meals were common in many of the Mystery Cults.[1] In the end, the teaching of Jesus and Paul was transformed out of all recognition by that very formalism and " paganism " which it was intended to replace.

Does " God " require all this ceremonial worship which still obtains? Does he—if we *must* use the personal pronoun— require any ceremonial worship at all? William James in his classical work, *The Varieties of Religious Experience*, says:

" Ritual worship in general appears to the modern transcendentalist, as well as to the ultra-puritanic type of mind, as if addressed to a deity of an almost absurdly childish character, taking delight in toy-shop furniture, tapers and tinsel, costume and mumbling and mummery, and finding his ' glory ' incomprehensibly enhanced thereby " (p. 330).

" Whatever sort of a being God may be, we *know* to-day that he is nevermore the mere external inventor of ' contrivances ' intended to

[1] Cf. Angus, *The Mystery Religions and Christianity*, pp. 127 ff. On p. 128 Dr. Angus says: " We have abundant evidence that in the cult meals of the Graeco-Roman age the deity was viewed sometimes as guest and sometimes as host, or indefinitely, as both guest and host, as in the religious conception, ' I will come in and sup with him, and he with Me ' " (*Rev.* iii. 20).

make manifest his ' glory ' in which our great-grandfathers took such satisfaction, though just how we know this we cannot possibly make clear by words either to others or to ourselves " (p. 74).

But of a truth the " inner chamber " to which Jesus referred is not any three-dimensional outward structure. It is the " inner chamber of the heart," wherein the lower self, the *personality*, having " shut the door " of the senses on all external objects, and, further even than that, the " door " of the mind which occupies itself with " the things of this world," now communes with " the Father in secret." But this is no new teaching. It is simply the Raja Yoga of Eastern philosophy, and the invariable practice of the Initiates of all ages. Nor has this communion any resemblance to the petitionary prayers of our Churches or of the individual Christian. In its highest aspect it is realization of *oneness*, at-one-ment; and one might perhaps say that in its lower aspects it is practice, practice, practice: practice of some one or other of the numerous methods of attainment which are taught in the esoteric schools; but never—*pace* the " Lord's Prayer," which is intended for " spiritual babes "—petitions for material benefits. In this and in other statements of a like nature, Jesus shows himself to have been an Initiate. His work was to transmute the formal *moral* religion of the Jews into the higher *cosmic* religion. Paul continued the same effort, but extended his mission to the " gentiles " also. Both efforts were a failure so far as both the Jews and the world at large were concerned. In the one case both the teacher and the teaching were rejected by the Jews as a race; in the other case the fearful monstrosity of sacerdotal " Christianity " arose to exterminate the Gnosis, to plunge Europe into the awful ignorance and cruelty of the Dark Ages, and to substitute for the pure teachings of Jesus those materialistic dogmas which are happily being so widely repudiated to-day: on rational grounds on the one hand, and also because there is to-day a genuine revival of the Gnosis for the many minds who are now ready to appreciate the principles of *cosmic* religion.

The essence of the ancient Gnosis, I repeat, is the oneness of the human soul with the Universal Soul, no matter by what name that *Principle* may be called to suit the apprehension of those whom the teacher addressed. That oneness gives the individual the right to call himself a " Son of God." It enables his present *belief* to pass into absolute knowledge (Gnosis); a knowledge which enables him to overcome every human disability, and confers upon him the freedom of the universe. Such are the great Initiates, the Masters of Wisdom, who to-day are once more making known their existence.[1]

Jesus never speaks of Jehovah, and there is not one of his references to God which may not be interpreted in a *cosmic* sense. In using the term " Father " he simply endeavoured to bring down the conception of the ONE (God) with whom he had realized his oneness, to the level of the intelligence of his Jewish hearers, since the Jews had been accustomed to think of God (Jehovah) as a *person*—and a very human one at that. But even so, the term " Father " has a legitimate use in cosmic religion so long as we speak of individual souls as being derived from and dependent on the Universal Soul. In those systems, such as the Egyptian, in which natural forces are personified as gods, there was always a one supreme " Father of the Gods " in the sense of being their Creator: he himself being self-created.

At various times and in different localities various names were given to this one supreme God. He was identified with Nu, with Tem or Atmu, with Ptah, with Khnemu the god of the First Cataract, and with Khepera. Thus philosophically or esoterically the religion of the Egyptians, like that also of the Hindus, was monotheistic, the various " gods " being merely personifications of natural forces conceived of as having great *Intelligences* behind them. Inevitably perhaps, the ignorant masses worshipped these lesser gods, just as to-day worship and intercession is made to the Virgin and to Saints in the Roman Catholic Church.

" *Nu* is the name given to the vast mass of water which existed in primeval times, and was situated presumably in the sky; it formed the material part of the great god Tem, or Atmu, who was the creator of the universe and of gods and men. In this mass, which was believed to be of fathomless depth and of boundless extent, were the germs of all life, and of all kinds of life, and for this reason the god who was the

[1] See Philo's description of them, pp. 105-6.

personification of the water, i.e., Nu, was called the ' Father of the Gods,' and the ' producer of the Great Company of the Gods.' "[1]

Here we have precisely the same idea as that expressed in the second verse of the first chapter of *Genesis*.

" And the spirit of God moved (was brooding) upon the face of the waters " (Primordial Substance).

In a *Hymn of Praise to Rā when he riseth in the Eastern Part of the Heavens* we read:

" Homage to thee, O Heru-Khunti (Harmachis), who art the God Khepera, the self-created."[2]

Also in chapter xvii, p. 116, of the *Book of the Dead*:

" Hail, Khepera in thy boat, the two-fold company of the gods is thy body! "[3]

There can be no question as to the depth and power of the religious instinct in man. Religion is a tremendous *urge*: from primitive man with his fetishes and totems onward through history to its highest expression in saint and mystic, and in such teachers as Gautama Buddha and Jesus Christ, and in such Scriptures as the *Upanishads*, the *Bhagavad Gītā*, the Egyptian *Book of the Dead*, or the Jewish and Christian Scriptures, known to us as the *Old* and *New Testaments*.

I have said that the root of all religions is the *instinct* in man that he possesses a spiritual nature. Now instinct is not necessarily a conscious recognition; indeed the primary meaning of the word is that of a natural spontaneous impulse moving without reasoning. Many so-called " rationalistic " writers, who regard all and every form of religion as being irrational, would have us believe that man has no such religious instinct, but that all religions have developed from ignorant superstitions and a dread of the " supernatural." The tirades of these " rationalistic " writers have been mainly directed against the dogmas of the Christian religion, and here they certainly have a very strong case.[4] But being thus directed

---

[1] Budge, *The Papyrus of Ani*, vol. i, p. 162.

[2] Budge, *The Book of the Dead*, p. 72.

[3] Ibid., p. 108.   See also the quotation from *The Laws of Manu*, pp. 125–6 *infra*.

[4] Vide *The Churches and Modern Thought*, by Vivian Phelips.

against *a* religion they fail to recognize the necessary distinction between Religion and religions; between the religious *instinct* which is so deeply implanted in human nature, and the *forms* to which that instinct gives rise, and in which it is expressed. Moreover most of these " rationalistic " writers are—or perhaps we should rather say *were*—simply materialists.   It is not in the lowest aspects of Religion, but in the highest, that we are able to perceive what really lies at its root.   However irrational may be many of the forms of Religion which come under the second category, that of the religion of *morality*, the third category, *cosmic* religion is in the highest degree rational: not in the sense of being able to explain everything by means of the intellect—no " rationalist " can do that—but rather perhaps in the negative sense of rejecting everything that is clearly *irrational* in so far as the legitimate use of the intellect is concerned.   And what more irrational than the materialism of last century on which the " rationalists " principally relied? One might almost say that the most *rational* thing to-day—as it has always been in the Schools of Initiation—is to recognize the limitations of the rational faculty.

> " The Mind is the great Slayer of the Real.
> Let the Disciple slay the Slayer."[1]

Broadly stated, and apart from any question as to the nature of *Spirit*, and apart altogether from the question as to the existence and nature of " God," we might say that man instinctively feels that he is something very much more than a mere physical being, and that he instinctively endeavours to realize that *more*—and this notwithstanding that there are some, even to-day who will assert that they are nothing more. The absence of the instinct in a few individuals, or even in a few communities, does not disprove its practically universal existence.   That *more* must necessarily lie in the superphysical —so often wrongly called the *supernatural*.   Thus one of the fundamental concepts of Religion is the survival of bodily death.   We may claim that that survival is a definitely proved scientific fact to-day, even though our " rationalists " may still deny it.   But beyond that, the student of Occultism knows

[1] *The Voice of the Silence.*

that it is possible to function consciously on the superphysical planes while still possessing a physical body.

Religion is an *urge* and also a *quest*. The urge comes from *within*; the quest, in the first instance, is an outward one. Up to a certain stage in the history of religion we find man seeking to ascertain his relation to some outside and unseen Power or Powers which he supposes to be operating to control the course of nature and his own destiny. Thus even to-day we find prayers for rain offered in our churches, and prayers for blessings on all sorts of our material interests, not excluding war. Hence also is it that we find that the definitions which are given in our Dictionaries to-day illustrate this particular stage: the stage in which man invents his gods and demons who need to be propitiated.

The word *religion* is commonly considered to be derived from the Latin *re*, back, and *ligo*, to bind; or, possibly from *re*, back, and *lego*, gather. Thus we find in the *Standard Dictionary* the following definition:

" A belief binding the spiritual nature of man to a supernatural being on whom he is conscious that he is dependent."

Would it not have been better here to have said " on whom he *thinks* that he is dependent "? For we see that such a definition as this rules out Buddhism as a religion; for Buddhism does not recognize any " supernatural being " or " God " on whom the individual is dependent. Buddhism certainly recognizes a higher Power or Powers above and beyond the *material* world; but it recognizes this rather under the aspect of immutable *Law*, operating in man's own subjective moral and spiritual nature as well as in the objective or physical world. Thus in the words of Sir Edwin Arnold's *Light of Asia*:

" Before beginning and without an end,
   As space Eternal and as surety sure,
Is fixed a Power Divine which moves to good,
   Only its laws endure."

"There is one eternal Law in nature, one that always tends to adjust contraries and to produce final harmony. It is owing to this Law of spiritual development superseding the physical and purely intellectual, that mankind will become freed from its false gods, and find itself finally—SELF REDEEMED."[1]

[1] H. P. Blavatsky, *The Secret Doctrine*, vol. ii, p. 420. O.E.

Which are we to believe in, (*a*) a *personal* God who will send or stop rain on request, and who "sends" his devoted worshippers toothaches, or even the most loathsome diseases, or deprives them of their children in order to "chasten" them; or (*b*) Deity as *Immutable Law*, operating in the spiritual and moral as well as in the material world, i.e. the Law of *Karma?*

In the definition given above from the *Standard Dictionary* the term *supernatural* is itself in question. Where does *Nature* begin or end? We have in this definition simply a survival of the idea which has dominated the Western world for centuries, that *Nature* is limited to that little aspect of the Universe which we can appreciate with our physical senses. The above definition also excludes any philosophical religion, such as the Vedanta, which recognizes the *immanence* of an Absolute PRINCIPLE—whether called God or otherwise—which, or who, IS the Universe in all its conditions and aspects.

A somewhat better definition is given in the *New English Dictionary*, or *Oxford Dictionary*, which has been so many years in course of preparation. The definition here is: "*Recognition on the part of man of some higher unseen power as having control of his destiny, and so being entitled to obedience, reverence and worship.*"

I think, however, that this definition also would be exclusive of Buddhism. It does not appear to be altogether free from the theological bias of Western Religion. Is it essential to religion that the individual should recognize "*some higher unseen power as having control of his destiny*"? Certainly not in the sense here intended if we are to recognize Buddhism as a religion—and how can we possibly exclude it?—for Buddhism teaches that:

> " Within yourselves deliverance must be sought,
>   Each man his prison makes."

This, as most students know, embodies the principle of *Karma*: or the law of cause and effect operating in the moral world.

Sir J. G. Frazer in *The Golden Bough* defines religion as: "*A propitiation or conciliation of Powers superior to man which are believed to control the course of Nature and of human life.*" He explains that by "Powers" he means conscious or personal agents. Here once more, then, we have a definition which does not cover the philosophical religions of the East, and these religions certainly present a further stage in the development of religious concepts than that of our Western ideas as given in the definitions I have just quoted.

Religion in its highest development is the realization of the *oneness* of man in his spiritual nature—of that which is *innermost* in himself—with that which is *innermost* in the Cosmos; with that which I will here call COSMIC SPIRIT, or the ABSOLUTE —the term *God* having rather too many theological concepts associated with it.

Of course when we speak of SPIRIT as being the *innermost*, and as being in some sense opposed to *Matter*, we are talking in terms of Appearance not of Reality. The Universe is SPIRIT through and through and Matter is only an *aspect* of that absolute PRINCIPLE—as even our physicists are now beginning to discover.

But between Spirit and Matter stands *Mind*—Cosmic Mind, the reflection of which in the physical man is perhaps better known as *intellect*.

Bergson, the philosopher of *Intuition*, says of intellect:

" Intellect has detached itself from a vastly wider reality. . . . We compare intellect to a solid nucleus formed by means of condensation."[1]

That "vastly wider reality" we should say is Cosmic Mind. A good analogy would be that of the physical atom as a nucleus formed in the substance of the all-pervading Ether. *Qua* atom it is an individual and limited thing; but *qua* substance it is the Ether itself. Thus what we know as mind or intellect in our present limited brain consciousness is as it were an atom of Cosmic Mind acting reciprocally with those atoms of Cosmic Substance which we call physical matter.

Bergson tells us that intellect and material objects are reciprocal adaptations.

" The same movement by which mind is brought to form itself into intellect, that is to say, into distinct concepts, brings matter to break itself up into objects excluding one another."[2]

[1] *Creative Evolution*, p. 203. [2] Ibid., p. 199.

On this basis Bergson clearly perceives that the intellect can never be the faculty by which we can cognize *Reality*.

" The intellectual tendencies innate to-day, which life must have created in the course of its evolution, are not at all meant to supply us with an explanation of life: they have something else to do."[1]

The importance of this to our present subject is simply this: that all formulated religions, all creeds and dogmas, are found to lie in the limitations of the intellect. We *cannot* formulate beyond those limitations.[2]

When we endeavour to bring down into terms of intellect that which transcends intellect, there is necessarily contradiction, antinomy. Theology, being precisely this effort, presents ever a mass of disputable and insoluble problems, and has to fall back on assertion, dogma. Hence the interminable systems and disputes of " theologians."

How then are we to transcend the limitations of intellect? The reply which Bergson gives us is by what he terms *intuition*. This is far from being a satisfactory word, but we do not appear to have any other to replace it. Intuition would still appear to be an operation of the mind, though a higher one than that of intellect. It is generally defined as a direct or immediate perception of truth without reasoning or analysis; but what is to check such a perception in matters transcending our normal consciousness?

The answer which we must give to this question is broadly this; that we shall find a certain *unanimity*, a certain consensus of teaching concerning first principles, among those who are generally classed as seers or mystics.

Now the mind, in its aspect as a rational *faculty*, is essentially *dualistic*. It cannot transcend the " either-or " aspect of things. Indeed I should say that it is the *function* of the mind —even of Cosmic Mind—to create this duality, to set things in contrast and opposition. Thus we have such pairs of opposites as Spirit and Matter, Good and Evil, God and Devil, etc., etc.

---

[1] *Creative Evolution*, p. 22. See also the quotation from Wm. James, p. 19 *supra*.

[2] *Creeds in the Making*, by Alan Richardson, well discloses the vain efforts of the intellect to formulate that which transcends intellect.

But we find in the experience of Seers and Mystics that this duality of the mind can be transcended, and an underlying fundamental *unity* perceived. This unity of all in the *Absolute* is in fact not merely a philosophical proposition—I had almost said a philosophical necessity—but it is the one supreme fact of religious experience: an experience which belongs to no one particular formulated religion.

Many of my readers will be familiar with the eloquent passage relating to this mystical experience of *union* in William James's classical work, *The Varieties of Religious Experience.*

It is the following:

" This overcoming of all the usual barriers between the individual and the Absolute is the great mystic achievement. In mystic states we both become one with the Absolute and we become aware of our oneness. This is the everlasting and triumphant mystical tradition, hardly altered by differences of clime or creed. In Hinduism, in Neoplatonism, in Sufism, in Christian Mysticism, in Whitmanism, we find the same recurring note, so that there is about the mystical utterances an eternal unanimity which ought to make a critic stop and think, and which brings it about that the mystical classics have, as has been said, neither birthday nor native land. Perpetually telling of the unity of man with God, their speech antedates languages, and they do not grow old."

We have to make a broad distinction between those religions which are dualistic and those which are monistic. It is the latter which constitute the highest development of the religious instinct in man, but that development is by no means a matter of the latest form of religion; indeed Christianity, although supposed to be a monotheistic religion, is essentially dualistic. We go back to the *Upanishads* for the highest concept both of a monistic universe and of man's *oneness* with the Absolute. Thus we have as the keynote of these Ancient Scriptures:

" What that subtle Being is, of which this whole Universe is composed, that is the Real, that is the Soul, *That art thou.*"[1]

In his work on *Theosophy of Psychological Religion,* Professor Max Müller speaks of this as:

" The highest summit of thought which the human mind has reached, which has found different expressions in different religions and philosophies, but nowhere such a clear and powerful realization as in the ancient Upanishads of India."

[1] *Chandogya Upanishad*, vi. 14, 3.

In the Egyptian *Book of the Dead* we find the same thesis in a somewhat different form. In general it is represented in that Scripture that the deceased who possesses the necessary occult knowledge to pass successfully through the various regions of the underworld, finally arrives in the presence of Osiris, and becomes one with the god. We may, however, I think, recognize that this work is not merely one which was largely used in connection with the burial of the dead, but that underneath its strange symbolism we have a profound cosmology and anthropology, and some of the deepest secrets of the ancient Mysteries of Initiation. Notwithstanding its Pantheon of gods, it is at root monotheistic.

For instance, as already stated, the principle known as *Nu* represented the watery mass out of which the gods were evolved: in other words *Primordial Substance*, coupled with the teaching of emanation and evolution therefrom.

Then we have *Thoth*, the divine intelligence which at the creation uttered the words which resulted in the formation of the world. In other words he is the equivalent of the *Word* or *Logos* of the Christian Scriptures; these being, as I hope presently to show, undoubtedly derived from the earlier mystery teachings. We might say also that he represents Cosmic Mind—Sanscrit *Mahat*, from which man derives *Manas*.

Or take the question of the origin of evil, and the impossibility of conceiving that it can originate in a God who is postulated to be both all good and all powerful. This difficulty is due simply to the natural duality of the mind. But here again intuition transcends intellect. Even in one verse in the Bible we find the deity declaring:

" I form the light and create darkness; I make peace and create evil; I am the Lord that doeth all these things " (*Isa.* xlv. 7).

No one in Christian Mysticism has perceived more clearly that God is the source and origin of what we call evil as well as of what we call good than that incomparable Seer, Jacob Boehme.

Thus he says:

" All is through and from God himself, and it is his own substance, which is himself, and he hath created it out of himself; and the evil belongeth to the forming and mobility; and the good to the love."[1]

Now I find in the *Book of the Dead* an absolute parallel to this passage.

" Who, then, is this? . . . It is Horus when he riseth up with a double head, whereof the one beareth right and truth and the other wickedness. He bestoweth wickedness on him that worketh wickedness, and right and truth upon him that followeth righteousness and truth " (chapter xvii. 28, 29).

Let us take some of the affirmations from this Book which are the equivalent of the " That art thou " of the *Upanishads*.

" Hail, Lord of the Shrine which standeth in the middle of the earth. He is I, and I am he " (lxiv. 7, 8).
" I came into being from unformed matter (i.e. Primordial Substance). I came into existence like the god Khepera, I have germinated like the tortoise. I am of the germs of every god " (lxxxiii. 3, 4).

This is the equivalent of the Kabalistic saying the Man is the microcosm of the Macrocosm.

Again:

" There is no member of my body which is not the member of some god " (xlii. 10).

The gods, as previously said, are simply personifications of natural forces.

" I am Osiris, the lord of eternity " (xliii. 4).
" In very truth I am Rā himself " (xliv. 4).

There are innumerable similar affirmations; and we may say, indeed, that notwithstanding the difficulty of translation, and the undoubted corruption of much of the texts, we have in this ancient Scripture—some of which is pre-dynastic, that is to say pre-historical—undoubted proof that this " highest summit of thought which the human mind has reached " is no product of the later and historical developments of religion, but has always existed alongside of the more primitive beliefs, customs, and rituals.

There is only one explanation of this. It is that of the existence of a Hierarchy of Initiates in all ages; men who had already achieved the full knowledge of their spiritual and

[1] *The Three Principles of the Divine Essence*, Preface.

divine nature and powers—not as a mere philosophical concept, but in all the knowledge of the nature of the Cosmos, of Cosmic Law, and of a supreme power over the forces of nature which such a knowledge gives.   Thus the Egyptians had their tradition of the divine King-Initiates or demi-gods who preceded the historical dynastic period; and initiation into the Egyptian *Mysteries*—from which the Greek *Mysteries* were later on derived—was eagerly sought after by many of the ancient philosophers whose writings have come down to us.   Moses himself is said in the *Acts of the Apostles* (vii, 22) to have been " instructed in all the wisdom of the Egyptians ";[1] and I do not think that it would be altogether too difficult to show that the same cosmological and anthropological ideas underlie the symbolism of both the Books of Moses and the *Book of the Dead*.   In other words, they are both derived from the same source: the supreme knowledge of the Hierarchy of Initiates. I have dealt further with this, however, in chapter IV.

We have information of the existence of this Hierarchy from many sources, and I deal with some of these in chapter III.

I take it then to be the fundamental fact of Religion that the real immortal Self in man is *one* with the Absolute.   Even thus have Sages and Initiates taught in all ages.   The ancient Aryans knew it, as witness the *Upanishads*.   The ancient Egyptians knew it, as witness the *Book of the Dead*.   It is also, as I hope presently to show, the root teaching of the Christian Scriptures, however much the Church may have obscured it by a literal interpretation of those Scriptures.

Thus I might sum up by saying that in that view of the nature of Religion which I am here presenting, Religion is the finding of the real *Self*: that spiritual Self which is inherently and intrinsically immortal, " eternal in the heavens," as being *one* with Cosmic Spirit, or the Absolute.

In the beautiful words of Sir Edwin Arnold in his verse rendering of the *Bhagavad Gītā*:

" Never the spirit was born; the spirit shall cease to be never;
   Never was time it was not; End and Beginning are dreams!
 Birthless and deathless and changeless remaineth the spirit for ever;
   Death hath not touched it at all, dead though the house of it seems!"

[1] See p. 77 *infra*.

And if a comparative study of religions does not lead us to acquire at the very least a profound intellectual conviction of this supreme truth of man's immortal spiritual nature—not to speak of the god-like powers which a practical realization of it can give—then I am afraid I must say that in a merely intellectual or scholarly study of religious beliefs and practices, we shall only be partaking of dead sea fruit.

Religion is nothing if it is not intensified life; aye, even to that which " eye hath not seen, nor ear heard, nor hath it entered into the heart of man to conceive."

Practical religion is the absolute conquest by the power of the Spirit—the " Christ in you " of St. Paul—of sin, suffering, and death *here and now*, in *this* world. Over and over again we must insist that practical religion is *conquest*, not *escape*. It is conquest through real knowledge, *Gnosis*. Your " Christianity " will not save you, or your child, or your loved one from physical harm and disease if there is ignorance of the causes of these, and a lack of the power to control those causes. Neither will you be saved from other and more subtle evils if you have not the knowledge of their causes, and the will to conquer them. We have every proof that that knowledge and power can be achieved, in the modern records—not to go back to ancient ones—of the powers, both physical and psychic, of the Eastern Yogis and Mahatmas. These do not achieve through belief in creeds or dogmas, but through belief in their own inherent powers—in short, belief in the *unity* of man with " that subtle Being of which this whole Universe is composed,"[1] and the *natural* powers which are the result of an ever increasing realization of that unity. In the first instance *Yoga* is control of the *Mind*. Our " New Thought " practitioners are taking the first steps in a more or less understanding manner towards this ancient science of Mind. In the higher stages, however, mind is altogether transcended. This conquest of the " world "[2] the individual must achieve through repeated reincarnations until he becomes the Initiate, the Adept, the Buddha, the Christ. But let no one imagine

---

[1] See p. 93 *infra*.

[2] *John* xvi. 83. " I have overcome the *world*." (Gr. *Kosmos*, order, orderly arrangement; thus *Natural Law*.)

that he can conquer the " world " until he has conquered himself. This we say is the inner *esoteric* meaning of the teachings of Jesus and of Paul, clearly to be recognized as underlying the outer and often corrupted form of their doctrine as given in our present documents.

" And the last enemy that shall be abolished is death "— the necessity for further reincarnations.

> " As one who stands on yonder snowy horn
>   Having nought o'er him but the boundless blue,
> So, these sins being slain, the man is come
>   NIRVANA'S verge unto.

> " Him the Gods envy from their lower seats;
>   Him the Three Worlds in ruin should not shake;
> All life is lived for him, all deaths are dead;
>   Karma will no more make

> " New houses. Seeking nothing, he gains all;
>   Foregoing self, the Universe grows ' I.' "[1]

But alas! how slowly, how very *very* slowly do these lower temporary personalities of ours which we are pleased to call *ourselves*, learn to become *at-one* with our real immortal spiritual Self, so as to manifest *here and now* the conquest of sin, suffering, and death which such an at-one-ment would bring about.

It is that at-one-ment which I take to be the essential nature of Religion—an at-one-ment *here and now*, in our present physical bodies, and not some after-death pardon and redemption.

For it is only as we as individuals accomplish that regeneration, that " second birth," that Humanity as a whole can accomplish it, and the golden age which prophet and seer have foretold can dawn in the world; for it is *we*, as integral units of Humanity from beginning to end of its great cycle of evolution, who must accomplish it.

How should it be accomplished by the Race if not by us as individuals? We *are* the Race; and the Race can only progress as the individuals progress through repeated reincarnations.

Let us finally, then, glance very briefly to this wider cosmic aspect of the nature of Religion as it affects Humanity as a

[1] *Light of Asia,* book viii.

whole. Let us endeavour to look upon Religion in a much larger light than as a mere matter of personal attainment of " salvation." Nay: has it not been taught that only as the lower personal self is *lost* can the higher immortal Spirit be found? It is in the wider interests of Humanity as a whole that the spiritual man will first of all merge or " lose " his personal interests, and even any thought of personal salvation. Far earlier than Christianity it was taught in the East that the Buddhas of Compassion renounced Nirvana in order to work for the salvation of Humanity.

The cosmic aspect of Religion is this—Humanity as a whole is a Unitary Cosmic Entity associated with the cosmic function of this particular globe as a unit in the Solar System: that System being a still larger cosmic unit whose life-history is represented by the Sun; or, spiritually, by the Solar Logos.

The great cycle of Man's evolution on this globe is a " fall " and a recovery; an *outgoing* from Spirit into Matter, and a *return* to Spirit.

Humanity reaches forward to a spiritual consummation when the whole Earth will be peopled with a Race of men fully conscious of their god-like nature and powers; and sin, sickness, and death will have been banished for the remaining period of the Earth's cosmic cycle.

The Cosmic Process is an *outgoing* from the ONE, and a *return* thereto; and Man—like everything else in the Cosmos— must return to his Source. It is the great Cosmic systole and diastole, called in the East the Days and Nights of Brahma.

If, then, Religion is for us as individuals the finding of the real spiritual Self—that transcendental Self which is the root and source of all these temporary *appearances* which are our little temporary personal selves—so also is it with Humanity as a whole; for it is our attainment as individuals which gradually accomplishes the attainment of Humanity in its *cosmic* aspect.

The return of Man, Humanity, to his spiritual nature is as certain as the outgoing therefrom, however long and bitter the process may seem. Far too much has been made of individual salvation, as if it had no reference to the salvation of the Race as a whole.

In that far distant future when the Earth will be peopled with a god-like Race of men—must not the members of that Race be those who, having gone through the great evolutionary process, have attained to the full knowledge of their spiritual nature and powers? Who else can constitute that Race? *That* humanity must be *this* humanity now evolving towards it. In short, it will be *ourselves*.

This I believe to be the root teaching of the Christian Scriptures, as well as of other and more ancient ones, however much these Scriptures may have been corrupted and overlaid with the doctrines and decrees of a priestly hierarchy of lesser knowledge and vision.

Thus Jacob Boehme writes, looking at the wider cosmic aspect:

" Such a man as Adam (Humanity) was before his Eve (before his fall into physical generation) shall arise, and again enter into, and eternally possess, Paradise."[1]

That is the consummation, here on this Earth, of that gradually dawning realization by man of his true spiritual nature, which now takes so many and varied forms of expression under the term *Religion*.

[1] *Mysterium Magnum*, chapter xviii, par. 3.

CHAPTER II

THE BIBLE

WHAT has been known for so many centuries as the *Bible*, or the " Canon of Scripture," is a collection of miscellaneous writings which were selected from a large number of similar documents by the early Church Fathers as embodying what at that time, i.e. the second and third centuries of the Christian Era, was considered by these same " Fathers " to be the revelation of a personal God, the Jehovah of the Jews, concerning his dealings with man. The Scriptures which were rejected came to be known about the fifth century as " Apocryphal " in the sense of not being considered worthy of being included in the Canon of Scripture. But the original meaning of the Greek word *apokruphos* was that of a work which contained a secret knowledge too excellent to be communicated to ordinary mortals.[1]

The Canonical Scriptures gain nothing by having been thus selected, nor do those which were rejected lose thereby; indeed, it is rather the contrary, for, as I have just said, these documents were selected because they were supposed to conform to an already formulated theology; in other words, because they were *orthodox* in respect of that dogmatic theology which was then being formulated, and which has survived in the Creeds. Clement of Alexandria and some other Church Fathers made considerable use of such apocryphal works as the *Epistle of Barnabas*, the *Preaching of Peter*, the *Gospel according to the Hebrews*, and the *Revelation* (or *Apocalypse*) *of Peter*. This latter appears at one time to have been reckoned as a canonical work.[2] There were many Apocalypses in circulation in the first two or three centuries, but that of John is the only one that has survived in the Canon of Scripture, though even so not without its authority being disputed. The Old Testament apocryphal books formed part of the *Septuagint* Bible, which was a translation of the

---

[1] See *Encycl. Bibl.*, i. 249.
[2] Cf. Smith and Wace, *Dict.*, art. "Apocalypses," vol. i., p. 130.

Hebrew Scriptures into Greek sometime between the years 280 and 130 B.C.

Yet despite the fact that the Books of the Old and New Testaments were selected—and not merely selected but also edited and overwritten—to conform to an already hardened creedal system, it was not possible for these historicizing and literalizing Church Fathers to exclude all indications of their derivation from that Ancient Wisdom or Gnosis which became such a heresy for these same " Fathers " towards the end of the second century, and the records of which in documents and monuments they did their best to destroy utterly.

But these founders of that priestly hierarchy which later on plunged the Western world into the profound darkness, ignorance, and superstition of the Middle Ages, could not altogether extinguish or overcloud that Light which has always existed in the *Mysteries*, and has always been accessible to those who diligently seek it. The expositors of those Mysteries, so well recognized in the palmy days of Greece and Alexandria, retired into the background, knowing well that what was about to befall the Western nations was simply *Karma*, and that it had to be allowed to run its course.

But now happily in these nineteenth and twentieth centuries, the mystery teachings of the Ancient Wisdom are emerging once more, and eager souls, reincarnations of those who have had a previous knowledge of the teachings, are once more taking up their quest where they laid it down in those far-back days. Not merely so, but the teachers, the Initiates, the high Masters of this Wisdom, are once more proclaiming their existence, and becoming the personal guides of those who are ready and fitted to receive those deeper secrets of Man and of Cosmos which cannot be disclosed to those who have not the preliminary qualifications. So has it ever been, so is it now. Here are three statements of the fact.

" This book is indeed a veritable mystery. Let no stranger any where have knowledge of it. Do not speak about it to any man. Do not repeat it. Let no other eye see it. Let no other ear hear it. Let no one see it except thyself and him who taught it to thee. Let not the multitude know of it except thyself, and the beloved friend of thy heart. . . . It is indeed a mystery. The dwellers in the swamps of the Delta and everywhere there shall not know it."[1]

" This therefore is manifested by the mandate of the Mysteries, which orders that they should not be divulged to those who are uninitiated. For as that which is divine cannot be unfolded to the multitude, this mandate forbids the attempt to elucidate it to anyone but him who is fortunately able to perceive it."[2]

" Unto you it is given to know the mysteries of the kingdom of heaven, but to them (the multitude) it is not given " (*Matt.* xiii. 11).

Jesus even forbade his disciples to disclose his real nature as the *Christos.*

" Then charged he the disciples that they should tell no man that he was the Christ " (*Matt.* xvi. 20).

In *The Laws of Manu* (xii. 117) we read:—

" Thus did the all-wise MANU, who possesses extensive dominion, and blazes with heavenly splendour, disclose to me, from his benevolence to mankind, this transcendent system of law, which must be kept devoutly concealed from persons unfit to receive it."

Even Jacob Boehme, who was under no obligation by any pledge of secrecy, finds it necessary to withhold certain truths which were revealed to him. Thus in his *Mysterium Magnum* (x. 2) he says:

" Here we have hinted enough to the understanding of our school-fellows: further we must be silent."

Dr. Angus, in his work on *The Mystery-Religions and Christianity*, writes (p. 78):

" An awful obligation to perpetual secrecy as to what was said and transacted behind closed doors in the initiation proper was imposed—an obligation so scrupulously observed through the centuries that not one account of the secrets of the holy of holies of the Mysteries has been published to gratify the curiosity of historians."

Thus all that we read about the initiations and ceremonies of the Mystery Cults is exoteric merely; and most of it, indeed, is merely a popularized echo of the real inner teaching. And what is ecclesiastical Christianity itself but such a popularized echo?

[1] *Book of the Dead, Papyrus of Ani*, Budge, ii. 648.
[2] Plotinus, *Enn.* vi. 9, 11.

As it was in ancient times so is it to-day. Thus **Mrs.**
Adams Beck in her instructive work *The Story of Oriental
Philosophy* says (p. 58):

> " It must never be forgotten that in the Eastern philosophies there is
> an open meaning for the many and a hidden meaning for the few who
> are thus initiated and instructed. This is emphatically so with the
> Vedanta and certain teachings of the Buddha.
>
> " Moving about in India, Ceylon, Burma, and Japan, one is much
> struck with the fact that these esoteric meanings are most carefully
> guarded and seldom meet the observer except in the most favourable
> circumstances. Yet they are none the less there and known to those
> who are able to penetrate beneath the surface."[1]

Looking broadly at our present age it is seen to be a return,
on a higher level, of those palmy days of eager philosophical
enquiry, and of a recognition of the existence of the *Mysteries*
to which I have just referred, which existed during the height
of Roman and Grecian civilization. The dark cycle has run its
course and humanity emerges once more into a cycle of
intellectual activity and discovery. That is simply because,
broadly speaking, the Egos now coming into incarnation are
those who lived in that previous light-cycle.

Nor is it mere chance that certain documents are being
" discovered " which enable us to penetrate to some extent
into the nature and teachings of those *Mysteries* which the
early framers of the " Christian " creeds so strenuously
endeavoured to destroy. One might refer perhaps more
specifically, as bearing upon the Gnosis in the Christian
Scriptures, to what are known as the Askew, Bruce, and
Akhmim Codices; and of these three the Askew Codex,
more generally known as the *Pistis Sophia*, is of such an
illuminating nature that it may almost be said to surpass in
importance any of the Canonical Gospels.

To return now, however, to these Canonical Scriptures:
for those who are students of the Ancient Wisdom these
Scriptures disclose plainly their origins in that Wisdom
notwithstanding the sad manner in which they have been
overlaid with " the precepts and doctrines of men." They
disclose quite plainly that they were written by *Initiates*.

---

[1] See also Paul Brunton's work, *A Search in Secret India*.

There is no question here of any " inspiration " by a personal God. I leave all disputes as to the nature of " inspiration " to those theologians who still wish to maintain—in spite of the facts which scholarship is now forcing them to recognize —that the Bible is the veritable " Word of God," disclosing to man by " revelation " what he could not have otherwise known. He *did* know what is therein disclosed of Man and the World he lives in, long before a single word of the Bible was written.

For what are the facts? The Bible commences with a cosmogenesis and anthropogenesis said to have been written by Moses. Now Moses, it is said, " was instructed in all the wisdom of the Egyptians " (*Acts* vii. 22). He learnt his cosmogenesis and anthropogenesis in the Temple Initiations of Egypt; therefore the knowledge existed there before ever he wrote his *Genesis*. It is to be found in the *Book of the Dead*. Some of the earlier chapters of that Script were long prior to Moses's period; indeed some scholars would attribute these earlier chapters to a pre-dynastic period, and in one of them the claim is made to have been " in the handwriting of the god (Thoth) himself "[1]—one of the pre-dynastic " Divine Kings," or King-Initiates, sometimes identified with Hermes.

With reference to this knowledge which Moses possessed, Fabre d'Olivet writes:[2]

" Moses had penetrated into the sanctuaries of Egypt, and he had been initiated into the Mysteries; one easily discovers this on examining the form of his cosmogony."[3]

" Moses, obedient to a special impulse of Providence, followed the way of sacerdotal initiation, and displaying a constancy which perhaps Pythagoras alone has since had, submitted to all the proofs, surmounted all the obstacles, and braving the death presented at each step, he attained at Thebes to the final degree of the divine science."[4]

The question, then, as to the proper place which the Christian Scriptures—that is to say the Old and New Testaments— should occupy in the religious literature of the world, and as to their authority as being the infallible Word of God: is

[1] Chapter cxxxvii a.
[2] *La Langue hébraïque restituée*, vol. i, p. xxvii.
[3] See p. 122 *infra.*
[4] Ibid., vol. ii, p. 8.

one which to-day, in the light of our modern knowledge, assumes a very different aspect from that which was hardly questioned somewhat less than one hundred years ago.

Our modern scientific knowledge and the researches of our scholars, which have disclosed not merely so much concerning the various books of the Bible which was previously unknown, but also the existence of other great religious literatures, the value of which in their relation to man's search for spiritual enlightenment cannot be ignored—all this has made it impossible for any well-informed man to-day to accept the Christian Scriptures in their literal word and form as being the veritable " Word of God." The very presentation and conception of " God " which those Scriptures embody in their literal word is repugnant to those of us who are no longer overawed by the traditional doctrines and dogmas of the Christian Church, and can thus examine these Scriptures on their own merits instead of accepting them on mere authority.

I need hardly dwell upon the very widespread rejection to-day of the traditional Christian doctrines and dogmas. It is true that the Roman Catholic Church is still inflexible in upholding them; and the same may possibly be said of one half of the Anglican Church—not to mention certain other sects. Nevertheless we have in the Modernist Movement some kind of an attempt within the Church itself to bring Christian doctrines more into line with our modern knowledge and our modern concepts as to the nature of Man and the Universe in which he lives.

But can Christian doctrine be thus reconstructed if the Bible is to be taken in its literal narrative and word?

Setting aside the question of its historical veracity in the numerous miraculous stories which it contains, can we—to go to the root of the matter—any longer accept such a " God " as is therein presented to us? Is it not abundantly evident that that God, the Jehovah of the Jews, is a purely human concept; a God conceived of in the likeness of man, and conceived moreover in the likeness of the Jew? When we study other religions and other Scriptures, it is abundantly evident that the concepts of " God "—that is to say of a

Supreme Being—never rise any higher than the intelligence of the peoples or community to which those religions and Scriptures belong; neither can any " revelation " of the nature of such a Supreme Being be given beyond that mark.

It has been clearly perceived by innumerable great teachers and philosophers in all ages that in very truth no concept whatsoever can be formed of such a Supreme Being or Absolute Principle. Nothing can be predicated of IT; for, since IT is ALL, to predicate any one particular thing or quality of IT is to exclude the opposite, and is therefore in itself contradictory. Let me give a few quotations.

We will take first of all a modern writer, Williams James in his *Varieties of Religious Experience* (p. 416):

" He, the Self, the Atman, is to be described by ' No! no! ' only, say the Upanishads—though it seems on the surface to be a no-function, is a denial made on behalf of a deeper yes. Whoso calls the Absolute anything in particular, or says that it is *this*, seems implicitly to shut it off from being *that*—it is as if he lessened it. So we deny the ' this ' negating the negation which it seems to us to imply, in the interests of the higher affirmative by which we are possessed. The fountain-head of Christian mysticism is Dionysius the Areopagite. He describes the absolute truth by negatives exclusively."

Next, a Christian mystical work of the fourteenth century, the *Theologia Germanica*:

" The things which are in part can be apprehended, known, and expressed; but the Perfect cannot be apprehended, known, or expressed by any creature as creature. Therefore we do not give a name to the Perfect, for it is none of these. The creature as creature cannot know nor apprehend it, name nor conceive it."[1]

And Eckhart:

" According to St. Augustine, what we say about God is not true; what we say that God is he is not; what we say he is not that he is rather than what we say that he is. Nothing we can say of God is true."[2]

Then Plotinus:

" Hence, it (the One) is in reality ineffable. For of whatever you speak, you speak of a certain thing. But of that which is beyond all things, and which is beyond even most venerable intellect, it is alone true to assert that it has not any other name (than the ineffable), and

[1] *Theologia Germanica*, p. 2, by S. Winkworth, Golden Treasury Series.
[2] *Meister Eckhart*, C. de B. Evans, p. 54.

that it is not some one of all things.   Properly speaking, however, there is no name of it, because nothing can be asserted of it."[1]

And the *Upanishads*:

> " Other, indeed, is IT than the known,
> And moreover above the unknown,
> Thus have we heard of the ancients
> Who to us have explained IT.
> That which is unexpressed with speech,
> That with which speech is expressed—
> That indeed know as Brahma,
> Not this that people worship as this."[2]

Dozens of other similar quotations could be given.   How comes it about, then, that our Christian theology can postulate this, that, and the other about this Supreme Being?   It is because that theology, as given in the Creeds, is merely a survival of those primitive concepts of " God " which we find in the Jewish Scriptures, and in terms of which both Jesus and Paul found it necessary to present their teachings to the multitude, otherwise they would not have been understood at all.   But both expressly say that they have other teachings reserved for the initiated—in other words, the *Gnosis*.

We are sometimes told that the nature of God was revealed in and by the *personality* of Jesus Christ, and is not Jesus himself reputed to have said, " he that hath seen me hath seen the Father "?   (*John* xiv. 9.)   Yes, but he is also reputed to have said, " No man knoweth the Son, save the Father; neither doth any know the Father, save the Son, and he to whomsoever the Son willeth to reveal him "   (*Matt.* xi. 27). Concerning which saying Meister Eckhart says: " In truth, to know the Father we must *be* the Son."[3]   " Revelation " is, as is the capacity of the individual to receive.   Maybe the whole nature of God was disclosed in Jesus Christ; but so it is in every blade of grass had we but the power to perceive it.   We would rather say that what Jesus *partially* disclosed was what a *man* can be who has realized his divine sonship; has realized that in his real esssential *Self* he is *one* with

---

[1] *Enn.* v. 3, 13.   [2] *Kena Upanishad*, 1, 3, 4.
[3] *Meister Eckhart*, p. 43.

" That subtle Being of which this whole universe is composed."[1] The exclusive Logos doctrine which subsequently became attached to the *man* Jesus is, as I have shown, obviously derived from other sources. What the Church made of Jesus Christ was only so much as the makers of the Creeds were able to perceive. Moreover there is a vast difference between the personal Jesus and the mystical Christ.

If then, this " Christian " concept of the nature of " God " has to be rejected, how are we to regard these same Scriptures which are supposed to reveal his nature and dealings with Man ? Are we to reject these Scriptures altogether, or is there some other means of bringing them into line, not merely with our modern knowledge, but also with the other great Scriptures of the world, which, indeed, happily present the relation of Man and of the individual to the Supreme Being in a manner much more acceptable to our modern knowledge and concepts of the universe.

Those of us who have fortunately been able to come into contact with and study these other Scriptures, have recognized that there is a body of teaching running through them all, back to the most ancient times of which we have any literary records, and which we have found to be consistent and uniform in all its fundamental principles in whatever form it may have been presented at different times and to different peoples: those of us, I say, who have been thus fortunate have been able to recognize that the Bible is mostly made up of *allegories*, put into a semi-historical form, which belong to this same Ancient Wisdom or *Gnosis*; taught, indeed, in those *Mysteries* of the existence of which we have so much reliable historical information, but of the teachings of which so very little is known outside of the circle of their Initiates: such teachings having always been wrapped up in allegory and symbol, as not being suitable, as already stated, for the hearing of the uninstructed masses.

The Bible, then, along with other Scriptures, having its origin in this same Ancient Wisdom or Gnosis, though sadly mutilated and garbled in our authorized version: its proper

[1] See p. 93.

interpretation lies in what we can gather from other sources of those great fundamental principles concerning Man's nature and destiny which have been taught for ages past, and long before the Jews were ever heard of. It lies in these same *Mysteries*—the " Mysteries of the Kingdom of Heaven " which Jesus is said to have disclosed to his Disciples, but refused to the common people; thereby merely following the traditional practice of all great teachers in this connection. Paul also speaks of the " Wisdom in a mystery " which was only disclosed to the " full-grown " (1 *Cor.* ii. 7).

Such an interpretation of the Christian Scriptures in the light of the Gnosis not merely gives to them an entirely new value—new, that is to say in so far as the common or exoteric interpretation is concerned—but also it is in no wise at variance with our modern discoveries, either in science or in any other direction. Let me now, therefore, endeavour to elucidate this to some extent.

In the *Zohar*, one of the books of the Jewish *Kabala*— which, by the way, is itself one of the keys to the esoteric interpretation of the Old Testament Scripture—we read:

" The narratives of the doctrine are its cloak. The simple look only on the garment, that is upon the narrative of the doctrine; more they know not. The instructed, however, see not merely the cloak, but what the cloak covers " (iii. 152, Franck).

As confirmation of this from Christian sources we have the following statement by Origen, when speaking of the Garden of Eden allegory:

" Who is so foolish as to believe that God, like a husbandman, planted a garden in Eden, and placed in it a tree of life, that might be seen and touched. . . . And if God is said to have walked in a garden in the evening, and Adam to have hidden under a tree, I do not suppose that anyone doubts that these things figuratively indicate certain mysteries, the history being apparently but not literally true. . . . Nay, the Gospels themselves are filled with the same kind of narratives " (*De Princip.* i. 16).

But not merely were these Old Testament allegories—the Garden of Eden one in particular—accepted as literal history in Origen's own time, but they are accepted literally by thousands even to-day. Nay, it was just precisely this

acceptance by Origen's own confrères that was the foundation of that traditional dogmatic " Christianity " that has
come down to us through the centuries accompanied by such
unspeakable intolerance, cruelty, and bloodshed.[1]

It it any wonder that those who could thus historicize the
Genesis allegory should also historicize the profound allegory
of the *Christos* underlying the Jesus story of the New Testament, as Origen also intimates?   See also how Paul recognizes
and uses allegory in *Galatians* iv. 23–31:

> " Which things contain an allegory," etc.

Now we have in both of these quotations, from the *Zohar*
and from Origen, a clear statement, well understood by the
" instructed " at the time that they were made—and well
understood also by the instructed to-day—that both the
Old and the New Testament Scriptures contain, hidden
beneath the mere narrative, an *esoteric* meaning, a *Secret
Doctrine*, a *Gnosis*.

As I have already said, when I speak of the *Gnosis*, I do
not refer specifically to the Greek or Coptic variety, but to that
Ancient Wisdom which can be discovered as a thread of gold
running through allegories and myths and fables from the
very earliest times of which we have any literary records,
and which has more recently been somewhat more fully
expounded to us by some of the existing Masters of that
Wisdom.

As regards the Greek variety—which, however, we have
principally known until recently through the attacks made
upon it by some of the early Church Fathers—we must
remember that not merely were there many sects of this,
but also that many of these sects were spurious and even
debauched, and had no right to the title of *Gnostic*.   They

---

[1] Even to-day such stuff as the following is put forward by such like literalizers or " fundamentalists." " The serpent, when it first appeared to Eve, was
not the writhing reptile, such as we connect with the word serpent to-day.
That condition was the effect of the curse pronounced upon it for lending
itself to Satan in order to tempt man.   Previously it may well have been
one of the most graceful and beautiful creatures in the Garden of Eden, second
only to man as the most ' subtil ' of created animals " (Basil Stewart, in *The
Witness of the Great Pyramid*, p. 191).

professed to teach " Mysteries " without having any real knowledge of them: just as to-day there are many spurious Societies professing to teach Rosicrucian, Kabalistic, and other " occult " secrets—for a consideration. Paul also speaks of " false apostles, deceitful workers, fashioning themselves into apostles of Christ " (2 *Cor.* xi. 12). How, then, are we to distinguish the true from the false? Must we not say, indeed, that all those teachers in the Church who still base their teachings on the literal word of the Scriptures belong to this class, and are simply " blind leaders of the blind "?

But how comes it about at all that these Biblical allegories and figurative stories were taken, and have been accepted for so many centuries, and are even so accepted to-day, in their literal and narrative form as the basis of the traditional Christian doctrines and dogmas? Were not those the " false apostles " who thus originally moulded them into this traditional form?

The study of Christian origins is a very large and controversial question into which I do not intend to enter here except indirectly; but it is quite evident that the literalization of these narratives was due to the fact that those who ultimately obtained the ascendency in the Church Councils, and were the framers of the Creeds which have been current for so many centuries, were *not* those who were instructed in the Gnosis. They were in fact miserably ignorant, not merely of that Gnosis which, as I shall presently show, lies at the root of all these allegories, myths, and fables in the Christian as in other ancient and pre-Christian Scriptures, but also of geographical, astronomical, and anthropological facts well known to other peoples for thousands of years prior to the Christian Era, and which, when known—as they were to the *initiated* Church Fathers, who were, however, declared to be *heretics* by these same creed-makers—entirely alter the whole structure of the traditional Creeds.

Thus, although many of the early Church Fathers were instructed in this Gnosis, their teachings were gradually eliminated by the more ignorant and fanatical framers of the Creeds who ultimately attained ascendency in the

Church, and Gnosis teachings were finally declared to be heresies; and heresies they have remained to this day.

If we want to understand somewhat of those " Mysteries " which Jesus is said to have disclosed to his Disciples only, we must go to such a Gnostic Scripture as the *Pistis Sophia*, which purports to be the teachings of Jesus to his Disciples eleven years after his resurrection; though even in that Scripture a symbolism is employed which it is not easy for the uninstructed to penetrate. There are, however, several things which are quite plainly taught therein: reincarnation, for example. Thus we have the following passage in which Jesus tells his Disciples that the good and blameless man who was not fortunate enough to become acquainted with the mysteries, would have the opportunity of doing so in his next incarnation.

" She (the ' Virgin of Light ') sealeth it (the soul of that man) with a higher seal and letteth it be cast down into the body . . . which will be good to find the signs of the mysteries of the Light and inherit the Light-Kingdom for ever.

" If on the contrary he hath sinned once or twice or thrice, then will he be cast back into the world again according to the type of the sins which he hath committed " (m.p. 262–3).[1]

In these Scriptures, God is called " the One and Only," the " Ineffable " and " The First Mystery which looketh within," while Jesus is called " The First Mystery which looketh without." It treats of all the grades and degrees of *emanation* from this " One and Only "; the outgoings from and the return to this ONE. Instead of the foolish teaching that all who " believe " will be lumped together in one heaven at the " last day," we have the following very rational statement by Jesus.

" They who have received the mystery of the Light, if they come out of the body of the matter of the rulers, then will every one be in his order according to the mystery which he hath received. Those who have received the higher mysteries, will abide in the higher order; those who have received the lower mysteries will be in the lower orders. In a world, up to what region every one hath received mysteries, there

[1] The quotations are from the revised edition (1921) of G. R. S. Mead's work, *Pistis Sophia*; and the references are to the marginal pagination (m.p.) which he has adopted from the Schwartze-Petermann translation.

will he abide in his order in the Inheritance of the Light.   For which cause I have said unto you aforetime: ' Where your heart is, there will your treasure be '—that is up to what region every one hath received mysteries, there shall he be " (m.p. 202).

It is only by *knowledge* of these " mysteries "—which, however, are simply the *natural laws* of our own being and nature and those of the cosmos—that the individual can in any sense be " saved," that is to say, can liberate himself from the powers of this lower world of matter and illusion.

But the knowledge of these " Mysteries " is simply the knowledge of Self in all its phases; for man is *one* with the " One and Only " in his inmost nature, in his *higher* self, his real immortal eternal nature; while his present "self," his *lower* self, is merely a passing phase.   Thus the ancient Greek philosophers said, " man, know thyself."   Thus also the great aphorism of the Upanishads, " THAT art Thou."   And thus also Jacob Boehme, and many another enlightened seer:

" For the book in which all mysteries lie is man himself; he himself is the book of the Being of all beings; seeing he is the likeness (or similitude) of God; the great *Arcanum* lieth *in* him " (Epistles, ix. 3).

This was the root principle of the Alchemists also, concealed in their chemical symbolism.   Thus the Arabian alchemist Abipili:

" I admonish thee, whosoever thou art, that desireth to dive into the inmost parts of nature; if that thou seekest thou findest not *within thee*, thou wilt *never find it without thee*. If thou knowest not the excellency of thine own house, why dost thou seek after the excellency of other things? . . . O MAN, KNOW THYSELF! IN THEE IS HID THE TREASURES OF TREASURES."[1]

And this also we say is the teaching of the New Testament when that teaching has been stripped of the " precepts and doctrines of men "; for this root " mystery " is the mystery of the " Christ in you " of St. Paul.

In the *Pistis Sophia* there is no mention of " salvation " by any " atonement " by blood sacrifice on the Cross.   It is only by a knowledge of the " Mysteries " that men can be raised out of this lower Kingdom of matter.   Thus Jesus says:

[1] Quoted from *Isis Unveiled*, ii, p. 617.

" Amen, amen, I say unto you: Even if a righteous man hath committed no sins at all, he cannot possibly be brought into the Light-Kingdom, because the sign of the Kingdom of the Mysteries is not with him. In a word, it is impossible to bring souls into the Light without the Mysteries of the Light-Kingdom " (m.p. 263).

And so, as aforesaid, the individual reincarnates again and again until such time as he may happily find such a body (such general circumstances and parents) " which will be good to find the signs of the mysteries of the Light."

Much might be written here as to the intermediate condition of the individual between one incarnation and another, but that is rather outside of our immediate subject. Suffice it to say that here also the *natural laws* of cause and effect hold good, and the man " goes " into that state of consciousness which is appropriate to the dominant note of his past earth-life as reflected in the actions, good or evil, which he has committed. There is a " heaven " for those whose dominant note was love; a " hell " for those whose dominant note was hate—and innumerable intermediate mixtures.

Doubtless for the great majority of professing Christians who might possibly read this Gnostic Scripture the *Pistis Sophia*, it would have no value as compared with the Canonical Gospels in their literal word and interpretation. It would probably appear to be merely a jumble of meaningless terms. But then, is not a symphony a mere jumble of sound for those who cannot penetrate the *idea* which the composer is endeavouring to express? For some of us the *Pistis Sophia* suggests *ideas* that lie too deep for words; ideas which are, indeed, *mysteries* which can in no wise be disclosed to the " uninstructed," or expressed by the intellect. They are the mysteries of the why and wherefore of this great manifested universe; mysteries of our outgoing from the ONE, and our return thereto; mysteries of our being and nature in its *oneness* with that ONE. Let me quote:

" O Mystery, which is without in the world, for whose sake the universe hath arisen—this is the total outgoing and the total ascent, which hath emanated all emanations and all that is therein and for whose sake all mysteries and all their regions have arisen—come hither unto us, for we are thy fellow-members. We are all with thyself; we are one and the same.   Thou (Jesus) art the First Mystery, which existed from the beginning in the ineffable before it came forth; and the name thereof are we all " (m.p. 16).

But how can we disclose to those who have no knowledge of the Gnosis—and who, indeed, in most cases do not *want* to have any such knowledge—the deeper laws of the universe and of our own being which is concealed in the allegories and symbolism of that Gnosis? Did not both Jesus and Paul find themselves up against this same inability to teach the deeper mysteries? Verse after verse might be quoted. But you must not tell those who are thus stubbornly ignorant that they *are* ignorant, otherwise they will turn again and rend you, even as the Jews crucified Jesus.

" God's wisdom is a mystery . . . which none of the rulers of this world knoweth; for had they known it, they would not have crucified the Lord of Glory " (1 *Cor*. ii. 7–8).

It is no different to-day. It has often been said that if Jesus were to come to-day, the Church would be first to reject him.

Nevertheless, there are to-day an ever-increasing number who, having already rejected the traditional Christian doctrines and dogmas, can approach this question of the existence of a real *Gnosis* (Knowledge of the Mysteries) with an open mind, and can catch some glimpse of those glorious heights of spiritual achievement to which the individual can rise through that knowledge, and to which he certainly will not rise without it.

For example, read in the *Pistis Sophia* of that " Vesture," that " Robe of Glory " which Jesus says that he left behind when he came down to earth, and which he is described in chapters three and ten as resuming. And having read that, try to realize—since, as just quoted, " we are all with thyself one and the same "—that each one of us possesses such a Robe of Glory but " left it behind " when we incarnated; and that what we must aim to achieve is to resume that " Robe " even here and now.[1] That " Robe " is what, in theosophical language, is called the " Higher Self "; or in

[1] See the quotation from *The Book of Dzyan* given on p. 121 *infra*, in which Man is said to " don his first clothing."

St. Paul's language, the " Christ in you." It is also that
body or " habitation which is from heaven " which he says
in 2 *Corinthians* v. 2 he "longs to be clothed with." It is the
spiritual " Buddhic " body which overshadows each individual, and which we have to bring into full manifestation
here and now, in *this* world, so that we ourselves become
Christs and Buddhas. This cannot be accomplished by any
mere profession of " belief " or " faith," as the *exoteric*
Christian doctrines teach. It can only be accomplished by
a real knowledge of what we *are*, both as separate personalities here in this lower world, and as being, on the higher
planes of the Cosmos and in our immortal *spiritual* nature,
one with " that subtle Being of which this whole universe is
composed."[1]

But we can only resume that " Robe " when, as in the
allegory of the crucified Christ, we also have " crucified " this
lower personal *self*, which we so constantly think of only as
separated from the ONE LIFE, or " God." Like Jesus, our
" resurrection " can only take place after our " crucifixion."
It is only then that the " Christ in us " can " rise from the
dead "—which things I say once more are, as represented in
the Scriptures, an allegory. But I will deal with this later on.

Let us see what some Scriptures and knowers of the Gnosis
have asserted concerning this higher *Self* in man.

" Verily he who hath seen, heard, comprehended, and known the
Self, by him is this entire universe known."[2]

And again:

" Him 'neath whose feet the mighty tide of days and years rolls past,
  In whom the five-fold host of things and space itself stands fast,
  Whom gods as light of lights adore, as immortality,
  The Brahman know I as my deathless Self, for I am he."[3]

And Chuang Tzu, 3rd century B.C., Chinese Mystic of the
School of Lao Tse:

" The perfect man is a spiritual being. Were the ocean itself scorched
up, he would not feel hot. Were the Milky Way frozen hard, he would

---

[1] See p. 65 *supra*.　　　　　　　　[2] *Brihad-aranyaka Upanishad*, ii. 4, 5.
[3] Ibid., iv. 4, 15, 16, 17.

not feel cold. Were the mountains to be riven with thunder, and the great deep to be thrown up by storm, he would not tremble."[1]

And from the Book of Hermes:

" Joined to the Gods by his cognate divinity, a man looks down upon the part of him by means of which he is common with the Earth."[2]

And Meister Eckhart:

" Now mark this well! I said of old, and say again, that I have now all that I shall possess eternally, for God in his felicity and in the fullness of his Godhead is enjoyed by my supernal prototype, though this is hidden from the soul " (in its present condition).[3]

In the Egyptian *Book of the Dead* the initiate who has thus learnt the nature of his real Self is said to realize his identity with Osiris, and he becomes the " Osirified one." Thus we have the following:

" I am the firstborn of the primeval God, and my Soul is the Soul of the Eternal Gods, and my body is everlastingness " (lxxxv).

" Hail, Lord of the Shrine which standeth in the middle of the earth. He is I, and I am he " (lxiv. 7, 8).

" I came into being from unformed matter (i.e. Primordial Substance). I came into existence like the god Khepera, I am of the germs of every god " (lxxxiii. 3, 4).

This, of course, is equivalent to the Kabalistic saying that man is the microcosm of the Macrocosm; or of Jacob Boehme's, " Man is the likeness (or similitude) of God; the great *Arcanum* lieth *in* him" (Epistles, ix. 8).

" There is no member of my body which is not the member of some god " (xlii. 10).

The " gods," though simply personifications of natural forces, we have also to consider as being differentiations of the ONE LIFE, and therefore in a certain sense as being *persons, Intelligences*; and as such they have at all times been worshipped by the ignorant populace. Again:

" I am Osiris, the lord of eternity " (xliii. 4).

" In very truth I am Rā himself " (xliv. 4).

---

[1] *Musings of a Chinese Mystic*, p. 86.   Wisdom of the East Series.
[2] *The Perfect Sermon*, vi. 1.   [3] *Meister Eckhart*, C. de B. Evans.

It is when we find these and similar sayings in such a variety of Scriptures, and at such remote and varying times, that we begin to realize the extent and universality of these teachings of the Ancient Wisdom or Gnosis. The Christian Scriptures belong to and teach that Gnosis; though in the form in which we have them they are overlaid with much that obscures and even appears to negative it.

The " higher criticism " to-day has destroyed the authority of the Christian Scriptures in their literal form, but has offered us nothing to replace that interpretation. We have to turn elsewhere for enlightenment as to the inner meaning of the " narratives of the doctrine "; and here we are fortunately not without guides. There is to-day a very large body of students of the ancient Gnosis and Mysteries from which these " narratives " are derived, and who are presenting to the world the results of their researches; nor are we without guidance from the present-day Adepts and Masters who belong to that Hierarchy of Initiates who have been for countless ages the custodians of this Ancient Wisdom. The principal body of these students is represented in the various Theosophical Societies, but there are many others also who are quite outside of those bodies, and who even look askance at them. Be that as it may, the principles upon which all are working are practically the same, and start from the same basis. That basis is, as I have already represented, the existence in all ages of a *Secret Doctrine* or *Gnosis*, wrapped up in allegory and symbol, the inner meaning of which was only disclosed to those who, as all great teachers have declared, were able or qualified to receive it.

It is no different to-day. There are thousands who are so uninstructed that they still cling to the literal interpretation of their Scriptures as given in the authorized version of the Bible; being, indeed, quite ignorant, and, in some cases, deliberately kept in ignorance by their teachers, who possibly, though not in every case, understand quite well the disputable nature and origin of that version.

The existence of the ancient Mysteries in Egypt, Greece, and elsewhere is of course well known as a matter of history; and many of the more *exoteric* ceremonies in connection with these have survived to this day in the ritual of Freemasonry and of the Church itself.[1]

What I wish, therefore, to emphasize now is this: that when we examine the Christian Scriptures in the light of this Ancient Wisdom we find that underlying the narrative we have a disclosure of the same fundamental principles concerning Man's origin and destiny which are given to us in many other forms in other Scriptures and by other great Teachers; so that it is not necessary to treat these Scriptures as being something *sui generis*, and superior to all other Scriptures, neither is it necessary to reject them as being in the nature of unbelievable fables.   The world has never been without those Teachers who have taught according to the capacity of their hearers to understand the great principles to which I now refer.

Instead, therefore, of regarding the Jewish and Christian documents as being the work of men inspired by the personal God therein represented, and whose character as there represented is surely too human to be accepted as anything but a concession to a people who could rise no higher in their ideas: we ascribe their authorship in the main, though by no means entirely, and certainly not as we have them in our authorized version, to that general body of teaching which I am here referring to as the Ancient Wisdom or Gnosis.

In the second place, I wish to represent that the *esoteric* interpretation which can be given in the light of that body of teaching has nothing to fear from those discoveries of science and of scholarship which are so perplexing to the defenders of the orthodox " faith "; but that, on the contrary, every such discovery goes to confirm the origin and interpretation which I am now outlining.

Let us now consider broadly what have always been the fundamental teachings of the Ancient Wisdom, and then proceed to trace it more in detail in the Canonical Scriptures.

---

[1] I commend here to the notice of students the work by the learned Egyptologist, Arthur Weigall, entitled *The Paganism in Our Christianity*.   Also the work by Edward Carpenter, *Pagan and Christian Creeds*.

CHAPTER III

THE ANCIENT WISDOM OR GNOSIS

In all ages of which we have any literary records we find the tradition of a recondite knowledge which could not be disclosed to any save to those who had undergone the severest tests as to their worthiness to receive it. This knowledge was very generally known under the term of the *Mysteries*, and it was concerned with the deepest facts of Man's origin, nature, and connection with supersensual worlds and beings, as well as with the " natural " laws of the physical world. It was no mere speculation; it was real knowledge, *Gnosis*, knowledge of " the things that are," knowledge of *Reality*; a knowledge which gave to its possessor powers which at one time or another have been regarded as pertaining only to the gods, and which are, indeed, widely denied to-day as possibilities of human achievement.

The basis of this knowledge, the fundamental principle on which all the teachings rested, was the essential inherent divine nature of man, and the consequent possibility of becoming by self-knowledge a god-like being. The final goal, the final objective of all the *Mysteries*, was the full realization by the Initiate of his divine nature in its oneness with the Supreme Being—by whatever name called—who IS the Universe in all its phases and in its wholeness and completeness.

Nowhere, as already stated, has this been more clearly set forth than in the ancient *Upanishads* of India.

" What that subtle Being is, of which this whole universe is composed, that is the Real, that is the Soul, That art Thou, O S'vetaketu " (*Chandogya Upanishad*, vi. 14, 3).

Also:

" Verily he who has seen, heard, comprehended, and known the Self, by him is this entire universe known " (*Brihad-aranyaka Upanishad*, ii, 4, 5).

It is my endeavour in this work to show that this teaching

is also fundamental in the Christian Scriptures, notwithstanding that Christian doctrine in its traditional form
separates eternally God and man as Creator and created, and
has no room for this super-knowledge of oneness. How it
appears in the Christian Scriptures will presently be
pointed out.

The broad outline of Man's nature, history, and destiny
according to the Mystery teachings is simply this: that Man
—Humanity as a whole—is one of a Hierarchy of Celestial
Beings, *emanated* " in the beginning " from the ONE. That
having to play his part in the great Cosmic Process, Spiritual
Man " descends into matter," and becomes the physical
race of beings as we now know him—or ourselves. But the
whole Cosmic Process being an outgoing from and a return
to the ONE, Man must inevitably return to his Source; he
must re-become that spiritual Being or Race which he' was
" in the beginning," but *plus* the knowledge gained by
his great pilgrimage through the manifested worlds of the
Cosmos.

This grand conception of the origin and destiny of Man,
that is to say of the Race as a whole, is the keynote of that
Ancient Wisdom or Gnosis which we shall presently endeavour
to trace in the Christian Scriptures, but which is not special
to those Scriptures, and indeed was taught ages before those
Scriptures came into existence. They only re-affirm it in a
certain form: a form which is mostly presented in allegory of
a semi-historical character.

But although the Race as a whole has thus " fallen into
matter " and physical generation, and has thereby entirely
lost sight of its divine origin, nature, and powers, we are
taught that certain individuals did not participate in this
" fall," but, retaining the full knowledge of their " divine
sonship," which they had acquired in previous evolutionary
experiences, they became the " divine instructors " of early
Humanity, and constituted the highest grade of that Hierarchy of Initiates who have always been the custodians of the
supreme knowledge or Gnosis. From time to time one of
these divine Instructors would incarnate, and would give to
the world in a form appropriate to the age and the race with

whom he had to deal some of those fundamental principles by an understanding of which the individual might be led to enter the real path of knowledge which would enable him to become an Initiate of the Mysteries, and to realize step by step his own divine nature and powers.

Now although the Race as a whole accomplishes this return process only through cycle after cycle of effort and renewed effort, extending over millions of years, in which, as we clearly see—even in the short period of a few thousands of years of which we have any records—nations and races have their birth, maturity, and death: yet there is always the possibility for the individual to step out in advance of the Race and achieve that real knowledge of his own nature and powers which liberates him from the " fate sphere " of this lower world of physical life. Indeed, it is only by such actual knowledge that he can be liberated. Until he has achieved that knowledge he is the helpless sport of cosmic laws which he can no more command than can the ignorant savage those physical laws which the civilized man utilizes to produce phenomena absolutely incomprehensible to the savage. Yet the " civilized " man, with all his modern science, has no real saving knowledge. He does not even know enough to save his fellows from the scourges of disease. His knowledge of physical laws is a mere surface knowledge, derived solely through his physical senses, and necessarily limited thereby. True, he is beginning to have some apprehension of the vast power of mind over matter, and a certain science of psychology is beginning to assert its importance in pathology and therapy; but here again he is only touching the fringe of a knowledge which has been taught in the *Mysteries* and in Eastern *Yoga* for untold ages.

I am merely tracing now in broad outline the fundamental teaching of this Ancient Wisdom or Gnosis, and the possibilities which it offers for the individual. The details will be filled in to some extent in subsequent chapters.

But so far as the individual is concerned in his connection with the Race, we must note here the fundamental teaching that the individual belongs to the Race from beginning to end of the great Cycle of outgoing and return. The Race is made up of the individuals, and it is only as the individuals progress that the Race as a whole can progress.

But how can this be accomplished if—as in the orthodox Christian teaching—the individual has only one life here on earth? How very very little the best of us can learn of our spiritual nature and powers in any one lifetime; whilst of millions it must be said that they not merely learn nothing at all, but are wholly given up to the pursuit of " the things of this world," which are precisely those which militate absolutely against that higher knowledge which alone can save them from " this ocean of incarnation and death."

How, then, does the Race progress through the progress of the individual—or, indeed, at times appears even to retrogress?

It does so because the individual comes back to earth, or *reincarnates* again and again after periods of rest, to take up the great task where he left off in his last incarnation. Death and rebirth are but a larger cycle of that process of sleep and reawakening which we experience in our present physical bodies. This is a fundamental teaching of the Ancient Wisdom, and it was taught in the Christian Church in the early centuries, but was subsequently made a heresy.

It is not possible here to go into details as to the working of this cyclic law, but some of these will appear in subsequent chapters of this work.

Returning now to the subject of initiation, and those " divine instructors " who are said to have guided early humanity, or who have appeared as *Avataras*[1] from time to time: we have what is perhaps the earliest tradition of these in the Egyptian records of a pre-dynastic line of Divine Kings, foremost among whom was Thoth, sometimes associated with Hermes, and afterwards identified as the Scribe and Recorder of the Gods.

In one of the chapters of the Egyptian *Book of the Dead*,[2]

---

[1] A Sanskrit word meaning the incarnation of some great spiritual being.

[2] *The Papyrus of Ani*, chapter cxxxviia, Budge's edition. *The Book of the Dead* is not the proper title of this Scripture. It is a conventional name for a collection of miscellaneous ritual texts of various periods, and used largely in connection with burial ceremonies. Copies of various parts are commonly found in mummy wrappings. Sir Wallis Budge translates the title as given

which is one of the records of the Ancient Wisdom, we are
told that it was " in the handwriting of the god (Thoth)
himself," and that it was discovered by Prince Herutātāf—a
son of Khufu the Great Pyramid builder, the second King
of the fourth dynasty—" in a secret coffer in the temple of
the goddess (Unnut)."

As a survival of the ideas associated with these pre-dynastic
Divine Kings, the dynastic Pharaohs were also regarded as
directly descended from the gods, and were accorded divine
honours; and doubtless the idea of the divine right of kings
which has come down to our own day is a survival of the same
tradition.

In India, again, or ancient Aryavarta, we have traditions
of the ancient Rishis and Avataras.   Persia, Chaldea, Babylon, China also, have similar traditions of divine Instructors;
and certain great names appear on the pages of history—
Krishna, Gautama Buddha, Sankaracharya, Zoroaster, Confucius, Lao-Tze—as being, if not all of them Avataras, at
least great Initiates in the supreme knowledge and wisdom.

But it is only when we come to the first five or six centuries
B.C., and to the palmy days of Greece and Alexandria, that
we obtain a definite knowledge of the existence of the Mystery
Schools, and of some of their more detailed teachings.   This
period is associated with such names as Anaxagoras, Pythagoras, Socrates, Plato, Aristotle, and later on, before the
dominance of ecclesiastical Christianity had suppressed the
Gnosis, and had plunged the Western world into the darkness
and horrors of the Middle Ages, we have such names as Philo
Judæus, Clement of Alexandria, Valentinus, Origen, Proclus,
Basilides, Iamblichus, and Plotinus,[1] all speaking openly of
the existence of the *Mysteries* and Mystery Schools, claiming
initiation therein, and openly teaching as much of it as it
was permitted for them to make public.

in the Rubric to chapter clxii as *The Book of the Mistress of the Hidden Temple.*
Marsham Adams gives it the title of *The Book of the Master of the Hidden
Places.*   It certainly deals in the main and *esoterically* with the Initiation
Mysteries, though *exoterically* it appears to deal principally with after-death
states.

[1] Hatch, in his work on *The Influence of Greek Ideas and Usages upon the
Christian Church*, remarks that " the true Gnostic, though he repudiates the
name, is Plotinus " (p. 132).

It was at this time that some part of the Ancient Wisdom became definitely known as the *Gnosis,* and its followers as *Gnostics,* though there were also other schools known by other names.

Here I might give the following quotation from the work of that great scholar Fabre d'Olivet.[1] It is from his best known work, *La Langue Hébraïque Restituée,* from which I give some further quotations later on. He is speaking of the ancient religions, and above all that of the Egyptians.

" They (these religions) were composed of a multitude of images and symbols admirably composed, the sacred work of an uninterrupted succession of divine men, who, reading page by page in the book of Nature and in that of Divinity, translated thus the ineffable language into that of the human. Those who regarded these sacred symbols and images as stupid, without seeing anything beyond them, stagnated, it is true, in ignorance, but their ignorance was voluntary. From the moment that they were willing to depart therefrom, they had only to speak. All the sanctuaries were open to them: and if they had the necessary constancy and virtue, nothing hindered that they should go from knowledge to knowledge, from revelation to revelation, even to the most sublime discoveries. They could, living and human, descend among the dead, rise even to the gods, and penetrate everywhere in elemental nature. For religion comprised all these things, and nothing of that which composed religion was unknown to the sovereign pontiff. He of the famous Egyptian Thebes, for example, only arrived at this culminating point of the sacred doctrine after having passed through all the inferior grades, having successively mastered all the science unfolded in each grade, and having been shown worthy to arrive at the most elevated " (vol. ii, p. 7).

Unfortunately for our knowledge of the Gnostic Schools of the pre-Christian and early Christian centuries, the fanatical dogma-makers, hereseologists, and " history " makers who ultimately gained the ascendancy in the " Christian " Church, destroyed every document which they could lay their hands upon which refuted or appeared to run counter to their interpretation of the mission and work of Jesus as a fulfilment of Old Testament narrative and supposed prophecy, literally and verbally. Is it not a fact that to this very day the central Christian doctrine of the Atonement rests on the acceptation

[1] He was a Chinese, Sanskrit, Hebrew, Phoenician, and Arabic scholar, and his method of reconstituting the Hebrew grammar was by comparing the roots of the words with those of other languages.

of the Garden of Eden story as literal history? When the evidence of the existence of their " history " in pre-Christian systems was too strong to be refuted, these creed-makers ascribed the fact to the subtlety of the Devil, who "plagiarized by anticipation." This theory appears to have originated with Justin Martyr. But Tertullian, writing probably about a century later, says of the rites of Baptism and the Eucharist:

" The Devil, whose business it is to pervert the truth, *mimics the exact circumstances* of the Divine Sacraments, in the Mysteries of idols. He himself baptizes some, that is to say, his believers and followers; he promises forgiveness of sins from the *Sacred Fount*, and thereby initiates them into the religion of Mithras; thus he *marks on the forehead* his own soldiers: there he celebrates the *oblation of bread*: he brings in the symbol of the Resurrection, and wins the crown with the sword. . . . Let us therefore acknowledge the craftiness of the Devil; who copies certain things of those that be Divine, in order that he may confound and judge us by the faithfulness of his own followers."[1]

By " his own followers " this fiery " Church Father " refers to the religion of Mithras, which was so closely associated with Christianity in the first few centuries. But must we not rather recognize *his* " craftiness " than that of the Devil, in endeavouring to make it appear that these rites were a *copy* of the Christian rites, whereas the real truth is that they were much older, and the " copy " is the other way about.

Even at the commencement of the last century, when the science of Geology was beginning to be understood, and the significance of the fossils as bearing upon the age of the world was seen to be inimical to the Genesis " history "—did we not even then find this same " plagiarizing " theory repeated, and the fossils declared to have been put there by the Devil in order if possible to refute the word of Scripture? To be a geologist at that time was looked upon as almost synonymous with being an atheist.

We have only fragments of many of the Gnostic Scriptures whose titles are known, these fragments having mostly been quoted, and often misrepresented, by the heresy-killing " Church Fathers " for the purpose of holding them up to ridicule. Thus in many cases the presentations of the Gnostic

[1] Quoted from King, *The Gnostics and Their Remains*, pp. 122–3.

teachings which we thus hear of are mere parodies of what we know from other sources must have been their real import. Chief among these hereseologists we must probably reckon Eusebius, and perhaps next to him Justin Martyr or Tertullian. They not merely misrepresented the Gnostic teachings, but did not hesitate to attribute base motives to the teachers. Thus, for example, Tertullian attributed the " apostasy " of Valentinus from the orthodox Church to his having been passed over in favour of another as a candidate for the Episcopacy.[1] Commenting on this we read in Smith and Wace's *Dictionary of Christian Biography*:

> " This narrative, it must be allowed, is, like so many other imputations of unworthy motives laid by the Fathers to the charge of their heretical opponents, subject to the suspicion of having been a malicious invention."[2]

Thus we see already, by the middle of the second century, the foundation laid for that bigotry, intolerance, and deliberate deception which reached its zenith in the dark ages of the dominance of the Church of Rome, and which prevails in certain quarters even to-day.

It is now beginning to be understood by scholars that the real Christology belongs to the Gnostic Schools, not to the Church " Fathers " who established the Hierarchical or Apostolic succession of Bishops and Popes; indeed, many of the Gnostics claimed to be the true Christians, and it was not until about the middle of the second century that the Christian Gnostics began to be definitely considered as heretics.

In the Introduction to the translation of the Gnostic work, *The Gnosis of the Light*[3] (*Codex Brucianus*), the Rev. F. Lamplugh writes as follows:

> " Recent investigations have challenged the traditional outlook and the traditional conclusions and the traditional ' facts.' With some to-day, and with many more to-morrow, the burning question is, or will be—not how did a peculiarly silly and licentious heresy rise within the Church—but how did the Church rise out of the Great Gnostic movement, how did the Dynamic ideas of the Gnosis become crystallized into Dogmas? "[4]

[1] *Adv. Valent.*, 4.   [2] Art. " Valentinus," vol iv, p. 1077.
[3] See Bibliography.
[4] This view is supported by Dr. J. C. McKerrow in his recent work, *Religion and History*.

But here it is necessary to utter a word of warning. In the first place, there are necessarily many stages, many degrees of initiation, and there always have been, even as there are to-day many Schools, many Societies or Communities which could take the aspirant a certain distance but no farther. Each of these would have a system of its own more or less specialized. Thus we hear among the Gnostic sects of the period we are now dealing with, of the Therapeuts, the Ebionites, the Essenes, the Ophites or Naassenes, the Valentinians, the Marcionites, etc., etc., to name only a few. The Marcionites are usually classified with the other Gnostic Sects, but we should hardly be inclined to grant them the title. The system of Marcion is very different not merely from those of the other Gnostic sects, but also from the fundamental principles of the Ancient Wisdom. It is doubtful whether any of these Orders can be considered as being more than alcoves, so to speak, in the outer courts of the Temple of Wisdom; capable, indeed, of giving a very necessary intellectual and moral training to the aspirant, but by no means able to give him that *practical* knowledge, that power to command the forces of nature, which the real Gnosis confers upon the *Master*.

Further, each of these main Groups of the Gnostics had sub-groups or sects who differed among themselves, just as the early Christians did, sometimes very radically, both in their fundamental teachings and in their interpretations of Scripture. Thus we have the following sects of the Ophites mentioned by Hippolytus: the Naassenes, the Peratae, the Sethians, and the Justinians. But though each Gnostic sect had a more or less well defined system of its own, Gnosticism as a whole was eclectic, like modern Theosophy, which is a revival of the Gnosis in many of its aspects.

Our point, however, is this, that all these *exoteric* communities and doctrines were merely *echoes* of the real inner Gnosis, the knowledge of the transcendental *Reality* underlying this world of *Appearances*, and which—as has been repeatedly stated by all great teachers, including Jesus and Paul—*cannot* be communicated to any but those who have undergone a special training, physical, mental, and moral, to receive it. Some, but by no means all, of this special preparation finds its way into the practices of these exoteric communities; and in general takes on the form of a more or less strict asceticism.

In the second place, there always have been, as there are to-day, spurious schools, professing to teach " Mysteries," or to confer powers, but which are mere pretensions and delusions. Many of the Gnostic Sects of the time to which we are now referring were of this nature, and were even debased and licentious. All, therefore, is not genuine Gnosis that goes by that name; just as to-day all is not " Occultism " that is so called. Moreover, it was an age of great superstition. Divination by astrology, by sacrifices, and by other means was common practice, and the sale of talismans and charms was a profitable business. This developed later on in the Christian Church into a worship of relics, which has continued to this day.

Most of the so-called Gnostic Schools or Sects were distinguished by an elaborate Cosmology or Æonology, the fundamental principle of which was a succession of emanations from the ONE of a series of Creative Powers in descending order, each having its appointed sphere of action in the economy of the Cosmos as a whole, from " Spirit " to " Matter." The names and functions of these Powers varied very considerably in different systems, and in many cases were associated with the most superstitious of beliefs and rites. Demons, antagonistic to God and to Man, figured very largely in some of them; but all this we must regard as excrescences on the true Gnosis, yet clearly taken over by the framers of the so-called " Christian " Creeds, who were themselves great believers in " demons." Eusebius, for example, constantly attributes all that was opposed to *his* Christianity to the work of demons. Even to-day the Roman Catholic Church denounces so-called Spiritualism as being of the Devil and his demons.

The Church Fathers who ultimately framed the Creeds were indeed incapable of understanding anything beyond the most materialistic concepts of " creation." They endeavoured to reduce everything to their flat-earth level.

What strikes one most, indeed, about these early creed-makers—as also about our modern orthodox Christians—is their utter lack of what we may call a *cosmic* sense. The whole history of Humanity was thought by them to be covered by a few thousand years, and the end of the world, when all the saints would go to heaven for ever and ever, and all the sinners to hell for ditto ditto, was confidently believed to be near at hand. The outlook on the world, not to speak of the Cosmos, was hardly even three-dimensional. It was limited to a superficies, both physically and mentally, both as regards history and the interpretation of Scripture. They had no conception of any third dimension in Scripture, let alone the consciousness of a fourth dimension in the Cosmos. In short, and to go to the root of the matter, our outlook on the Cosmos to-day is so totally different from that of those uninstructed creed-makers that we cannot conceive of the world as being either built or governed by such a God as they imagined to be its " Creator." Yet there are millions of Christians to-day whose outlook rises no higher than the level of these crude realists; and it is in the interests of a priestly caste to keep them at that level. Thus all doubt, all questioning, is with them a sign of " unbelief," and unbelief is the one deadly sin. As it was at the beginning of the formulation of the Christian Creeds, so it is to-day; the appeal of all the numerous sects and sections is still to the literal word of Scripture as the inspired mandate of " God," notwithstanding that the whole history of Humanity, both before and after the formulation of the Christian Creeds, falsifies their whole basis, let alone the history of the evolution of Religion itself as distinguished from that of any one religion in particular.

Yet the larger *cosmic* sense was prevalent ages before Christianity, and it may even be said to have been a distinctive feature of the communities and times in which Christianity appeared. Thus Dr. Angus in his work on *The Mystery Religions and Christianity*, to which I have already referred, says (p. x):

" Never was there an age which heard so distinctly and responded so willingly to the call of the *Cosmos* to its inhabitants. The unity of all Life, the mysterious harmony of the least and nearest with the greatest and most remote, the conviction that the Life of the Universe pulsated in all its parts, were as familiar to that ancient Cosmic Consciousness as to modern biology and psychology."

How came it about, then, that " Christianity " lost this cosmic consciousness, and has not merely been its bitter opponent all down the " Christian " centuries, but to-day finds itself the opponent of modern biology and psychology, not to speak of that revival of the Ancient Gnosis under the term *Theosophy*, of which this Cosmic Consciousness is a distinctive feature?

One of the characteristic teachings of the Ancient Wisdom or Gnosis is that of the existence of Hierarchies of " Builders," or subsidiary " Creators," graded from the Logos or Demiurgos downwards.   Hence the many systems of classification of these Hierarchies of Æons in some of the Christian Gnostic teachings.   The creed-makers rejected this concept with the exception of the Logos teaching; which, however, as is well known, they retained as being only applicable to the incarnation of the historical Jesus.

It is true that Christian doctrine tells us of Angels and Archangels, but these do not appear to have any real cosmological functions; they simply fulfil the behests of a *personal* God, who can be entreated by prayer to favour the individual, or to interfere in the course of nature for the benefit of a few individuals who either want to have rain, or who want the rain to cease, or who conceive themselves to be entitled to victory over their " Christian " enemies in battle, however *worldly* may have been the cause for which they have gone to war.   Yet, strange to say, this " God " appears at the same time to have no compunction in destroying at one fell swoop thousands of human beings by earthquake, tornado, fire, or flood.

We will not deny that there are " invisible helpers " who can and do protect the individual; but the individual must have earned the *right* to such protection; and: " All they that take the sword shall perish with the sword "—whereby, indeed, many more things than swords are implied, for this is simply a statement of the law of *Karma*.

It is, then, the great distinction of the Ancient Wisdom that its principles are *Cosmic*, in contradistinction to the narrow geocentric principles of the Christian doctrine, centred wholly on the things of this Earth and the " salvation " of a few favoured individuals thereon—witness the doctrine of " Grace " or " Election."

In the Ancient teachings Man and his Globe are regarded as a *cosmic unit*. As such, Man, Humanity as a whole, is merely one unit in the larger unit of the Solar System, with the Solar Logos as its informing Principle. Even our modern scientists are very far as yet from thinking cosmically as regards *Life*. They speculate as to whether there is " life " on the other Planets only as regards those physical *forms* of life which belong to this particular physical Globe, not understanding that LIFE is universal, and can and does have its appropriate forms in every state of " matter " in the manifested universe, both visible and invisible to the physical eye. Thus each Planet has, equally with the Earth, its appropriate unitary life as well as its appropriate physical forms of life. It is a unit in the larger cosmic unit of the Solar System. And since the Solar System is a unitary *Life*, Humanity and the Beings on these other units are linked in one evolutionary scheme and destiny, and also act and react on each other just as do the various organs of our individual physical bodies. This is the basis of the *real* science of Astrology, of which our modern astrologers have only a smattering. I shall give some further hints as to this cosmic outlook, and as to how the individual may achieve this genuine Gnosis, in my final chapter. Meanwhile it may be useful here to give the testimony of a first-century philosopher as to the existence of the supreme Hierarchy of Initiates to which I have referred, the nature of their lives, and their work in the world.

Philo Judæus, the learned Helenistic Jew, who was a contemporary of Jesus—but who, strange to say, never mentions him, although he taught the Logos doctrine—wrote as follows:

" Most excellent contemplators of nature and all things therein, they (the ancient sages) scrutinize earth and sea, and air and heaven, and the natures therein, their minds responding to the orderly motion of the moon and sun, and the choir of all the other stars, both variable and fixed.   They have their bodies, indeed, planted on earth below; but for their souls, they have made them wings, so that they speed through æther and gaze on every side upon the powers above, as though they were the true world-citizens, most excellent, who dwell in cosmos as their city; such citizens as Wisdom hath as her associates, inscribed upon the roll of Virtue, who hath in charge the supervising of the common weal. . . . Such men, though (in comparison) few in number, keep alive the covered spark of Wisdom secretly, throughout the cities (of the world), in order that Virtue may not be absolutely quenched and vanish from our human kind " (*De Sept.*, §§ 3, 4).

There are some magnificent lines from the Oracle of Apollo, quoted by Eusebius:

> " The path by which to Deity we climb,
>   Is arduous, rough ineffable, sublime;
>   And the strong massy gates thro' which we pass,
>   In our first course, are bound with chains of brass;
>   Those men the first who of Egyptian birth,
>   Drank the fair water of Nilotic earth,
>   Disclosed by actions infinite this road,
>   And many paths to God Phoenicians showed;
>   This road the Assyrians pointed out to view,
>   And this the Lydians and Chaldeans knew."[1]

At the close of the 18th century, Louis Claude de Saint Martin again disclosed the existence of this Hierarchy, and gave out some of their teachings.   The following are his words:

" For such an enterprise as that which I have undertaken more than common resources are necessary.   Without specifying those which I employ, it will be enough to say that they connect with the essential nature of man, and that they have always been known to some among mankind from the prime beginning of things, and that they will never be withdrawn wholly from the earth while thinking beings exist thereon. . . . The principles here expounded are the true key of all the allegories and all the mysterious fables, of every people, the primitive source of every kind of institution, and actually the pattern of those laws which direct and govern the universe, constituting all beings.   In other words, they serve as a foundation to all that exists and to all that operates, whether in man and by the hand of man, whether outside man and independently of his will.   Hence, in the absence of these principles there can be no real science, and it is by reason of having

[1] Quoted by Mary Ann Atwood in her work *A Suggestive Inquiry into the Hermetic Mystery*, p. 181.

forgotten these principles that the earth has been given over to errors. But although the light is intended for all eyes, it is certain that all eyes are not so constituted as to be able to behold it in its splendour. It is for this reason that the small number of men who are depositories of the truths which I proclaim are pledged to prudence and discretion by the most formal engagements."[1]

In the last quarter of the 19th century these teachings or " principles " were again put forward, but in much greater detail, by another messenger of the Hierarchy, Mme H. P. Blavatsky, and became known all over the world and very widely accepted under the term *Theosophy*.[2]

One of the great Teachers behind this modern movement writes as follows of the great Hierarchy of Initiates:

" For countless generations hath the adept builded a fane of imperishable rocks, a giant's Tower of INFINITE THOUGHT, wherein the Titan dwelt, and will yet, if need be, dwell alone, emerging from it but at the end of every cycle, to invite the elect of mankind to co-operate with him and help in his turn enlighten superstitious man. And we will go on in that periodical work of ours; we will not allow ourselves to be baffled in our philanthropic attempts until that day when the foundations of a new continent of thought are so firmly built that no amount of opposition and ignorant malice guided by the Brethren of the Shadow will be found to prevail " (*Mahatma Letters to A. P. Sinnett*, p. 51).

It is necessary to distinguish very clearly between the positive knowledge of an *Initiate* of the Mysteries and what is more generally known nowadays as *Mysticism*. It is true that broadly speaking both have the same end, the same goal and achievement in view, i.e. union with the Supreme, the ONE. But the means of achieving that union is totally different in the two cases. The Initiate climbs carefully that " arduous path " which leads to the final goal; making sure of the ground beneath his feet at each upward stage. This he does by learning the laws which govern the various " planes " of the universe. He learns to conquer and command on each plane in succession. First of all he learns the

[1] *Des Erreurs et de la Vérité*, part I, pp. 5, 6, 7, 8, 10, Edition 1782.
[2] Since these teachings were first given out in the work of Mme Blavatsky, there has been a great deal of spurious " Theosophy " put forward by other writers, and a good deal of discrimination needs to be exercised in dealing with these later pronouncements.

laws of the physical plane and of his own physical nature, so
that he has absolute command of his physical body, at a
later stage he can prolong his life indefinitely.   Next he learns
the laws and conquest of the etheric or " astral " plane.   He
learns to command the semi-intelligent beings, or " elementals " as they are sometimes called, which have their
existence and function in the inner invisible plane.   He
learns also the use of his own astral body, and how to function
in that independently of his physical body.   Then there are
still higher planes on which to function consciously, so that,
as Philo says, " they speed through the æther and gaze on
every side upon the powers above."   We have no language
in which to describe these higher planes, or the laws which
operate there.   Indeed, we have scarce language to describe
the laws and conditions of that next plane above the physical,
i.e. the " astral," some phenomena of which are being forced
upon the attention of the community to-day in so-called
spiritualistic phenomena, and which are the subject in a more
or less scientific manner of psychical research.

But now, how fares it with the *mystic*?   In the first place,
and as a rule, instead of having and cultivating a perfect
physical body, he is more or less of a physical wreck and a
neurotic, even when he does not deliberately torture and
macerate his body, as so many Christian mystics have done.
He has little or no knowledge of any of the laws of nature;
indeed, he cares nothing for them.   He is wholly concerned
with the effort to *force* an ecstatic state of consciousness of
blissful union with the Supreme.   This he does achieve; it is
the universal testimony of all mystics of whatever age, clime,
or religion, that this supreme consciousness of *union*, or
oneness, can be and is achieved.[1]   But it is only achieved
sporadically.   It is only achieved as a kind of emotional
tour de force—at least we must say this of the great majority
of religious mystics.   It is true there have been also some
philosophical mystics who have achieved this supreme
experience in a less forceful and more rational manner.
Plotinus, for example, writes of the " flight of the alone to
the alone," and is said to have achieved it four times during

[1] See the quotation from Wm. James on p. 65 *supra*.

his life. But the ordinary religious mystic not merely fails to conquer the ground as he proceeds, but his forced flight generally results in that terrible reaction in the opposite direction known as " the dark night of the soul."

We have seen that the real knowledge which was to be learnt in the *Mysteries* was a carefully guarded secret; and, indeed, the penalty for any disclosure of it was death. In his work on *The Mystery Religions and Christianity*, Dr. Angus says (p. 78):

> " An awful obligation to perpetual secrecy as to what was said and transacted behind closed doors in the Initiation proper was imposed—an obligation so scrupulously observed through the centuries that not one account of the secrets of the holy of holies of the Mysteries has been published to gratify the curiosity of historians."

What, then, do we learn in any of those Gnostic teachings which have been more or less openly given to the world?

Apart from the invariable *moral* teachings, we find in general a cosmology and anthropology set forth in a symbolical manner. How, indeed, can things which are *super*-physical be set forth otherwise than by some kind of analogy with things physical?

When we are told, for example, in the first chapter of *Genesis* that " the spirit of God moved (or was brooding upon) the face of the waters," we are using symbolism and analogy; and many other different kinds of symbolism have been used in different systems for this first beginning of things. One of the commonest and most universal of these has been that of the " world-egg "; the process being likened to the gradual differentiation of the substance of the egg (Primordial Substance) from the fructified germ-cell. We have a reflection, indeed, of this symbolism in the alternative reading of the passage just quoted, " the spirit of God was *brooding* upon the face of the waters." Water also has been commonly used as the symbol for Primordial Substance. A vivid light has been thrown upon this ancient symbolism in its many various forms by Mme H. P. Blavatsky in her great work *The Secret Doctrine*.

These cosmological systems are so numerous and varied in their *exoteric* forms that we need a synthesizing key whereby we may recognize a similarity of teaching underlying them all; and this key is given to us in the work just referred to.

When once we have that key, we can trace a uniformity of teaching running like a thread of gold through all the ancient Scriptures, myths, and allegories. They all teach the same principles as regards the great World-Process and Man's connection therewith—MAN, outgoing from the ONE, a " Divine Son "; descending into Matter—that is to say, participating in the great Cosmic Process—and thereby losing the consciousness of his divine nature and sonship, but finally turning back to his " Father's home," gradually regaining the lost consciousness of his spiritual nature and powers by a quickening of the latent " divine spark," the " Christ *in* you " of St. Paul, and so in due course becoming the Initiate, the Master, the Christos, the Buddha.

It being my endeavour in this work to show how this fundamental teaching of the ancient Wisdom or Gnosis is embodied in the Christian Scriptures, let us first of all examine what we are told in *Genesis* of the beginning of things.

CHAPTER IV

THE GENESIS NARRATIVE

I AM dealing principally in this work with the interpretation of the New Testament Scriptures, but it is necessary in the first instance to glance at the *Genesis* narrative as to the creation of the world and of Man; as to his first estate in the " Garden of Eden "; and as to his " Fall." The fundamental Christian doctrine of the Atonement is based on this narrative as being literal history, and in fact the whole structure of Christian doctrine is based on this *Jewish* cosmogony in the first instance, and on the belief that this and the subsequent history of Man as given in *Genesis* and the other books of the Pentateuch are a special divine revelation of what had not been, and could not have been, otherwise known.

I have sometimes been told when I have referred to this *literal* acceptation of the *Genesis* narrative that nobody accepts it literally to-day; but that is not so. It is still the orthodox teaching—not to mention the " Fundamentalists." There are several writers who profess to give you the exact date of Adam; while the location of the Garden of Eden as a geographical place is still believed in or speculated upon by the great majority of professing Christians.

If, then, the narrative is not to be taken literally, if it is *allegory* pure and simple, what is the *esoteric* interpretation thereof?

Before that question can be answered we must have a clear understanding of some fundamental principles, and more particularly of what is involved in any statement whatsoever which can be made about the *commencement* of a manifested universe: that is to say, of what is involved in the words " In the Beginning."

Observe in the first place that we have to distinguish between the *manifested* and the *unmanifested*.

The manifested implies that there is an unmanifested; in other words, it implies not merely a *Cause* which is concealed as a *Source* of the manifested which is perceived, but also which existed before the manifested came into existence.

Even from a purely physical point of view we know that there are subtle planes of Substance—the Ether in the first instance—which are extremely active as causes of physical phenomena. The *activities* of the substance of these more subtle planes are certainly *things* on their own plane—etheric waves for example—which can conceivably be objects of perception did we but possess the necessary faculties to perceive them, while psychology shows us—apart from the more definite teachings of occult science—that super-physical faculties do exist and sometimes come into play whereby perception *is* obtained on these superphysical planes, though for the most part these faculties are latent in the great majority of individuals. Moreover we may be said to have definite evidence that we actually possess " bodies " composed of the substance of these planes; and though it is difficult for the ordinary individual to conceive of a " body " of any other sort than that which is composed of physical matter, there is no inherent difficulty when the matter is fully thought out—and more particularly with our new knowledge of the extreme tenuousness of physical matter—of conceiving that modes or forms of motion can be " atoms " on these more subtle planes of substance, and that these " atoms " can just as well combine to form " bodies " there as here on this physical plane. To the possessor of such a body, and with his consciousness acting in or through that body, the objects or *things* on that plane will be as real and " solid " as are the things on this our present plane of perception. In fact, and very briefly, the One homogeneous Root Substance can differentiate into any number of conceivable *forms*—which are simply *modes of motion* in or of that Substance—which we may conceive of as increasing in complexity in a descending scale of which physical matter is *for us* the " lowest."

There is a profound Eastern doctrine of Illusion, *Maya*, concerning the nature of these externally cognized planes or " worlds." Briefly, the mind as *subject* creates its own *objective* world. Our most familiar experience of this is in dreams, but psychology also gives us many examples of similar projections of subjective thought forms as a visible object when in the waking state: though these are commonly referred to as " hallucinations."

Well, what if from the point of view of the ONE REALITY—or shall we say the *Logos*—this whole *manifested* universe is such a projection?—the " Eternal Thought in the Eternal Mind " projecting Itself to Itself as a (temporary) *object*, which may be said both to have and not to have a " reality " of its own.

The whole aim of Eastern *Yoga* has for its object the transcending of the *illusion* of the objective world in a knowledge of the real nature of the SELF as being the ONE, the birthless and deathless *Cause* of all that ever has or can exist as a *manifested* universe. This realization of the SELF is called in Hinduism and in Buddhism *Nirvana.* It has been supposed by some writers to mean extinction of consciousness, total annihilation. Well, in one sense it is that; but what is extinguished is the illusion of a separate personal self as distinct from the ONE SELF. Sir Edwin Arnold in *The Light of Asia* has well put it in a single phrase:

" Foregoing self, the Universe grows ' I.' "

This is a profound teaching which has many aspects, and which is dealt with in many ways in Eastern Scriptures. I shall hope to show, however, that it comes into line with the *esoteric* interpretation of the New Testament Scriptures also, though it is certainly too profound for the ordinary Christian who only reads those Scriptures *exoterically.* I do not think, however, that it is too profound for those to whom this work is more particularly addressed.

Mr. Edmond Holmes, in his useful and stimulating work *Self-Realization,* puts the difference between the ordinary idea of the *self* and this deeper philosophy of the *Self* very clearly in the following words (p. 54):

" This philosophy (of the *Self*) makes great demands on those who accept its teaching. If we would be true to the spirit of it we must rid our minds of two great delusions—the delusion of the intrinsic reality of the material world and the delusion of the intrinsic reality of the individual self. These two delusions are, as it happens, the fundamental assumptions which underlie the philosophy of popular thought. The average man takes for granted the reality of his own individual self, of his self as it is known to him; and, having placed himself (as so interpreted) at the centre of the Universe, he guarantees reality, on the one hand to the world which he looks out upon and which he miscalls Nature, and on the other hand to the magnified and glorified replica of himself which he miscalls God. And as he knows of no degrees in reality, the guarantees that he gives are absolute, not relative; final, not provisional. The characteristic features of this philosophy are dualism, staticism, the logic of Yes *or* No, a God who takes sides, a legalistic morality, the pursuit of the minimum, salvation through machinery.

" The philosophy of the Upanishads, like the philosophy of popular thought, takes the reality of the self for granted and places it at the centre of the Universe. But it is a different self. It is a self which transcends our experience of self; a self whose depths and heights, whose mysteries and secrets are unknown, a self with limitless possibilities; a self in whose all-embracing being there is room for Nature, for Man, and for God. ' What that subtle being is, of which the whole universe is composed, that is the real, that is the soul, that are thou, O S'vetaketu.'[1]

" By comparison with this inner self, which is at once the spirit of God, and the soul of Nature, and the soul of the soul, the self of the self of man, the outer or material world is unreal. . . . Our assumption that it is in itself what it seems to be when we perceive it is gratuitous and fallacious."

This touches the whole matter as between Appearance and Reality, as between a common or crude realism and an idealism which penetrates beneath the mere appearance of things. In the Christian Scriptures it is the difference between the *exoteric* and the *esoteric* interpretation.

F. H. Bradley, in his classical work *Appearance and Reality*, speaks as follows of the common idea of the *self* (p. 75):

" A man commonly thinks that he knows what he means by his self. He may be in doubt about other things, but here he seems to be at home. He fancies that with the self he at once comprehends both that it is and what it is. And of course the fact of one's own existence, *in some sense*, is quite beyond doubt. But as to the sense in which this existence is so certain, there the case is far otherwise. . . . So far is the self from being clearer than things outside us that, to speak generally, we never know what we mean when we talk of it."

Now what we have to realize is simply this, that the whole of Religion—as distinguished from *a* religion—and in fact

[1] *Chandogya Upanishad*, vi. 14, 8.

the whole of our life-experience through cycle after cycle and incarnation after incarnation, and whether as religion or otherwise, is an effort of self-realization which can only find its goal, its term, its consummation in a return to that ONE REALITY from which it has *apparently* gone out, but from which in *reality* it has never been separated.

The *Genesis* narrative deals with this apparent *going out,* or the separation of the *manifested* universe from the *unmanifested* Reality. Our authorized version commences with the words " In the beginning." Let us see what is meant by the " beginning."

I have already referred to the fact that there are, according to the esoteric teaching, an endless succession of periods of manifestation or objectivity succeeded by periods of withdrawal into the ONE unmanifested ROOT CAUSE.[1] The " beginning," therefore, is the commencement of one of these periods of out-going; the beginning of a *Manvantara*, or " Day of Brahma."

Now in using the word *Beginning* we are introducing the concept of *time*; and time, like space also, is part of that mind-created illusion which, in our present consciousness, takes the form of an *objective* world. The ROOTLESS-ROOT, the ONE, the ABSOLUTE is beyond time and space; IT is timeless and spaceless: in short, ETERNAL.

But here, again, we must guard against a misconception. *Eternity* is no mere extension of " time," either backwards or forwards. It is not *extension* at all. It is non-existence of these creations of the mind which we call " time " and " space." It is the mind—the Cosmic Mind, the Logos, in the first instance—which projects its own content as an *objective* universe, and this, reflected into the individual mind, is spread out, so to speak, in time and space. The Eternal Thought in the Eternal Mind is timeless and spaceless. Did not Plato enunciate this quite clearly in his doctrine of innate or archetypal *Ideas*? We shall see presently that this is also to be found in the opening verses of the first chapter of *Genesis* when that is more literally translated from the Hebrew.

[1] See p. 27 *supra.*

Nothing is more foolish in Christian teaching, nothing discloses more clearly its naïve ideas and utter lack of a sound
philosophical basis than the distinction which it makes
between " time " as being this our present life, and " eternity "
as being an endless continuation of that life after physical
death, while at the same time it conceives of the individual
as *commencing* his existence when he is physically born.   It
has no teaching of the pre-existence of the soul.

It is a fundamental axiom which must be clearly grasped
if we would pass beyond the crude realism which regards
things as being what they *appear* to be, that *what begins in
time must end in time*.   Since, then, in any cosmogony which
commences with the words " In the Beginning," or with any
equivalent words, we are introducing the concept of *time*,
we must be prepared to treat what follows as a *time-process*
which must have an ending as well as a beginning.   It is the
great World-Process, spread out as it were as a panorama, a
cinematograph projection in time and space—or space-time,
shall we say.   We call this process to-day " evolution " and
" involution "; the outgoing and the return.   In the Cosmic
Mind, the Mind of the Logos, it exists archetypally as one
complete Whole, just as in the mind of the artist the picture
exists as a complete whole before he spreads it out in time
and space as an *object* on his canvas.   The canvas may be
destroyed—will be destroyed—but the Eternal Thought in
the Eternal Mind—and the artist's thought is only a reflection
of that—remains.

Our universe—only one of innumerable universes—is but a
single thought in the incomprehensible ALLNESS of the
Eternal ONE.   Man, the microcosm, did he but know it, is a
reflection of the Macrocosm: even as Jacob Boehme, and
many an ancient philosopher and seer before him, had clearly
perceived.   " The book in which all mysteries lie is man
himself. . . . The great Arcanum lieth *in* him."[1]

" In the Beginning."   What was there, then, before the Beginning ? "

There was THAT which is neither Being nor Non-Being,
and can therefore only be described in negatives.

[1] See p. 86 *supra*.

There are several ancient Scriptures which commence their cosmogony with some statement as to the pre-existence of the *unmanifested* ONE. Even in the *Genesis* account as given in our authorized version we have an indication of this:

" The earth was waste and void; and darkness was upon the face of the deep (the ' waters ' of space); and the spirit of God (the as yet *unmanifested deity*) moved upon the face of the waters."

I will comment upon this more fully presently, but let us first of all see what some other Scriptures say.

In what is perhaps the oldest known Scripture in the world, the *Rig Veda* (x. 19), we have the following, which may be best given in the beautiful verse translation by Colebrook:

" Nor Aught nor Nought existed; yon bright sky
Was not, nor heaven's broad roof outstretched above.
What covered all? what sheltered? what concealed?
Was it the water's fathomless abyss?
There was not death—yet there was nought immortal,
There was no confine betwixt day and night;
The only One breathed breathless by Itself,
Other than It there nothing since has been.
Darkness was there, and all at first was veiled
In gloom profound—an ocean without light—
The germ that still lay covered in the husk
Burst forth, one nature, from the fervent heat.

·   ·   ·   ·   ·

Who knows the secret? who proclaimed it here?
Whence, whence this manifold creation sprang?
The Gods themselves came later into being—
Who knows from whence this great creation sprang?
THAT, whence all this great creation came,
Whether Its will created or was mute,
The Most High Seer that is in highest heaven,
He knows it—or perchance even He knows not."

We might note here in this earlier Scripture several correspondences with *Genesis*—for example: " Nor Aught nor Nought existed "; " The earth was waste and void "; " Darkness was there " ... " an ocean without light "; " And darkness was upon the face of the *deep*." " The spirit of God "; " THAT."

From the *Veda* we might turn to the *Upanishads*. Here

we have again as in *Genesis* several references to " water " as being the primal condition of the universe before manifestation. " Water " we may consider as being either abstract *Space*, or as *Primordial Substance* practically indistinguishable from Space. Thus in the *Brihad Upanishad* we have (v. 5. 1):

" In the beginning this world was just Water. That Water emitted the Real—Brahma (being) the Real—; Brahma, Prajāpati; Prajāpati, the gods."

Note here, also, that " the gods came later into being." In the above, Brahma is the first Being out of Non-Being. Prajāpati is a secondary creative Being who emits or emanates the " gods "—which term includes " devils." Thus in *Brihad* i. 3. 1 we read:

" The gods (*deva*) and the devils (*asura*) were the twofold offspring of Prajāpati." In the same *Upanishad*, v. 2. 1, we read:

" The threefold offspring of Prajāpati—gods, men, and devils (*asura*) —dwelt with their father Prajāpati as students of sacred knowledge (*brahmacārya*)."

Clearly we must here disabuse our minds of the popular idea as to the nature of devils.

In the *Chandogya Upanishad*, i. 9. 1, we find " space " used instead of " waters."

" Verily all things here arise out of space. They disappear back into space, for space alone is greater than these; space is the final goal."

We must always look for the abstract *Principle* behind all the various terms which are used to *symbolize* it. In this quotation " space " is once more used to signify the abstract undifferentiated primal ONE, which is neither Being nor Non-Being. Later on in this Upanishad, however, we read, vi. 2. 1:

" In the beginning, my dear, the world was just Being (*sat*), one only, without a second. To be sure, some people say: ' In the beginning this world was just Non-being (*a-sat*), one only, without a second; from that Non-being Being was produced.' "

The speaker then goes on to contest the idea that Being

could arise from Non-being. This we may grant in the ordinary use of the two terms as signifying opposites or contrasts as understood by the *intellect*; but, as previously said, we should consider the ONE, the ABSOLUTE, to be beyond all these duality concepts of the intellect, and therefore as being neither Being nor Non-Being—and yet both. *Sat*, we might say, is rather Be-ness than Being.

When we turn from the Hindu philosophy to that of the Egyptians as contained in the *Book of the Dead*, we find again the same conception of one primal Being from whom everything manifested comes forth, and of " water " as that which existed as the primal state: This " water " is called *Nu*. Thus Sir Wallis Budge in the Introduction to his edition of the *Papyrus of Ani*, vol. i, p. 171, says:

" The story of the Creation is entitled ' The Book of knowing how Rā came into being,' and is told by the god Nebertcher, the Everlasting God of the Universe. Where and how this god existed is not said, but it is clear that he was supposed to have created himself and to be self-existent. The desire to create the heavens and the earth arose in his heart, or mind, and he assumed the form of the god Khepera, who from first to last was regarded as a form of Nu, or the Creator *par excellence*. At this time nothing existed except the vast mass of Celestial Waters which the Egyptians called Nu, and in this existed the germs of all living things that subsequently took form in heaven and on earth, but they existed in a state of inertness and helplessness."

We can easily recognize in this latter sentence, in the " germs," the archetypal *Ideas* of Plato, and, as we shall see presently, a correspondence with a similar concept in the first verse of *Genesis*. Khepera is here, as the *creative* god, the Demiurgos, or Logos. He is sometimes identified with the god Rā. In a *Hymn to Rā* we read:[1]

" 'Thou art the God One who came into being in the beginning of time. Thou didst create the earth, thou didst fashion man '—and so on with other ' creations.' "

Note here, again, the beginning of *time*. The god Rā, as a *personal* god, only comes into existence with *time*, like all the rest in this *phenomenal* universe.

[1] Budge, *The Book of the Dead*, p. 4.

In the *Book of the Dead*, as in the *Veda*, " the gods came later into being." Thus in chapter xvii we have:

" Who, then, is this?
" It is Rā, the creator of the name(s) of his limbs, which came into being in the form of the gods who are in the train of Rā."

Also in a *Hymn to Rā*:

" Homage to thee, O thou who hast come as Khepera, Khepera the creator of the Gods."[1]

In another passage in *The Book of the Dead of Nesi-Khonsu* we read:

" Khepera who createth every evolution of his existence, except whom at the beginning none other existed; who at the dawn of primeval time was Atennu, the prince of rays and beams of light; who having made himself (to be seen, caused) all men to live."[2]

But we find in this Papyrus a still deeper metaphysical concept of this God. He is *manifested* in his creations, but yet he remains the ever-concealed Cause.

" The god Khepera who is unknown and who is more hidden than the (other) gods, whose substitute is the divine Disk; the unknown one who hideth himself from that which cometh forth from him . . . who maketh decrees for millions of double millions of years, whose ordinances are fixed and are not destroyed, whose utterances are gracious, and whose statutes fail not in his appointed time."

Do the Hebrew Scriptures show any higher conception of " God " than that?

We might find similar concepts and symbolisms in many other cosmogonies, those of Babylon, Assyria, and Chaldea, for example; but what I have here given is sufficient to show that underlying all these varied accounts of " Creation " there are to be found certain fundamental concepts which are common to all; and it is these concepts, we say, which constitute the Ancient Wisdom or Gnosis from which they one and all derive.

Before I leave these cosmogonies, however, I must refer to the very latest exposition of this ancient doctrine as given to us last century in that astonishing work by Mme H. P. Blavatsky,

[1] Budge, *The Book of the Dead*, p. 4.   [2] Ibid., p. 651.

The Secret Doctrine. Here we have in the first instance some
magnificent Stanzas from *The Book of Dzyan*—a work not
as yet known to our scholars.   It describes in greater detail
than any other Scripture the successive stages in the evolution of the universe; and secondly it gives a voluminous and
learned commentary on the Stanzas, and on ancient myths
and fables in their relation to the Wisdom-Religion.

Let me quote from the first Stanza describing the pre-
existing state before the evolution of the manifested world
commenced, of which I have just given some descriptions
from other Scriptures.   I omit some of the Slokas.

" 1. The Eternal Parent (Space) wrapped in her ever invisible robes
had slumbered once again for seven eternities.

" 2. Time was not, for it lay asleep in the infinite bosom of duration.

" 3. Universal Mind was not, for there were no Ah-hi (Celestial Beings)
to contain it.

" 5. Darkness alone filled the Boundless All, for Father, Mother, and
Son were once more One, and the Son had not awakened yet for the
new Wheel (*Manvantara*, or period of Manifestation), and his pilgrimage
thereon.

" 7. The causes of existence had been done away with; the visible
that was, and the invisible that is, rested in eternal Non-Being—the
One Being.

" 8. Alone the one form of existence stretched boundless, infinite,
causeless in dreamless sleep; and life pulsated unconscious in universal
space, throughout that all-presence which is sensed by the opened eye
of the Dangma (the inner spiritual eye of the perfected Seer)."

The agreement of this with what I have already illus-
trated from other Scriptures will readily be seen, so let us
turn now to the *Genesis* narrative and note the correspondences therein.

It must already have been seen that the *Genesis* narrative
or cosmogony is only *one* of numerous others, all dealing with
certain fundamental principles of the Ancient Gnosis, but in
a more or less incomplete and broken manner; but who is
there who can maintain in the face of these other records
which I have so briefly indicated, that the *Genesis* narrative
is the one and only God-revealed account as to how the world
and Man came into existence?   Humanity has never been
without its Divine Instructors, who have taught *esoterically*

to those able to receive the " Wisdom in a mystery," but *exoterically* only, and mostly in allegory and myth, to the masses. Whether it was Moses or some other *Initiate* who originally wrote the *Genesis* cosmogony, it most evidently derives from the Ancient Wisdom source.

I cannot stay to deal with the more recondite meaning which lies behind the real Hebrew text, so very incorrectly translated in our English version, as for example the difference in the names given to the Deity in the first and second chapters, and representing different stages in the evolutionary process, but believed by most Christians to be one and the same person. Readers must be referred to the *Kabala* for these more recondite meanings. Very broadly, however, the esoteric interpretation is as follows:

Man, the Human Race—the Adam of *Genesis*—is one of the great Hierarchies of Celestial Beings emanating from the ONE " In the Beginning." In his first estate in the " Garden of Eden " he was a " heavenly " being, wholly *spiritual* in his nature. He contained within himself the potentiality of what was to be *his* world. He had " dominion " (chapter i. 26) over the whole of that " creation." In this state also he was innocent of any knowledge of that duality which constitutes for us what we call " good and evil." It is represented that he could only acquire that knowledge by eating the fruit of " the tree of the knowledge of good and evil." But this is anticipating somewhat. Let us see first of all in what manner the cosmogenesis is set forth.

" The spirit of God moved (or was brooding) upon the face of the waters."

Here the " waters," as we have already seen in other cosmogonies, are the Primordial Substance, indistinguishable from Space, fecundated by the moving (or brooding) Spirit.

Fabre d'Olivet, the learned author of *Le Langue Hébraïque Restituée*, translates these first verses as follows (vol. ii, p. 25 ff.):

" 1. AT-FIRST-IN-PRINCIPLE, he-created, Ælohîm, the-selfsameness-of-heavens, and-the-selfsameness-of-earth.

" 2. And-the-earth was contingent-potentiality in-a-potentiality-of-being: and-darkness-was-on-the-face of-the-deep and-the-breath of-HIM-the-Gods was-pregnantly-moving upon-the-face-of-the-waters,

" 3. And-he-said HE-the-Being-of-beings: there-shall-be light; and-there-became light.

" 4. And-he-did-ken, HE-the-Gods that-light as good; and-he-made-a-division HE-the-Gods, betwixt the-light-and-betwixt the-darkness."

Let us see what this means.

Fabre d'Olivet is careful to explain that he makes no endeavour to read any theological or other interpretation into the text, but that he translates strictly in conformity with the meaning of the Hebrew words and grammar as given in vol. i. of his work.

Now the first word is BERÆSHITH, and this, as will be seen, he translates " at-first-in-principle," whereas our English version gives it as " In the beginning." But " at-first-in-principle " means simply *archetypal*; and it strikes the key-note of the whole first chapter which differs so radically from the account given in the second chapter.

In the first place: the God-name is different in the two chapters. In the first it is Ælohîm, whereas in the second, from the fourth verse onwards, it is IHÔAH Ælohîm.

In the second place: in the first chapter (verse 26), " Man " is said to have been created after all the other creations, whereas in the second chapter (verse 7) he is created first of all. Fabre d'Olivet translates these two verses as follows:

(Chapter i. 26): "And-he-said, HE-the-Gods, We-will-make *Adam* in-the-shadow-of-us, by-the-like-making-like-our-selves: and-they-shall-hold-the-sceptre, in-the-spawn breeding-kind of-the-seas, and-in-the-flying-kind of-the-heavens, and-in-the-quadrupedly-walking-kind, and-in-the-whole-earth-born-life, and-in-all-moving-things crawling-along upon-the-earth.

(Chapter ii. 7): "And-he-formed IHÔAH, HE-the-Being-of-beings, the-selfsameness of-*Adam*, by-rarefying of-the-adamick; and-he-inspired into-the-inspiring-faculty-of-him, a-being-exalted of-the-lives, for-being-made Adam according-to-the-soul of-life."

Fabre d'Olivet has a great deal to say about the root-meaning of the word Adam, but it must suffice us here to say that he interprets it as " original similitude, collective unity, universal man." It is, in fact, the *prototype* of Man (Humanity collectively). It is the " Heavenly Man," the Logos, the Cosmic Christ, who *remains*, notwithstanding the creation—emanation rather—of the lower earth man.[1] Jesus, speaking as this " Man," says (*John* viii. 58): " Verily, verily, I say unto you, Before Abraham was (born), I am." We shall obtain more light on the connection between this Archetypal Man and our present Humanity when dealing with the New Testament Scriptures.

Philo Judæus makes this same distinction between the original " heavenly " or archetypal man as a copy or image of God, and the " earthly " man, the human mind or soul.[2]

We must note now, however, in the opening verse of chapter ii, where the god-name is still Ælohîm, that after this archetypal creation, the Creator retires from the scene. In our version it is said that he " rested "; but this is erroneous, what is really meant is that the Supreme Being, " He-the-Gods," is no longer the active principle. He " retires into silence and darkness," and it is now the Logos who becomes the active principle.   Thus Fabre d'Olivet translates the second verse thus:

" 2. And-he-fulfilled, HE-the-Gods, in-the light's-manifestation-the-seventh, the-sovereign-work-which he-had-performed; and-he-restored-himself (he returned in his former divine self) in-the-light's-manifestation the-seventh, from-the-whole-sovereign-work, which he-had-performed."

Also in the third verse he translates:

" 3. He-re-established-himself (he returned into his unspeakable self), from-the-sovereign-work whereby he-created, He-the-Being-of-beings, according-to-his-performing."

This is a root teaching of the Ancient Wisdom, that the Absolute, although in a certain sense IT may be said to create, or emanate, yet IT is not the *active* God of our universe. We have already seen a similar idea expressed in the Egyptian *Book of the Dead*.[3]

We find a similar teaching also with some of the Christian

---

[1] In the *Bhagavad Gītā, Krishna*, the Heavenly Man, the Logos, says: " I establish this whole universe with a single portion of myself, and remain separate " (chapter x).

[2] See Smith and Wace, *Dict.*, art. " Philo," vol. iv, p. 376.

[3] See p. 98 *supra*.

mystics in the distinction made between the Godhead and God. Thus Meister Eckhart says:

" All that is in the Godhead is one. Therefore can we say nothing. It is above all names, above all nature. The essence of all creatures is eternally a divine life in Deity. God works. So doth not the Godhead."

This great Cosmic Cycle of manifestation in which Man has thus to play his part is known in Eastern philosophy as the outbreathing and inbreathing of Brahma. In modern language we should call it evolution and involution; and, looking at it from the more material point of view, it is the evolution of a vast Cosmos out of some homogeneous Primordial Substance, to which it ultimately returns. Even physical science is now teaching that physical matter, the physical atom is evolved out of the Ether, and will presently " return " to that etheric state.

Some of our more philosophical modern scientists—having had to abandon the concept of indestructible physical matter —are even beginning to postulate that the Primordial *Substance* is not even the Ether, but may be in the nature of " mind-stuff."[1] The activity of this primordial mind-stuff— or, as I should prefer to call it, Cosmic Mind—might very well be called *ideation*; and it is only one step from this to the Gnostic concept of the *Logos* as the creative principle, the active *word*, or *Demiurgos*, *speaking forth* the manifested universe. The idea also embodies a concept of the occult power of sound.

In the *Pistis Sophia*, Jesus is represented as saying to Andrew:

" Know ye not and do ye not understand that ye and all angels and all archangels and the gods and the lords and all the rulers and all the great invisibles and all those of the midst and those of the whole region of the Right and all the great ones of the emanations of the Light and their whole glory—that ye all one with another are out of one and the same paste and the same matter and the same substance, and that ye are all out of the same mixture " (Second Book, chapter c).

We might go back to the ancient *Laws of Manu* for a parallel passage:

[1] See p. 27 *supra*.

" The divine spirit alone is the whole assemblage of the gods; all worlds are seated in the divine spirit; and the divine spirit no doubt produces, *by a chain of causes and effects consistent with free will*, a connected series of acts performed by individual souls " (xii. 119).

But whatever may have been the variations of language in which this ancient concept has been expressed, the fundamental idea is that of an emanation from the ONE, and —from our *objective* point of view—the gradual differentiation of the primordial substance into various *Planes* of increasing density and complexity until physical matter is formed, and the physical universe as it is disclosed to our physical senses comes into existence; though, be it noted, the previous or " higher " planes still exist. Thus although physical matter is a differentiation of the Ether of space, and in that sense a " lower " plane of the Cosmos, yet the Ether *remains*.

But here it must be noted that this evolution or outgoing from the ONE which, from this lower point of view, we look upon as *material*, has behind it as its informing principle in all its stages, a hierarchy of *Lives, Intelligences,* " *gods* " which, *pari passu* with the differentiation of Primordial Substance, are differentiations of the ONE LIFE which is the informing Principle of that Substance: and indeed is, in any ultimate analysis, indistinguishable from it.

" All is through and from God himself, and it is his own substance." [1]

And in like manner, in so far as we are entitled to consider a hierarchy of *Lives* as being differentiated from the ONE LIFE: each of those hierarchies carries with it both the life and the substance in its own special characteristic in the economy of the whole manifestation.

Planes of substance must also be regarded as planes of consciousness; and, indeed, it is an open question in philosophy whether what is objective is not entirely and wholly a construct of the subjective consciousness: even to the extent of being a pure illusion when seen in the light of the ever-abiding and eternal nature of the ONE REALITY which is both subject and object.

In this differentiation or outgoing concept, however, we

[1] See p. 134 *infra*.

trace the origin of all the *Trinities* of the various religions. And here, again, we may note that the Trinity was formulated long before it became a part of Christian doctrine. We have to remember, however, that all this formulation, all these cosmogonies and theogonies, are merely concessions to the human *intellect*. Reality transcends them all, and they must be held very lightly, must never be rigidified into dogmas by the seeker after fundamental Truth. The intellect is essentially the maker of opposites; it breaks up unity into discrete objects, and must needs have God *and* Man, whereas in Reality there is no such distinction.

Thus Plotinus says:

" Becoming wholly absorbed in Deity, she (the soul) is one, conjoining as it were centre with centre. For here concurring, they are one; but they are then two when they are separate. For thus also we now denominate that which is another. Hence this spectacle is a thing difficult to explain by words. For how can anyone narrate that as something different from himself, which when he sees he does not behold as different, but as one with himself " (*Enn.* vi. 9, 10).

In the formulation of the Trinity we have first of all the ONE LIFE (Father); then Primordial Substance (Mother) which, acted upon by its own inherent activity (Father)— but which we should perhaps now from a physical point of view call eternal *motion*—brings forth the manifested universe (the " Son ") in an archetypal form. In one aspect—since Father-Mother are ONE—this bringing forth is an Immaculate Conception, or Virgin Birth.

What I am now setting forth only gives a bare idea: in the first place of the inadequacy of our authorized version, and in the second place of the cosmological facts concealed in the original of Moses' work.

It may be fitting here to quote the following remarks of Fabre d'Olivet:

" Without troubling myself with the various interpretations, good or bad, that one could give to the word BERÆSHITH, I may say that this word, in the connection in which one finds it, offers three distinct meanings: the one literal, the other figurative, the third hieroglyphic. Moses has employed all three, as is proved by the context of his work. In this he has followed the method of the Egyptian Priests; for I would say above all that these Priests had three ways of expressing their ideas. The first was clear and simple, the second symbolic and figurative, the third sacred and hieroglyphic."

We are, in fact, taught in *The Secret Doctrine* that there are *seven* keys to the interpretation of these Books of Moses, and that each key must be turned seven times. The reader must be referred to the *Kabala* for some of those keys, more particularly the numerical and geometrical key as given in the number equivalents of the Hebrew letters.

Swedenborg appears to have known something about these various interpretations, for he says in his *Arcana Celestia* (vol. i, p. 61):

" If anyone could know how many arcana each particular verse contains, he would be perfectly astonished; for although there is but little evidence of their existence in the letters, they are too numerous ever to be explained."[1]

It is, in fact, only as one becomes acquainted in detail with the teachings of the Ancient Wisdom that one can commence to glimpse some of these hidden meanings.

Man, then, as one of the great Hierarchies of Spiritual Beings differentiated from the ONE, had to evolve *pari passu* with the evolution of the material universe. He had to descend or " fall " into physical matter and generation, he had to play his part in the great Cosmic Process of Manifestation. In doing so he not merely loses sight of his spiritual nature and origin, but he becomes enamoured with " the things of this world," and being thus enamoured he becomes subject to them instead of ruling over them, and thereby sin, sickness, and death reign in his mortal body.

The " fall " of man into physical nature and generation is represented in the first instance in the second chapter of *Genesis* as the " deep sleep " of Adam, i.e. the loss of his spiritual consciousness in the first place, and in the second place the physical separation of the sexes by the formation of Eve. There is every reason to believe that the earliest races of mankind were hermaphrodite, though not in the present physical anatomical sense. On Man's return journey, and as

[1] Those who wish to pursue this subject further should consult in the first instance *The Secret Doctrine* by Mme H. P. Blavatsky.

he regains his original spiritual nature, he must again combine both the father and the mother principle in himself, or, as Jacob Boehme says,[1] must re-become that which he was " before his Eve."

> " They that are accounted worthy to attain to that world (age of the world) and the resurrection from the dead (their present spiritual deadness) neither marry, nor are given in marriage: for neither can they die any more: for they are equal with the angels; and are Sons of God " (*Luke* xx. 35).

This is pure Gnosis. Note the statement about the resurrection. If, as the orthodox theology teaches, everyone has to rise from the dead at " the last day," why should Jesus here say that it is only those who " are accounted worthy " who thus rise? Clearly the spiritual resurrection from the deadness of the carnal nature which, as I show later, Paul taught, is here indicated, and is one more proof that the teaching of Jesus was the spiritual doctrine of the Gnosis, whereas that of the Church is the carnal doctrine of a crude realism.

As with the individual, so it is with the Race, simply because the Race is made up of the individuals. The child is both ignorant and innocent of good and evil, but he learns the nature of these as he grows. Reaching man's estate he becomes absorbed in material interests and pursuits; and, having constantly before him the choice between good and evil, he only too often turns a deaf ear to the promptings of his inner spiritual nature—the Christ within, which always overshadows the individual—and he *sins* by choosing the evil rather than the good.

> " For all have sinned, and fall short of the glory of God "—the god *within* (*Rom.* iii. 23).

But Man, having thus to play his part in the great Cosmic Drama, his return to his Source is as certain as his outgoing therefrom. Man " falls " in order that he may rise. Thus Paul:

> " Our light affliction, which is but for a moment, worketh for us more and more exceedingly an eternal weight of glory " (2 *Cor.* iv. 17).

[1] See p. 72 *supra*.

And again:

> " For I reckon that the sufferings of this present time are not worthy to be compared with the glory which shall be revealed to us-ward.
> " For the earnest expectation of the creation waiteth for the revealing of the sons of God.
> " For the creation was subjected to vanity not of its own will, but by reason of him who subjected it " (*Rom.* viii. 18, 19, 20).

Note that " the creation was subjected to vanity (or folly, i.e. departure from original saneness or spiritual wisdom) *not of its own will*." In other words, Man *had* to " fall " in order to play his part in " creation," the great Cosmic Process. Thus, viewing the matter from the cosmic point of view, the " fall " was no " sin."

I take the following from the commentary on the Stanzas from the *Book of Dzyan*, to which I have already referred (vol. i, p. 268):

> " Starting upon the long journey immaculate; descending more and more into sinful matter, and having connected himself with every atom in manifested *Space*—the *Pilgrim*, having struggled through and suffered in every form of life and being,[1] is only at the bottom of the valley of matter, and half through his cycle, when he has identified himself with collective Humanity. This, *he has made in his own image.* In order to progress upwards and homewards, the ' God ' has now to ascend the weary uphill path of the Golgotha of Life. It is the martyrdom of self-conscious existence. Like Visvakarman[2] he has to sacrifice *himself to himself* in order to redeem all creatures, to resurrect from the many into the *One Life.* Then he ascends into heaven indeed; where, plunged in the incomprehensible absolute Being and Bliss of Paranirvāna, he reigns unconditionally."

Note further in the above statement by St. Paul that "the creation waiteth for the revealing of the sons (plural) of God." Why " sons "? Because every individual is a potential " Son of God," a potential *Christ*; that potentiality being represented in the Gospels as having been actually manifested in the person of Jesus Christ; and Paul here anticipates the time when Man having returned to his

---

[1] See the lines by the Sufi poet, Jalalu 'd-Din Rumi, quoted on p. 168 *infra.*

[2] A Vedic god, described as the ONE, beyond the comprehension of (un-initiated) mortals. In the two hymns of the *Rig Veda* specially devoted to him he is said to " sacrifice himself to himself."

" first estate," " the earnest expectation of the creation " will be realized in deliverance " from the bondage of corruption into the liberty of the glory of the children (or sons) of God." We can link this up with statements in other Scriptures.

In the Stanzas from the *Book of Dzyan* we read:

" Then the Builders, having donned their first clothing, descend on radiant earth and reign over men—who are themselves."

This " first clothing " we shall identify with Man's original spiritual or " Garden of Eden " body; and also with the " Robe of Glory " of the *Pistis Sophia*. In this latter work we find Jesus represented as saying:

" Now, therefore, amen, I say unto you: Every man who will receive that mystery of the Ineffable and accomplish it in all its types and all its figures—he is a man in the world, but he towereth above all angels and will tower still more above them all. . . . And amen, I say unto you: That man is I and I am that man (228).

" And at the dissolution of the world, that is when the universe will be raised up and when the numbering of the perfect souls will be raised up all together, and when I am king in the midst of the last Helper, being king over all the emanations of the Light and king over the seven Amens and the five Trees and the three Amens and the nine guards, and being king over the Child of the Child, that is the Twin-saviours, and being over the twelve saviours and over the whole numbering of the perfect souls who shall receive the mysteries in the Light—then will all men who shall receive the mysteries in the Ineffable, be fellow-kings with me and will sit on my right and on my left in my kingdom.

" And amen, I say unto you: Those men are I, and I am they " (230).

It would take us too far out of our way to make any attempt to explain the symbolism employed in the above passage, but the main point is clear enough as to the rebecoming of the individual into oneness with the Logos through Initiation into the " mystery of the Ineffable." It is, in fact, Paul's " revealing of the sons of God," or those who have " donned their first clothing," and who then " descend on radiant earth and reign over men."

In the eleventh chapter of *Revelation* we read:

" And the seventh angel sounded; and there followed great voices in heaven, and they said, the kingdom of the world is become the kingdom of our Lord, and of his Christ; and he shall reign for ever and ever " (or " unto the ages of the ages ").

Here we have a reference to the occult teaching that there are seven major Cycles in this Cosmic Process of the Fall and Return of Man. It is at the end of the seventh that the final consummation takes place, and " the kingdom of the world " —of *this* world—re-becomes a spiritual kingdom. Man belongs to *this* world from beginning to end of the Cycles. It was *this* world that was originally his " Garden of Eden," and must become so again. That " Garden " was no isolated geographical spot—as so many good Christians still believe. It was the whole world in which the original *spiritual* Humanity—" Adam " before his " fall "—lived; only that world was not then this gross physical thing which it is now in consequence of that " fall." Man and his Globe are the subjective and objective aspects of one and the same thing: the Cosmic Hierarchy MAN.[1]

Christian theology finds no room for the evolution of either the individual or the Race; indeed, the very term *evolution* is anathema for it. It is neck or nothing for the individual; he is either "saved" through the atoning work of Jesus on the Cross, or he is for ever " lost," even if not— as some would still maintain—eternally damned to the torments of Hell.

What, then, we ask, becomes of the cave man, of prehistoric man, of the present-day primitive man, not to speak of the untold millions of individuals of pre-Christian ages who had a more or less highly developed religion—in some cases, indeed, quite the equal if not superior to the concepts of

---

[1] For an instructive discourse on the relation between the subjective and the objective universe, the student may be referred to the small work by Sri Aurobindo Ghose on the *Isha Upanishad*.

Note in this connection the words " *radiant* earth " in the above quotation from *The Book of Dzyan*. As man becomes a *spiritual* humanity, as he regains his ' first estate " and puts on his " first clothing," his *radiant* body, so also, *pari passu*, the Earth regains *its* first " Garden of Eden " condition and *its* radiant appearance, whilst the other planets of the solar system will also have undergone corresponding transformations. Man and his Globe are indissolubly linked up with the greater *Life* cycles of the whole solar system. It is one unitary *Logos*.

When we understand something of these vast *Cosmic* Cycles of Evolution, the parochial nature of Christian doctrine appears almost pathetic in its naïveté.

" Christianity "?   If the individual is only " redeemed " by belief in a particular historical event—or rather by belief in the *interpretation* which Christian theology gives to that event—we ask again, what is the fate of the countless millions who, if they are only granted one life here on earth, lived and died hundreds, thousands, nay, millions of years before that particular event?   Setting aside the horrible doctrine of the old theologians as to the fate of the " heathen " and the " unbeliever," have our modern theologians any answer to that question?   Were not all these pre-Christian individuals *human* beings?   Were they not a part of humanity?   *Are* they not part of humanity?   Is it only the individual who *happens* to be born after the said historical event who can have any chance of " eternal life "?   And if it is held to be really necessary to be a " Christian " in order to be " saved," one would think that at least reincarnation would be granted to give the pre-Christian individuals a chance.   But no!   The more we examine the Christian theory of Humanity in its relation to " God " and to what we know to-day of the history of humanity, the more we see how utterly inadequate it is to cover the ground of Humanity's great struggle to regain its spiritual heritage; not to mention the fact that it is an actual materialization and perversion of the deeper *Cosmic* knowledge which was taught in the *Mysteries*, or Schools of Initiation, and which is actually contained in its own Scriptures in an allegorical form.

Oh! poor suffering humanity; how few of you have as yet learnt, notwithstanding that the truth has been openly set before you over and over again, that the remedy for all your agony lies in your own hands, in the realization of your own inherent spiritual nature, the Christ principle within.   Nay, even without that, without any *spiritual* knowledge, does not the remedy for nine-tenths of the evil in the world lie in man's own hands?

In the *Pistis Sophia* the explanation which is given of the words of Jesus: " The first will be last and the last will be first," is that Man, having gone through his fall and return, will, at the consummation of the Age, be infinitely higher than those Hierarchies of Spiritual Beings who have not yet accomplished this cyclic experience. Does not Paul also say: " Know ye not that we shall judge angels "? thereby giving us one more clue to the fact that he was familiar with the *Cosmic* teaching. In the *Pistis Sophia* he is spoken of by Mary Magdalene as " our brother Paul,"[1] and thereby classed with those initiated disciples who were taught the mysteries by Jesus.

One of the most fundamental axioms of the Ancient Wisdom is, as already stated, that all things return to their Source. Perhaps the clearest statement of this from the Cosmic point of view which is to be found in the New Testament is the statement by Paul that:

" When all things have been subjected unto him, then shall the Son (the Logos) also himself be subjected to him that did subject all things unto him, that God may be all in all " (1 *Cor.* xv. 28).

Is not God, then, " all in all " *now*? As the Absolute, yes; but viewed from the point of view of the time-process, no. In the time-process of the manifested universe it is the " Son," the Cosmic Logos, who is the informing active Principle, and who thus has to be considered as differentiated from the " Father," the ONE. He is the creative power who speaks forth the " Word " which—by the power of *sound*— brings into existence the objective worlds. This is quite clearly stated in the opening verses of St. John's Gospel:

" All things were made by (or through) him (the Logos); and without him was not anything made that hath been made."

Paul also states the Logos doctrine in *Colossians* i. 15 ff.:

" Who is the image of the invisible God, the firstborn of all creation; for in him were all things created, in the heavens and upon the earth, things visible and things invisible, whether thrones or dominions or principalities or powers, all things have been created through him, and unto him; and he is before all things, and in him all things consist."

As regards the power of the *Word* in its aspect as the occult power of *sound*, we might here quote Jacob Boehme:

" Of what the Word is in its power and sound, of that the *Mysterium Magnum* is a substance; it is the eternal substantial Word of God."

[1] m.p. 294.

This doctrine of the *Logos* or *Word* clearly belongs to Greek philosophy. In the Preface to his work on Theosophy, or Psychological Religion, Professor Max Müller says:

" Whoever uses such words as *Logos*, the Word, *Monogenes*, the Only-begotten, *Prototokos*, the First-born, *Hyios tou theou*, the Son of God, has borrowed the very germs of his religious thought from Greek philosophy."

And yet it has been denied by some that either the Christian Scriptures or Paul in particular owed anything to that philosophy. Perhaps they do not owe anything *directly* to that philosophy, but both are in debt to the Ancient Wisdom. Greek philosophy at all events is known to have derived largely from the East, the home of that Wisdom.

It is interesting in this connection to note the close correspondence between this Logos doctrine in the Christian Scriptures as given in the above quotations, and that which we have in the corresponding Eastern Scripture, the *Bhagavad Gītā*. In chapter ix, Krishna, the Logos, speaks as follows:

" All beings, O son of Kuntī, go to My nature at the end of the age; and I put them all forth again at the beginning of the world-period.
" Establishing My own nature, again and again I put forth this host of being inevitably, by the power of nature."[1]

A somewhat freer translation in W. Q. Judge's edition of the *Gītā* reads as follows:

" O son of Kuntī, at the end of a Kalpa[2] all things return unto my nature, and then again at the beginning of another Kalpa I cause them to evolve again. Taking control of my own nature I emanate again and again this whole assemblage of beings, without their will, by the power of the material essence (*prakriti*)."

Note here in the first place how all things are said to return unto the being of the Logos; and in the second place that they are emanated " without their will," or " inevitably ": which is just the same as Paul's statement that " the creation was subjected unto vanity *not of its own will*."

Now as regards this Logos doctrine, we need not enter into the fruitless and endless theological controversies, which began to rage even in the first century, and more particularly

[1] Charles Johnston's translation.   [2] A manifested world-period.

as between Arius and Athanasius, as to the exact relation between the " Father " and the " Son." It lies simply in a metaphysical abstraction which the *intellect* is unable to transcend. God as the *Absolute*, as the " all in all," cannot have any *relation* to the parts. He is " not this, not that." An *active Principle* is therefore postulated as secondary to the Ever-concealed Causeless-Cause—Paul's " invisible God "— and that active Principle is the Logos. The *Bhagavad Gītā* represents " It " (or " Him ") as Krishna, the Christian Scriptures as Jesus Christ. Krishna says:

" I am the *embodiment* of the Supreme Ruler, and of the incorruptible, of the unmodifying, and of the eternal law, and of endless bliss " (chapter xiv).

Now the practical application of this to our " fallen " nature is clear enough. Humanity, like everything else in the universe, must *return to its source*. This simply means that it must regain, individually and collectively, that *spiritual* nature which belonged to it when it was first brought into being by the Cosmic Logos who, as the inner divine *Self* of each individual, is still an *active principle*—the " light that lighteth every man coming into the world," and the " Christ in you " of St. Paul, the " Ego which is seated in the heart of all beings " of the *Bhagavad Gītā*—giving to man, even in his lowest aspect, the *instinct* which makes him a religious animal, while in its highest aspect it manifests in such men as Gautama the Buddha and Jesus the Christ, and in many others of whom the world knows little or nothing.

This fact of Man's outgoing and return is stated by Jesus in the parable of the Prodigal Son. The parable is applicable both to the individual and to Humanity as a whole. What is Humanity to-day in bulk but a Prodigal, wasting his substance in riotous living, in attachment to the " things of this world," in wars and rebellions, in tyranny and greed and oppression? Is it not the very husks of life on which the great majority feed to-day in the feverish rush for excitement, or in the struggle for the wherewithal to obtain these?

Well, that is the lesson which Man, the Prodigal Son, has to learn, both individually and collectively through bitter experience. ' And, we repeat, it can only be learnt collectively as it is learnt individually.

Has not the experience of Humanity been bitter enough these millions of years past in which he has sunk from his spiritual estate into physical matter and generation? And is it not bitter enough to-day for the great majority, aye, and even for those who, from a worldly point of view, may be considered to be more fortunate? Yet there are perhaps to-day more individuals than ever before who have perceived the possibilities of their spiritual nature, and have girded up their loins for the return journey to their " Father's home." It is not merely to the Christian religion that these belong. They existed in their thousands before ever what is known as *Christianity* took form or shape in history; and by re-incarnating they carry forward both their own evolution and that of the Race.

Behind all the Cycles of Man's evolution on this Globe, behind the rise and fall of nations and races, there have always stood representatives of that great Hierarchy of Initiates, of the " Sons of God," gradually drawing into their circle in its various grades and degrees those who were able to receive the great doctrine of Man's divine origin and nature, and could apprehend what was required of them if they would enter the Path of return. Man—like everything else in the universe—is an outbirth from the ONE; and—like everything else in the universe—to that ONE he must return. But he returns " bearing his sheaves with him." He goes out as a spiritual " babe "; he returns as the full-grown " Son of God."

But here the Church, in its feeble imagination, has taught, and teaches to-day, nothing but individual salvation or damnation after one brief earth-life; and has supposed that the individual could only be " saved " by a profession of faith in its exclusive teachings. It teaches a physical resurrection at the " last day."

" At whose coming all men shall rise again with their bodies. . . . This is the Catholic Faith: which except a man believe faithfully, he cannot be saved " (Creed of St. Athanasius).

I have been told sometimes when I have commented on

such like statements in the Creeds that I am flogging a
dead horse. But am I? Why, then, are they not expunged
from the Prayer Book? At the recent Convocation of
York it was declared that no man could be called a Christian
who did not accept the " faith " as given in the words of
the Creed of Nicaea that:

" Jesus is very God of very God, who for us men and for our Salvation
came down from heaven and was made man."[1]

But the individual belongs to the Race from beginning to
end of the Cycle; and it is only as the individual progresses
that the Race can progress. Hence the necessity for reincarnation, which was clearly taught in the early Church
itself. Thus Origen says:

" Every soul has existed from the beginning; it has therefore passed
through some worlds already, and will pass through others before it
reaches the final consummation. It comes into this world strengthened
by the victories or weakened by the defeats of its previous life " (*De
Princ.*, 3, 1, 20, 21).

But this doctrine of a succession of lives was, like so many
other of the teachings of the Initiates, ultimately made a
heresy at one of the Church Councils in the 5th century.

In the *Pistis Sophia* Jesus says:

" And ye are in great sufferings and great afflictions in your being
poured from one into another of different kinds of bodies of the world "
(m.p. 248).

One by one the individuals composing the Race learn the
lesson of the Prodigal Son; and, though often with many
backslidings, the individual gradually comes to the point
where he may be regarded as one of the " elect," having his
feet firmly planted on the " Path " that leads to final liberation from " this ocean of incarnation and death," even as the
Buddha taught.

> " Enter the Path! There spring the healing streams
> Quenching all thirst! there bloom the immortal flowers
> Carpeting all the way with joy! there throng
> Swiftest and sweetest hours! "[2]

---

[1] See *The Hibbert Journal*, October 1934, p. 3.   [2] *The Light of Asia.*

Now, just as the Old Testament treats of the " Fall " of Man, so the New Testament treats of his Return; the return to his lost estate as a spiritual being. This is taught under the guise of his redemption by the *Christ principle*, the divine " Son," the " light which lighteth every man coming into the world," the " higher Self " of every individual.

That " light " is set forth as being specially manifested in a certain historical character, namely, Jesus of Nazareth.

" And the *Logos* became flesh, and dwelt among us (and we beheld his glory, glory as of the (or an) only begotten from the (or a) Father, full of grace and truth " (*John* i. 14).

This is the great distinctive claim made for Christianity by the early writers and apologists. In the person of Jesus of Nazareth there was a full and complete revelation of the Christ *principle* or *Logos*, which, though previously operative as the inspiring principle of many notable men, could only give through them a partial revelation of the eternal truths.

Thus Justin Martyr says that there were Christians before Christ; thereby confirming what St. Augustine says in the quotation I have given on p. 163 *infra*. He claims Empedocles, Pythagoras, Socrates, and Plato among others as having been inspired by the Christ or Logos; and he even says that Socrates was martyred for Christ.

" Christ who was known in part by Socrates, for he was and is the word which is in every man " (*Apol.*, ii. 10. 49, A).[1]

But the early Christian writers and dogma-makers can hardly have known of similar special incarnations of *Avatāras* of the " Word " or Logos as they are narrated in the ancient Eastern Scriptures now known to us; more particularly that of Krishna and his teachings—practically similar to those of Jesus—as contained in the *Bhagavad Gītā*.

Ascribe what perfections you like to the historical man Jesus; accept if you like all or any of his recorded miracles; let him be essentially a *divine* man, and what follows therefrom is simply this: that what he was each one of us may and can, nay, *must* become; and that simply because—as stated above in reference to Socrates—the *Christ principle* which he mani-

[1] Cf. Smith and Wace, *Dict.*, art. "Justin Martyr," vol. iii, p. 576.

fested in such perfection is that same " word which is in every man."

But we do not become Christs (*Christos*) because *he* was that. We shall never become it simply by *believing* that he was that, or that he did all that the Gospels record; or that he did something *for* us which washes away our sins and gives us a short cut to eternal bliss. No. We shall only achieve the same likeness when " that same mind (or ' word ') which was also in Christ Jesus "[1] has been " brought to birth " in us also, i.e. when we have realized that we, equally with him, are essentially divine in our deepest nature; that we are, equally with him, " sons " of the same " Father," and are thus able to manifest as he did that divinity in our very humanity.

This was his teaching and that of Paul the Initiate; and it has been the teaching of the Gnosis through other divine Avatāras from time immemorial. Unfortunately for the subsequent history of Christianity, it was too high a doctrine to be understood and *practised* by the narrow-minded disciples who looked for an immediate Second Coming of the *personal* Jesus to establish an earthly kingdom. And so, gradually, " Christianity " *fell* into its traditional dogmatic and materialized form, with all the squabbles and rancour and meannesses and persecutions which accompanied the settling of that form; not to speak of the devilish cruelties which have subsequently been associated with it.

Is the *mystical* doctrine of the indwelling Christ Principle, the *Cosmic Christ*, too high a doctrine for everyone to-day? Undoubtedly it is. We see the evidences of it on every hand in what is taught in our Churches and Chapels, and, one might add, in much of our modern theological literature also. Well, sufficient for each one for the time being must be the measure of understanding which he is able to reach.

In the light of the foregoing, let us now proceed to examine the New Testament Scriptures somewhat more closely.

[1] *Phil.* ii. 5.

CHAPTER V

THE NEW TESTAMENT SCRIPTURES

I. The Gospels

WE have seen that the fundamental teaching of the ancient Wisdom-Gnosis is the outgoing of the *manifested* universe from the ONE, the ABSOLUTE, the EVER-CONCEALED CAUSE-LESS-CAUSE, and its inevitable return thereto at the end of the great cycle of evolution and involution, the *Maha-Manvantara* or *Day of Brahma*.

We have seen that Man is necessarily a part of this great Cosmic Process; that he also has " come out " from the ONE, and must inevitably return thereto; and we have seen that this *outgoing* is allegorically set forth in the *Genesis* narrative, where it is represented as a " Fall."

All through the Old Testament, then, we have a representation in a more or less allegorical or semi-historical form of Man in his " fallen " condition. The semi-historical basis centres round one small tribal race out of the whole vast population of the world, and out of the innumerable races which preceded that one race; and we can easily translate such " history " as that of the Patriarchs, the sojourn of the Children of Israel in the " wilderness," etc., into the terms of Man's more universal evolution—which, indeed, they are intended to represent. As I shall presently show, this is somewhat more than hinted at both in the Gospels and in Paul's Epistles.

But mixed up with these fragments of the ancient Gnosis we have in the Old Testament the exceedingly anthropomorphic conceptions of the Jews with regard to the Supreme Being, or " God ": which conceptions have unfortunately been taken over—like the literal acceptation of the *Genesis* narrative—by *exoteric* or orthodox Christian doctrine.

It is only by a study of other Scriptures and other religions with an open mind that we can appreciate the real position of the Old Testament Scriptures in the sacred Scriptures of

the world, and discount the exclusive claims that have been
made for them by those who knew of no others, or who
classified all others as " heathen " and anti-Christian.   A
knowledge of the fundamental principles of the Ancient
Wisdom-Gnosis shows us that they all contain those teachings
in some more or less open form suited to the requirements,
that is to say, the mental capacities, of those for whom they
were written.   Broadly speaking, all the " sacred " Scriptures of the world, i.e. those which treat of Man's nature and
destiny, are the effort of *Initiates* to give to the peoples they
addressed some understanding of the fundamental principles
of the Divine Science; and hence it is that when once we have
grasped those principles we can trace them in all these
Scriptures notwithstanding the accretions and corruptions of
the texts to which they have been subjected by subsequent
editing and translation—not to speak of the *exoteric* and in
some cases grossly materialistic doctrines which have arisen
by taking their allegories literally, and thereby serving to
obscure their real intention and purpose for the ignorant
and superstitious masses of priest-ridden devotees.

Now, as the Old Testament treats broadly of Man's outgoing or " Fall," so the New Testament treats of his *return.*
It is thus naturally linked up with the Old Testament, more
particularly as both are Jewish in their origin and form.
Yet we might take the teachings of the New Testament *when
understood esoterically* quite apart from those of the Old
Testament; and indeed some of the earlier Christian sects did
so, as, for example, the Pauliciani to whom I have referred
on p. 35 *supra.*   Orthodox Christian theology cannot do
this; it is indissolubly tied to the anthropological God of
the Old Testament and his " plan " of Salvation owing to
the " sin of our first parents," and the supposed prophecies
relating to him.

Now the New Testament purports to give in the first instance a biography—or at least a partial biography—of the
man Jesus of Nazareth; and in the second place the beliefs
and teachings concerning him which were held by certain
men called Apostles.

Treating these records critically, just as we should treat

any other Scriptures or beliefs, we may note in the first place that whatever may have been the real history of the man called Jesus, or however much of it as recorded in the Gospels can be accepted as history, there is evidently much which, as myth or allegory, comes from pre-Christian sources, or at least if not directly derived from those sources must have some common ground of origin. Myths, allegories, and miraculous stories exactly similar to those recorded in the Gospels are found in connection with many other " World-Saviours," and we cannot accept their historical truth in any one case more than another, let alone their inherent improbability as history. A notable example of this is the Virgin Birth story, the immediate prototype of the Virgin and Child being the Egyptian Isis and Horus, while there are other similar representations to be found in India, China, and elsewhere.[1]

But the important point is, that for the *esoteric* interpretation of the Gospels we need not trouble ourselves in any way with the historical difficulties which are now so much in evidence. By the *esoteric* interpretation I here mean the interpretation in terms of that *Gnosis* which I am now endeavouring to show belongs to a deeply rooted ancient tradition of Divine Instructors of the human race. That Jesus or Jehoshua was one of those Divine Instructor-Initiates or *Avataras* we may very well believe, for we find in his *Sayings* the same teachings as those of Krishna, Buddha, and other Instructors of the historical period. As for the other contents of the Gospels, the miraculous stories that gathered round his reputed life, and the doctrinal *opinions* of the writers of the Gospels: some of these we find to be *esoterically* in line with the Ancient Wisdom, notably in St. John's Gospel, while others—such as the immediate Second Coming of the resurrected man Jesus which was such an enormous stimulus to the " faith " of the early Christians —were obviously entire misconceptions of the nature of the teachings.

I have already referred more or less explicitly to the endless theories and contradictions in which modern scholar-

[1] Cf. Doane, *Bible Myths*, chapter xxxii.

ship is involved in the effort to get at the real truth and origin of the narratives in the four canonical Gospels, even to the extent of denying altogether that there was any historical man Jesus. Well, as just said, we need not trouble ourselves even as to that question. It is only vital for *exoteric* Christian doctrine, which places everything on the actual sacrificial and atoning work of the incarnate God in the person of Jesus Christ.

But in every respect in which Jesus is represented as the Logos, or as speaking of himself as the " Saviour " of mankind, we have an exact parallel in that beautiful Hindu Scripture, the *Bhagavad Gītā*, where Krishna discourses in a similar manner to Jesus on the method of return or " salvation " by devotion to him. For example:

> " For those who worship me, renouncing in me all their actions, regarding me as the supreme goal and meditating on me alone, if their thoughts are turned to me. O Son of Pritha, I presently become the Saviour from this ocean of incarnations and death " (chapter xii).

Note the parallelism between this and many of the sayings of Jesus, speaking also as the Logos, for example:

> " Abide in me, and I in you. As the branch cannot bear fruit of itself, except it abide in the vine; so neither can ye, except ye abide in me " (*John* xv. 4).

Now we understand very well that it is not any personal or historical Krishna who speaks, but precisely that same *Logos* who is represented in the opening verses of St. John's Gospel as being the " light which lighteth every man coming into the world." Neither is it the personal man Jesus who speaks in the above and other sayings, such as " I am the light of the world." We all know that that " light " has been taken by the Church—in its mere literal interpretation of the Scriptures—to have been the historical man Jesus. But how could that possibly be? Untold millions of the pre-Christian inhabitants of the world could never hear of that light—unless, indeed, reincarnation be admitted. Untold millions since have never heard of the personal Jesus. No; Jesus, like Krishna, speaks thus as the Logos, the Cosmic Christ of St. Paul, the " Christ *in* you," the divine " Spark,"

now so dim in the great majority of the human Race in its
" fallen " condition; and it is *that* teaching that matters,
whether attributed to Krishna or to Jesus.

In the *Bhagavad Gītā* Krishna says:

" I am the Ego which is seated in the hearts of all beings; I am the
beginning, the middle, and the end of all existing beings."

It is not the historical man Krishna who makes these
affirmations about himself, neither is it the historical man
Jesus who makes such closely similar affirmations. These
words are put into the mouths of supposedly historical
characters by those who had a knowledge of the deeper mysteries of Man's nature, and perhaps with the distinct recognition that the great masses of the people must have some
person to adore as a divine Saviour.

An additional proof that Jesus does not speak in any
personal sense is seen in his statement that:

" Abraham rejoiced to see my day; and he saw it, and was glad. . . .
Verily I say unto you, before Abraham was, I am " (*John* viii. 56–8).

We shall not trouble ourselves, therefore, to ascertain
whether the historical man Jesus actually used the words
attributed to him in the Gospels. What is important is that
the *teaching* here given, as also that attributed to Krishna,
is that same profound and ancient Wisdom-Gnosis as to Man's
inherent divine nature, and the means by which he may
recover the consciousness of that nature, and so be " saved "
from " this ocean of incarnations and death," as we find in
many other Scriptures and as set forth in varying forms by
many other ancient Sages, Initiates, and Divine Instructors.
When once we have recognized the universality of this teaching, and its existence in all ages, we not merely understand
it in the *form* in which it is presented in the Gospels, but we
naturally reject the literalization of the narrative as well as
the exclusive claims which are made for these Scriptures by
Christian theologians.

Tracing broadly the evolution of Humanity as we know it
to-day, we see in the primitive man an individual just rising
out of the mere animal kingdom. His next stage of development is that of mind or intellect, and he becomes " civilized "

—which often means that his last state is worse than that of the first. Be that as it may, Man rises from the animal to the *homo sapiens*. Our " civilized " nations to-day represent broadly speaking the development of intellect. This should carry with it rational beliefs and rational conduct, which would include of necessity a high degree of ethical and moral considerations. But we are very far from finding this to be the case; indeed, the primitive man has often a far higher standard of morals than the so-called civilized man. Nor is it difficult to see what it is that is lacking in order to give to intellect the right objective. It is the *spiritual* basis that is lacking. Real religion, the things of Man's inherent spiritual nature, has as yet no hold on the masses. Look at the state of the world to-day, where multitudes are starving in the midst of plenty. Communism, Socialism—any amount of isms—are trying to alter this state of affairs *without any thought of altering human nature*. It is there that the root of the matter lies. Alter that, and external matters will adjust themselves automatically, for they are only the reflex of Man's thoughts and desires; nay, the very configuration of his Globe, its storms and its cataclysms are that. Atlantis went down thereby, and:

" Those eighteen, upon whom the tower in Siloam fell, and killed them, think ye that they were offenders above all the men that dwelt in Jerusalem? I tell you, Nay; but, except ye repent, ye shall all likewise perish " (*Luke* xiii. 4).

And so the next stage—still a very very long way off—in Man's *return* is the development of " religious " nations: that is to say, whole races who have reached the stage of awareness of their *spiritual* nature, and who regulate all their communal relations as well as their individual actions thereby. We have no such religious nations to-day, notwithstanding the claims of so many to be called " Christian," and mankind has as yet to go through many long cycles of bitter experience before a sufficient number of individuals have reached such a stage that that can become possible. In the occult teachings with regard to these cycles we are now said to be in the *Kali Yuga*, the black or iron age, the duration of which is 432,000 years. According to the Hindu chronology it began 3,102 years B.C., at the moment of Krishna's death.

Here we must clearly understand that nothing can possibly manifest itself in the individual—and thereby in the community—which is not in the first instance *cosmic* in its nature. The physical atom as an individual *thing* owes its properties to the more cosmic nature of the Ether. So in Man: he can develop mind or intellect because there is a Cosmic Mind: and he can develop *spirit* because there is a Cosmic Spirit. The development of that means the conquest of all that is " evil " in himself and in the community. Call that Cosmic Spirit God, or the Logos, or Christ, or Krishna, or Buddha, or what you will: it is that Cosmic Principle which, in Paul's language, you must " bring to birth " *in* you to be " saved "—not from the orthodox Hell, but from " this ocean of incarnation and death." It can only be brought to birth in the Race as it is brought to birth in the individual.

Now you can only be saved by *knowledge*, by growth, by actually *becoming*, here and now, the perfected spiritual man, of which Jesus is represented in the Gospels as our example. Whatever may have been his real history as a man, we have in his *Sayings* precisely the same teaching concerning the method of attainment, the *Path* to Salvation or Liberation by a *knowledge* of " the mysteries of the kingdom of heaven " which are to be found in so many other Scriptures.

These Mysteries, we repeat, are definite *knowledge*; a knowledge which brings definite *power* to conquer where the individual is at present, in his ignorance, the helpless victim of, and a sinner against, the natural laws of his being, physical, mental, and spiritual.

But where to-day in the Christian Church will you find the real Initiate, the real Master of the Divine Science of the *natural laws* of Man's spiritual nature? We have to go to the great spiritual Masters of the Far East, the Masters of *Yoga*, to learn these. Beyond those Masters who are accessible to-day are others whose attainment is still higher; indeed, there is no break in the scale of evolution, no lack of representatives from those who have only just set out on the return journey to those who have completed it, the Christs, and the Buddhas.[1]

An actual knowledge of the divine Mysteries is put forward over and over again in the *Pistis Sophia* as essential for " salvation." There is no teaching of any " atonement " by a blood sacrifice. Jesus came specifically to disclose the " Mysteries of the Kingdom of Light "; those Mysteries which the Adepts and Initiates and divine *Avataras* of all ages have taught to those who had " ears to hear." Reincarnation, in order that these *Mysteries* may be learnt, is one of the fundamental teachings of this work. Thus in chapter cxxxv Jesus says:

> " Of the patriarchs and of the righteous from the time of Adam until now. . . . I have made to turn into bodies . . . which will find the mysteries of the Light, enter in and inherit the Light-Kingdom."

In the canonical Scriptures, even as we have them now, overwritten as they have been for the express purpose of making them accord with an already formulated and materialistic theology, we have the direct statements of both Jesus and Paul that they would not disclose the " mysteries " to either the common people, or even to those in their own community who were not ready to understand them. This in itself shows these teachers to have been following the invariable rule of all Initiates. It shows that they were dealing in all their sayings and doings with the Ancient Wisdom or Gnosis, and this is easily recognizable by those who know what that Gnosis teaches. For the rest—well, " They have Moses and the prophets; let them hear them " (*Luke* xvi. 29).

The Gospels are replete with allusions to ancient initiation ceremonies and terms—Baptism, the " Second Birth " (Sanscrit *dwija*, " twice born "), Transfiguration on the " Mountain," Temptation in the " Wilderness," Crucifixion, Resurrection, Ascension—all these are borrowed from the " *Mysteries*," and once more attributed to the *Initiate* Jesus, as they previously were to Krishna and other " crucified Saviours."

Of the real history of this great spiritual teacher we know

---

[1] See the quotation *re* the *Silent Watcher* on p. 189 *infra*.

so little that many scholars who have gone deeply into " the search for the historical Jesus " have, as already said, been inclined to deny his physical existence altogether. The real historical problem—hardly as yet dealt with by critical scholarship—is as to how these myths, allegories, and symbolical rites belonging to the ancient Mystery Cults came to be attached to the personality of this great teacher, whoever he may have been, or whatever may have been his real history. There is even a certain amount of support for the Jewish tradition that he lived one hundred years earlier than the date usually ascribed to him.[1]

The " history " contained in the Gospels is at best only semi-historical. It was *made* in its present form largely in order that it might conform with the supposed prophecies in the Jewish Old Testament Scriptures concerning an earthly Messiah, as is well shown in the numerous statements " that the Scripture might be fulfilled," or " according to the Scriptures." But even so, what of that if these same Scriptures are also allegorical?

It is my own opinion that there was an actual historical character, Jesus or Jehoshua, an Initiate; but I shall not here advance any specific arguments in support of this. It is quite sufficient that the teachings ascribed to this personage, whether actual or mythical, are those of the Ancient Gnosis; and first and foremost, *the divine nature of Man*, and the possibility of recovering the consciousness and powers of that divine nature, as taught in many pre-Christian Scriptures.

Assuming, then, the man Jesus to have been an actual personality, where and how did he obtain his initiation knowledge? Every great Initiate, every divine *Avatar*, when incarnating in a physical body, has to overcome in the first instance the limitations of his physical instrument, and to train that instrument to be properly responsive to the requirements of the real Self, the immortal divine man. That is, in fact, what we all should be doing; but at our present stage of evolution we have neither the pure physical body nor the consciousness of a strong compelling spiritual Self which

[1] Cf. G. R. S. Mead, *Did Jesus Live 100 B.C.?*

belongs to the great Adepts in virtue of their attainments in previous incarnations. The Buddha had to spend many years of strenuous search before he attained to his Buddhahood (Enlightenment), and doubtless it was the same with the man Jesus before he became *Christos*, the Anointed, the Initiate, the man who had realized to a high degree his divine nature, his oneness with the " Father."

The prospective Adept is also *tempted* in every possible manner, and he must prove his power to resist. We have the allegorical presentation of the final temptation of Jesus in the Gospel narrative of the Temptation in the Wilderness.[1] This is one more evidence of the connection of those narratives—partly historical and partly allegorical—with the ancient hierarchy of Initiates and their initiation laws.[2]

We have no record of the life of Jesus between the story given by Luke of his appearance in the Temple at the age of twelve, and the commencement of his public teaching at the presumed age of thirty. The most likely supposition as to his life during that period was that he joined the community of the Essenes. Smith and Wace, in their *Dictionary of Christian Biography*, uphold this view in the following terms:

" When it is remembered that the whole Jewish community at the advent of Christ was divided into three parties, the Pharisees, the Sadducees, and the Essenes, and that every devout Jew belonged to one of these sects, it is natural to suppose that Jesus, who in all things conformed to the Jewish law, belonged to this portion of His religious brethren. He who was holy, harmless, undefiled, and separate from sinners, would naturally associate Himself with that order of Judaism which was most congenial to His holy nature, and it would be unlike Christ who taught us lessons from the sparrows in the air and the lilies in the field, and who made the whole realm of nature tributary to His teachings, to refuse to avail Himself of moral precepts and divine truths simply because they were more fully developed and more earnestly practised among the Essenes than among the rest of his co-religionists."[3]

But there is a great deal more to be said about the Essenes than that they were outwardly an exclusive ultra-Jewish community practising the most rigid observance of the

[1] Compare with this the beautiful verse description of the temptation of the Buddha as given in Sir Edwin Arnold's *Light of Asia*, book vi.

[2] See p. 207 *infra*.   [3] Vol. ii, p. 203, art. "Essenes."

Mosaic Laws, more particularly in reference to ceremonial purification. Our principal knowledge of them is derived from Philo and Josephus. Philo tells us that:

"They give innumerable demonstrations, by their constant and unalterable holiness throughout the whole of their life, their avoidance of oaths and falsehoods, and by their firm belief that God is the source of all good, but of nothing evil. Of their love of virtue they give proofs in their contempt for money, fame, and pleasure; their continence and endurance; in their satifying their wants easily; in their simplicity, cheerfulness of temper, modesty, order, firmness, etc. As instances of their love to man, are to be mentioned their benevolence, equality, and their having all things in common."[1]

It is readily seen how much the character and teachings of Jesus correspond with these characteristics.

Mr. Fairweather in his work *The Background of the Gospels,* p. 16, says of the Essenes:

"The sect cannot have originated later than the middle of the second century B.C. According to Friedlander, its beginnings go back to the golden age of the Wisdom literature, and Essenism is to be regarded as the development of one of the prevailing religious tendencies of the pre-Maccabaean Judaism, in short, as the ripe fruit of Jewish Hellenism."

It is easy to see in this work by Mr. Fairweather the difficulty which confronts the historian in his endeavour to explain this and other Gnostic sects if he is unacquainted with the deep and ancient source of the Gnosis.

Every candidate for admission to the Essene community had to submit to a noviciate extending over three years. Having successfully passed through this, he was admitted to a second stage, lasting two years, in which he was called an "approacher," but was still excluded from many of the communal practices of the Community, even from the common meal. If this stage was satisfactorily passed, the candidate became an "associate" or full member, when he took the oaths of the community to follow their practices, and moreover a strict oath of secrecy concerning those things which were not to be disclosed to the public, i.e. their secret teachings, for Josephus tells us (*War*, II, viii, 8) that they had

[1] *Dictionary of Christian Biography*, vol. ii, p. 198.

esoteric doctrines and ancient books on magical cures and exorcisms.

Here, again, we find " miracles " of healing and the casting out of demons—what we should nowadays call mediumistic obsession—to have been the principal demonstrations of the occult powers attributed to Jesus.

It is evident, however, that when Jesus commenced his public mission, he set aside all the practices of ceremonial purity to which the Essenes so strictly conformed. He came " eating and drinking," and that even with " publicans and sinners."[1] He heartily condemned the Pharisees, some sects of whom were only a little less strict in their ideas of ceremonial purity than were the Essenes. How is it that the Gospels never mention the Essenes, nor is there any reference to them in the whole of the New Testament? Have the original documents which would disclose the connection of Christianity with the Essene community and their inner secret occult and mystical teachings been destroyed by those precious Church " Fathers " who destroyed so many priceless documents which would have disclosed the real origin of their Cult? This must be at least a likely surmise.

Did Philo refer to the highest Initiates among the Essenes when he spoke of " the ancient sages " in the quotation which I have given on pp. 105–6? Perhaps; but also he must have been aware that the highest Adepts are absolutely unknown to the world at large, and are not to be found in any outward communities.

In this connection there is one problem which bears upon the question of the historical man Jesus. Philo was contemporary with his supposed date, yet he never mentions him. How was that if Jesus was such a great teacher and miracle worker, or if he was greater even than that, as claimed in the Gospels and in traditional Christian doctrine?

Setting aside now these controversial questions, we find that we have to make a very clear distinction in the first instance between the man Jesus and the appellation of *Christos* which was given to him, and which simply means *Anointed*. This is itself a term indicating the Initiate. It is the equivalent

[1] *Matt.* xi. 19.

of the term Buddha, *Enlightened.* It has become so cus-
tomary to use the term *Christ* as if it was a proper name that
the original meaning has been almost entirely lost sight of.

Now the most important key to the interpretation of the
Gospels lies in the distinction between the utterances of the
man Jesus speaking as a personal teacher, and the utterances of the Initiate *Christos* speaking as one who had realized
his divine " Sonship," his oneness with the " Father "—
speaking, in fact, as the *Logos* of St. John's Gospel, which is
essentially a *Gnostic* Gospel.

Paul understood well this distinction. He disregards
entirely any " Life " of Jesus apart from the Crucifixion and
Resurrection, which, as already said, are *mystery* allegories;
and surely if he attached any importance to the *man* Jesus
as a personal teacher, he would constantly have dwelt upon
both his living example and his teachings. But what Paul
preached was the indwelling Christos *principle* which had to
be " formed " or " brought to birth " *in* the individual. It
would obviously be absurd to speak thus of the personal
Jesus, save only in the injunction to: " Let that same mind
be in you which was also in Christ Jesus " (*Phil.* ii. 5). But
that " mind " is just precisely that which makes the man an
Initiate, a " twice-born," a " divine Son." Thus Paul says
(1 *Cor.* ii. 16), " But we have the mind of Christ." It is
Cosmic Mind. That " Christ in you " is the higher *spiritual
Self* of each individual: shining only as a dim spark in the
ordinary individual at the present stage of the evolution of
humanity on its way back to its Source in the ONE, but yet
recoverable in its full glory by a knowledge of " the mysteries
of the kingdom of heaven " which such men as the Christ
and the Buddha came to disclose to such as could receive it?
It is the Cosmic Logos of the opening verses of St. John's
Gospel, and, being also " the Light which lighteth every
man coming into the world," i.e. the Higher self, it is that
with which each individual must necessarily be at-oned if
he would be " saved," i.e. brought back to his original spiritual
consciousness and estate.

Paul clearly teaches this distinction between the lower and
the higher self. In *Romans* vii. 18 he says:

" For I know that in me, that is, in my flesh, dwelleth no good thing: for to will is present with me, but to do that which is good is not."

And in verses 22 and 23:

" For I delight in the law of God *after the inward man*: but I see a different law in my members, warring against the law of my mind (the mind of Christ), and bringing me into captivity under the law of sin which is in my members."

Also in chapter viii. 6, he makes the distinction between the lower and the higher *mind*.

" For the mind of the flesh is death; but the mind of the spirit is life and peace."

Now it is just this lower mind which we normally call " ourselves "; for we normally identify " ourselves " with our bodies. We easily link up this teaching with our modern knowledge of psychology, for this *lower self*, this " mind of the flesh " is nothing more or less than the backward pull of that lower animal stage through which we have passed, and which is now *active* as the subconscious of the individual and the Race. What we have to learn is to subject this lower mind to the dictates of the higher Self, the supra-conscious, the mind of the indwelling Christ principle; to dissociate the idea " I " from this mortal body and fix it on the immortal Self, so that we can say with Paul (*Gal.* ii. 20):

" I have been crucified with Christ; yet I live; and yet no longer I, but Christ liveth in me."

When the individual is thus at-oned with the Christ principle, his higher Self, he realizes to the full his oneness with the " Father," the supreme ONE, and can speak of that oneness as Jesus did, and as many had done before him. For this attainment of oneness was known ages before the Gospels were written—as witness the quotations I have given on p. 90 *supra*. There is not, in fact, a single disclosure of man's spiritual nature and " the way of return " set forth in the Gospels which can in any sense be called new. What is new—and not true—are those ideas and dogmas which the *unitiated* creed-makers subsequently imposed on those Scriptures.

" This is the Ennead with which he rewarded those that fled from matter; they became happy, they became perfect, they knew God and the Truth, they comprehended the mystery which works in Man; for what cause He has revealed Himself, that they might see Him, for He is in truth Invisible; and for their sakes He has revealed in words His Logos, so that they might know Him and become gods and perfect."[1]

It is quite easy to separate the two classes of sayings of Jesus as we have them in the Gospels. To the one class belong the moral teachings: in no wise different from those which had been given to the world over and over again by other teachers. To this class also belong the parables. To the second class, that in which Jesus speaks as the Logos, belong all those sayings in which he claims his divine Sonship and his oneness with the " Father "; though even here one might interpret some of them as being simply what an Initiate, one fully aware of his divine nature, might say, as already shown in quotations from the *Book of the Dead*.

These Logos sayings are particularly in evidence in the Gnostic Gospel of St. John.

" I and the Father are one " (x. 30).

" I am in the Father and the Father in me " (xiv. 11).

" I am the light of the world " (viii. 12).

" I am the way, and the truth, and the life; no one cometh unto the Father, but by (or through) me " (xiv. 6).

" I am the resurrection, and the life " (xi. 25).

In the *Bhagavad Gītā*, Krishna, speaking as the Logos, says:

" He, my servant, who worships me with exclusive devotion, having completely overcome the qualities (rajas, tamas, and sattva), is fitted to be absorbed in Brahma the Supreme. I am the embodiment of the Supreme Ruler, and of the incorruptible, of the unmodifying, and of the eternal law, and of endless bliss " (chapter xiv).

Also:

" Let a man, restraining all these (tumultuous senses) remain in devotion at rest in me, his true self " (chapter ii).

There is perhaps nothing that discloses more clearly the pre-Christian existence of this ancient doctrine of salvation

[1] *The Gnosis of Light*, p. 53.

through realization of the *divine. man*—the Christ principle
in each individual—than these and similar passages in this
ancient Scripture, which is part of the great Indian epic the
Mahābhārata. According to the best Hindu authorities, the
Mahābhāratian period was 5000 B.C.

Jesus and Krishna are interchangeable characters as human
personalities representing the divine in man. Fortunately
the teachings of Krishna have not been so flagrantly treated
in dogma as those of Jesus. In the *Bhagavad Gītā* he is
represented as the charioteer of Arjuna, but no one takes
that for a historical fact. Yet he has also a legendary
history which is almost an exact parallel of the Gospel story.
His mother was Devaki, who was overshadowed by Vishnu,
and thus gave birth to Krishna as that god's *Avatara.* Kansa,
the Indian King Herod, sought to slay him, and in doing so
slew thousands of newly born babes. His birth was an-
nounced by a star in heaven. He is also said to have been
put to death on *a tree*, and to have risen again. The tree
symbol appears to have been to a certain extent interchangeable with that of the cross. In *Acts* v. 30, Jesus is said by
Peter to have been hanged on a tree, and in *Galatians* iii. 13,
Paul also speaks of him as having been hanged on a tree.
These variants of the orthodox crucifixion story are significant as showing its derivation from earlier crucified Saviour
myths. Krishna is further said to have ascended bodily into
heaven after his resurrection, and there are numerous other
parallels between his life and that of Jesus.[1]

The distinction between the personal Jesus and the Cosmic
Christ or Logos *principle* is an important one in the interpretation of the *Sayings* in St. John's Gospel, which are
admittedly so different from those of the Synoptics. Ecclesiastical Christianity has interpreted these Sayings as applying in every case to the personal Jesus; hence all the creedal
assertions as to what we must believe about that supposed
or actual historical character. But the *esoteric* interpretation
is quite clear in the light of the fact that the Christ *principle*—
the " light which lighteth every man coming into the world "
(*John* i. 9)—is the *Higher Self* of each individual, as already

[1] Cf. Doane, *Bible Myths*, chapter xxviii.

explained; and it is only through the recovery by the lower self—our present personalities—of a full knowledge and consciousness of that Higher Self in its oneness with the ONE or " Father," that we can " come " or *return* to that " Father," that source from whence we have descended into these lower worlds.

And if any of our modern teachers of the Gospels will still adhere to the literal word of the Scripture, and to the efficacy of a belief in the *personal* Jesus as the Saviour, then we will ask them where to-day are the signs of that belief as given in the following passages:

" He that believeth on me, the works that I do shall he do also; and greater works than these shall he do " (*John* xiv. 12).

" If ye have faith as a grain of mustard seed, ye shall say unto this mountain, Remove hence to yonder place; and it shall remove; and nothing shall be impossible unto you " (*Matt.* xvii. 20).

" And these signs shall follow them that believe: in my name they shall cast out devils; they shall speak with new tongues; they shall take up servants, and if they drink any deadly thing, it shall in no wise hurt them; they shall lay hands on the sick, and they shall recover " (*Mark* xvi. 17, 18).

To-day—yes, and even while those words were being spoken, and ages before that—the great Masters of Wisdom in the East could, and did, and can accomplish such things;[1] not by any " belief " but by actual knowledge of their own innate powers. Yet your modern Christian has not even " so learnt Christ " that he can keep his own body free from sickness—not to mention sin and death. How can he when it is to the personal, historical Jesus that he is looking for help, and not to the Christ *within*? He will even attribute his sickness and misfortunes to " the Will of God," these being " sent " to him as trials of " faith." Doubtless from one point of view there is much in such a " faith " which is praiseworthy; and it does serve many as consolation in this world of sorrow and suffering. But it is based on a childish conception of " God " in the first instance, and, " we speak wisdom among the full-grown " (1 *Cor.* ii. 6).

[1] An illuminating work on this subject is the recently published volume by Paul Brunton, *A Search in Secret India*, as also *Tibetan Yoga*, by Dr. W. Y. Evans-Wentz.

It is significant that the same literalizing process which has taken place in connection with the legends about Jesus, took place also in connection with the birth and other stories about Krishna. Large numbers of Hindus of all castes and classes celebrate during the month of August the Natal Day of the Divine Man, Krishna, just as Christians celebrate Christmas as the Natal Day of the Divine Man, Jesus. The supposed events in Krishna's life as described in the *Mahābhārata*, in the *Puranas*, and in the *Bhagavad Gītā*, are taken as actual history and Krishna is regarded as the *personal* Saviour by these devotees. He has power to forgive their sins, and to send them health, wealth, and happiness. This is human nature in its spiritual childhood. It must have the definite, the concrete, the *person* to whom to look for guidance and salvation. It has not yet learnt its own powers. It is not yet the " full-grown " to whom St. Paul refers; those who have learnt that their real inner, eternal, immortal SELF is no other than this same Christ, or Krishna, or *Logos Principle: Cosmic* in its nature. When this has been clearly realized, all the spume and froth of " theological " controversy as to the relation of the " Father " to the " Son " is seen to be of no more account to the ocean of Cosmic Truth than that which the sea casts up on the ever-shifting sands to the great ocean itself.

I might remark here that possibly the Gospels, or the Sayings of Jesus—as also of Paul and other Apostles—were written round the idea of " Fatherhood " simply as the only way in which the teachings could be brought home to the minds of a community accustomed to the worship of a *personal* God of a very human nature. This " Father " idea has undoubtedly been, and is to-day, the consolation of countless simple souls who cannot possibly conceive of that oneness with God which is the real root teaching. But ages before the Gospels were written, the ONE had been understood and represented as *impersonal*, as THAT, not HE; yet at the same time as being that ONE LIFE in which all things that exist " live and move and have their being." It was so represented to a race, the early Aryans, who had quite a different mentality from that of the

Jews for whom the Scriptures we are now considering were written.

It should be seen then that when we have recognized this teaching of the inner divine nature of man as a universal teaching of the Ancient Wisdom, it is easily recognizable also in the Christian Scriptures; and those Scriptures become susceptible to quite a different interpretation from that which has been imposed upon them by the Church Creeds, or which they appear to bear in their mere literal word.

Scholarship has doubtless done much to destroy the blind belief in the infallibility of the Scriptures which has prevailed for so many centuries; but scholars are by no means agreed among themselves, and we cannot put our trust in scholarship. This, however, we can confidently assert, that what we have in the authorized version of the Scriptures has been selected, overwritten, and translated and re-translated to conform to an already hardened doctrine such as has come down to us in the traditional Church Creeds. Through all this selection and overwriting, however, enough remains to show those of us who are students of the Ancient Wisdom that the real origin of these Scriptures, as of many others, lies in this Wisdom teaching. Moses, as already said,[1] was an Initiate of this Wisdom. Jesus was *par excellence*, as hinted at in the Gospels and as disclosed in the *Pistis Sophia*, the great Initiator in that Wisdom. Paul also understood it well, but could not disclose it—"God's wisdom in a mystery, even the wisdom that hath been hidden " (1 *Cor.* ii. 6–7)—save to those who were " full-grown." How, indeed, *could* he disclose it to such people as the Christians at Corinth are represented to be in 1 *Corinthians* v and vi? Nor is it any different to-day.

The inevitable tendency of any disclosure of the esoteric doctrine to be misconstrued and materialized has been amply in evidence over and over again in history; and it is exemplified in Paul's Epistles.

" O foolish Galatians, who did bewitch you, before whose eyes Jesus Christ was openly set forth crucified? . . . Are ye so foolish? having begun in the Spirit, do ye now make an end in the flesh? " (*Gal.* iii. 1).

[1] See p. 77 *supra*.

" How turn ye back again to the weak and beggardly elements where-unto ye desire to be in bondage over again? Ye observe days, and months, and seasons, and years. I am afraid of you, lest by any means I have bestowed labour upon you in vain " (*Gal.* iv. 9–11).

In other words, having been taught the esoteric doctrine of the Spirit, the " Christ *in* you "—which Paul refers to a few verses farther on—why did they want to return to the *exoteric* teaching of " The Law "? Perhaps because the esoteric doctrine was still for them " strong meat " which they could not digest; indeed, he addresses them as " my little children, of whom I am again in travail until Christ be formed in you " (verse 19).

Thus in the earliest Apostolic times the process had already begun which ultimately resulted in the " orthodoxy " of a priestly hierarchy absolutely opposed to the teachings of Jesus and of Paul as to the freedom of the Spirit.

We know that the fanatical Christians endeavoured to destroy every trace of this pre-existing Gnosis that could be found in documents and inscriptions in Egypt and else-where. Gradually, however, documents are coming to light which disclose the real truth of the Christian origins. This origin of the Scriptures in the Gnosis is gradually coming to be recognized by independent thinkers and students, as witness the statement of the Rev. F. Lamplugh in his intro-duction to the Gnostic work, *The Gnosis of the Light*, which I have given on p. 100.

Those who do not know anything about the Gnosis—and how many Christian teachers to-day do?—cannot, of course, possibly recognize this fact.

If it be asked how " the Dynamic ideas of the Gnosis became crystallized into Dogmas? "—the answer is easily given. It is, that the ruling power in the Church gradually fell into the hands of ignorant and ambitious men, who did not fail to trade on the credulity and superstitions of the masses—as witness the rise of the temporal power of the Church of Rome and its subsequent history, stained with bloodshed and unspeakable cruelties. So has it ever been with priestcraft; nor is it much different to-day, save that the Church has, fortunately for humanity, lost its temporal power.

The wide, deep, all comprehensive teachings of the Gnosis was, and is still, the natural enemy of this proselytizing and exclusive so-called " Faith "; and the early framers of the Creeds were not slow to perceive it. And, indeed, it is little better to-day within the narrow limits of the Christian sects of whatever denomination, who know nothing of any other religion than their own, but regard all these as " heathen," standing in need of conversion to their own particular beliefs. How different is the statement in the *Bhagavad Gītā*, where Krishna says:

" In whatever form a devotee desires with faith to worship, it is I alone who inspire him with constancy therein, and depending on that faith he seeks the propitiation of that God, obtaining the object of his wishes as is ordained by me alone " (chapter vii).

We are, therefore, very far from saying that the orthodox " Gospel " is not, or cannot be, a means for salvation from the grosser temptations of this world to countless millions of sincere Christians. Sufficient unto each individual is that which he can receive. It is only the exclusive and proselytizing attitude which we condemn; the idea that the individual can only be " saved " by a belief in these outward doctrines.

The proper place of the Christian Scriptures in their relation to man's great effort to recover the knowledge of his own nature and its relation to the spiritual world, cannot be estimated so long as these Scriptures are regarded as something *sui generis*, as the only revelation granted to man, and so long as they are not studied in the light of our wider knowledge to-day.

Six hundred years before Christianity was ever heard of under that name, the Buddha taught a doctrine of salvation, of *attainment*, in a form suitable to a vastly different racial intellect than that of the Jews to whom the Christian Scriptures are primarily addressed. Yet these teachings of the Buddha are in no wise different from the teachings of these later Scriptures when they are *esoterically* interpreted. The Buddha also taught a morality in all respects the same as that which Jesus presented, and certainly more consistently practised by his followers.

In their *exoteric* form, and excepting Paul's Epistles, the Christian Scriptures were written exclusively and wholly for that peculiar and ultra-exclusive race the Jews. It speaks their language and appeals to their exclusive ideas of " God," whose character, however, as presented in the Old Testament is by no means acceptable to us now. That " God " has unfortunately been " fathered " on the Christian Church. Our ideas of a Supreme Being are vastly different to-day. They become more and more *impersonal* as we learn to think more and more cosmically.

But what are or were the Jews as a race in the countless races of Humanity which preceded them through the countless millions of years that Man has been on the earth, and will follow them through the countless millions of years which the Cycles of the Human Race have yet to run? How can we in any sense regard the Jews as a " Chosen People " when we consider the whole history of mankind?—or even such little of it as we know in our recorded historical period of a few thousand years. How, indeed, can we believe at all in a God who has *favourites*—either individually or nationally?

What did the Jews know of the great religious philosophies of the East? It is true that they had Moses and the Prophets who were instructed in this same Wisdom of the Ancients; but—as Jesus himself is reported to have said—" If they hear not Moses and the Prophets, neither will they be persuaded if one rise from the dead." Are our modern Pharisees any different?

The great mystery of all the Mystery Cults of all ages has been the mystery of *Man's inherent divine nature*; the mystery of his " Fall" or descent into this world; and the mystery of his " redemption " or return to his original spiritual estate as a part of the great Cosmic Process.

The method of that return was taught in the *Mysteries* ages before " Christianity " became a historical religion. Dean Inge in his work on *Christian Mysticism* tells us that:

" The conception of salvation as the acquisition by man of Divine attributes is common to many forms of religious thought. It was widely diffused in the Roman Empire at the time of the Christian revelation, and was steadily growing in importance during the first centuries of our era. The Orphic Mysteries had long taught the doctrine " (p. 256).

St. Augustine wrote:

" That which is called the Christian religion existed among the ancients, and never did not exist, from the beginning of the human race until Christ came in the flesh, at which time the true religion which already existed began to be called Christianity" (*Epis. Retrac.*, Lib. I, xiii. 3).

But surely this " Christianity " to which he refers was not that which has come down to us in an ecclesiastical form. No. It was this same ancient Gnosis which has always existed with the Hierarchy of Initiates. Yet it is curious to find such a writer as St. Augustine making a statement of this nature. It is true that at one time he was a Manichæist, and that subsequently he turned to Neoplatonism, and he must therefore have known something of the pre-Christian Gnosis: but after his conversion to orthodox Christianity under the influence of his mother, he violently advocated all the extremes of Roman Catholic dogma, and he could not possibly have found any correspondence between these and any pre-Christian teaching " among the ancients." He persecuted the Donatists who held that holiness was above all things the character of the members of the Church of Christ, and the characteristic of that Church itself; whereas he held that the Church of Apostolic Succession was the only Church of Christ; it alone had the Truth, and there was no salvation outside of it. He also maintained the right of the Church to persecute " heretics." This was in the fifth century (he died A.D. 430), and we all know what these dogmas led to in subsequent centuries. The shrieks of the tortured victims of this " Christian " Church still ring in our ears.

Yet there are passages in his *Confessions* which are purely mystical and Gnostic as, for example, where he describes his transcendental ecstatic experience: which reminds us of Plotinus, and even more of Eastern Yoga, since he not merely abstracted the mind from all sensuous objects, but passed beyond the mind itself.

" Thus step by step was I led upwards from bodies to the soul which perceives by means of bodily senses, and thence to the soul's inward faculty, to which bodily sense reports external facts. . . . And when this power also within me found itself also changeable, it lifted itself up to its own intelligence, and withdrew its thoughts from experience, abstracting itself from the contradictory throng of sensuous images, that it might find out what that light was wherein it was bathed, when it cried out that beyond doubt the unchangeable was better than the changeable, and how it came to know the unchangeable, which it must have known in some way or another, for otherwise it could not have preferred it so confidently to the changeable.   And thus, with the flash of one hurried glance, it attained to the vision of THAT WHICH IS " (Lib. VII, xvii. 2–3).

" And so we came to our own minds, and passed beyond them into the region of unfailing plenty, where Thou feedest Israel for ever with the food of truth, where Life is Wisdom by which all these things come to be, both the things that have been and the things that shall be; and the Life itself never comes to be, but is, as it was and shall be evermore, because in it is neither past nor future but present only, for it is eternal, for past and future are not eternal " (Lib. IX, x. 2).

This is pure Gnosis; and yet this same man can declare that God sent him a toothache as a trial! (Lib. IX, iv. 8). He goes on to say:

" But I could not sustain my gaze; my weakness was dashed back, and I was relegated to my ordinary experience, bearing with me nothing but a loving remembrance, cherishing, as it were, the fragrance of those viands which I was not yet able to feed upon."

Observe the difference between this forced emotional ecstasy and that of the trained Adept in *Raja Yoga*. The one cannot sustain his supra-conscious state, the other can sustain it (*Samadhi*) for hours and days at a time.[1]

How very early the materialization of the spiritual teachings of Jesus and of Paul set in, we have ample evidence in *The Acts of the Apostles* and in Paul's Epistles.   Paul found it hard to convey *spiritual* teachings, i.e. the Gnosis, to the early converts.   " And I, brethren, could not speak unto you as unto spiritual, but as unto carnal " (1 *Cor.* iii. 1). Divisions and disputes of doctrine arose even then, and evidently centred round differences of teaching by different Apostles.   " For it hath been signified unto me concerning you . . . that there are contentions among you. . . . Each one of you saith, I am of Paul; and I of Apollos; and I of Cephas; and I of Christ " (1 *Cor.* i. 11–13).

Later on Creeds began to be formulated which were more or less " orthodox " as being held by a majority, until finally " the Dynamic ideas of the Gnosis became crystallized into Dogmas,"[1] and the Gnosis became altogether a " heresy," while instead of a spiritual Church, setting an example of a renunciation of the world, a priestly hierarchy was established of proud, ambitious, worldly men, having often, even as their supreme Pontiff, horribly wicked men, claiming absolute power over both the bodies and souls of men. And yet apparently intelligent men accept those dogmas even to-day.

Most certainly the Christian Scriptures, even in their present over-written form, do present that " religion which existed among the ancients, and never did not exist, from the beginning of the human race "; but most certainly also not so when literally interpreted. It is only the *form* that is different, because, as already said, it had to be adapted to the Jewish mentality. In the first instance we find the form largely bound up with the idea of a *Messiah* who should deliver his " chosen people " and rule as an earthly king. When this Messiah was rejected and put to death, the story went about among his immediate followers—so at least the Gospel history would tell us—that he had been resurrected, and had been seen by a great many of them. Then there arose the idea of an almost immediate Second Coming.

" Verily, I say unto you, There be some of them that stand here, which shall in no wise taste death, till they see the Son of man coming in his kingdom " (*Matt.* xvi. 28).

" And they shall see the Son of man coming on the clouds of heaven with power and great glory. . . . Verily, I say unto you, This generation shall not pass away till all these things be accomplished " (*Matt.* xxiv. 30–5, *Mark* xiii. 26–30, *Luke* xxi. 27–32).

" Behold, I tell you a mystery: We shall not all sleep, but we shall all be changed, in a moment, in the twinkling of an eye, at the last trump: for the trumpet shall sound, and the dead shall be raised incorruptible, and we shall be changed " (1 *Cor.* xv. 51).

" For the Lord himself shall descend from the heaven, with a shout,

[1] See p. 100 *supra*.

with the voice of the Archangel, and with the trump of God: and the dead in Christ shall rise first: then we that are alive, that are left, shall together with them be caught up in the clouds, to meet the Lord in the air " (1 *Thess.* iv. 16–17).

Did there not seem to be ample warrant in these and other passages for an immediate " Second Coming "? Are we, then, dealing here with the infallible word of God, or are we only dealing with certain popular beliefs? As regards the Gospel narrative of the Prophetic words of Jesus respecting the great tribulation and his own Second Coming—repeated substantially in the same words in the twenty-fourth chapter of *Matthew*, the thirteenth chapter of *Mark*, and the twenty-first chapter of *Luke*, but not at all in *John*—since " these things " were *not* accomplished during that generation: we have here clearly a case of words attributed to Jesus merely to support the hope of an immediate Second Coming which was the prevalent belief of the Apostles and early converts. But if such a circumstantial statement could be attributed to Jesus by the Synoptics, we are faced with the choice of either accepting them as genuine, though falsified by subsequent history, or else accepting the unreliability of the Gospels in general. It is the latter alternative which we here accept. Whatever may have been their original form, they have been over-written to introduce material which only existed in the imagination of the writers, more particularly in connection with the idea of an earthly Messiah, as evidenced by the constant use of the phrase " that the scripture might be fulfilled," or " as it is written." An immediate Second Coming is indeed fervently believed in by thousands to-day, who imagine that they can read in modern events " the signs of the times " as given in the chapters above mentioned, and also in *Revelation*.

Did Paul also share in that popular belief in an immediate Second Coming, with its crude materialistic idea of a physical resurrection of the dead from their graves? We can hardly think so when we understand that Paul's teaching was that of a *spiritual* resurrection from the present deadness of the earthly man. Yet the words attributed to him as quoted above are explicit enough, and we must therefore say either that he spoke with two voices, or else conclude that his Epistles have been tampered with and over-written. It is the latter alternative which we prefer; and indeed it is more than doubtful whether some of the Epistles attributed to him were written by him at all. This idea of a " Second Coming " is, as said, very prevalent to-day with a certain sect. England and America have been placarded with posters stating that " millions now living will never die." But these are side issues. Christian doctrine centres round the idea of a blood sacrifice on the Cross of the " only begotten Son of God " as an atonement for the sins of the world—based on the literal acceptance of the allegory of man's " fall " as given in the *Genesis* narrative.

But if we reject the literal interpretation of the *Genesis* narrative, how can we accept the literal interpretation of the Crucifixion narrative? As in the case of the " Second Coming," so also as regards this *exoteric* doctrine of atonement by blood sacrifice, there are plenty of passages which, if taken literally, abundantly support it. Nevertheless, and as I have already said, most of these passages are readily seen to be symbolical in their use of the term " blood," or " blood of Christ." Paul well knew the inner meaning of the symbolism, but found that he had to teach a very *exoteric* doctrine to the great majority of his followers.

Now this " Christ in you " is, in a certain sense, the sacrificial victim of the lower personal self. Thus the author of *Hebrews* speaks of those who " Crucify to themselves the Son of God afresh, and put him to an open shame " (*Heb.* vi. 6).

This is one of the aspects of the allegory of the Crucifixion, which was a " pagan " allegory long before it became identified with the man Jesus. In another aspect of this allegory, however, it is the lower personal man who has to " crucify " his personality with its earthly passions and desires in order that he may be " resurrected " from the deadness of this lower nature. The animal must die that the god may be brought to birth.

"They that are of Christ Jesus have crucified the flesh with the passions and lusts thereof " (*Gal.* v. 25).

Hippolytus tells us that the Ophites, who were a Christian Gnostic sect, held that the saying " the dead shall rise from their graves " signifies that the Earthly Man shall be born again spiritual.[1]

This " dying " of the lower that the higher may be brought to birth is one of the deepest mysteries of the Cosmic Process. The divine *monad, spark, soul*—call it what you will— emanates from the ONE and has to pass through all the kingdoms of " Nature." It " descends "—we are compelled to use our common language—to the mineral, passes to the vegetable and thence to the animal; from the animal it passes to man, and from thence to the god. Who shall say what lies beyond that? Suffice it that what we would now regard as godlike is our next stage.

Nowhere, perhaps, has this progressive process been more beautifully expressed than by the Persian mystic and poet, Jalalu'd-Din Rumi:

> " I died from the mineral and became a plant;
> I died from the plant and reappeared in an animal;
> I died from the animal and became a man;
> Wherefore then should I fear?
> When did I grow less by dying?
> Next time I shall die from the man,
> That I may grow the wings of angels.
> From the angel, too, must I seek advance;
>   ' *All things shall perish save His face* '[2]
> Once more shall I wing my way above the angels;
> I shall become that which entereth not the imagination.
> Then let me become naught, naught; for the harp-string crieth unto me,
>   ' Verily unto Him do we return.' "

But as regards our present condition, this " dying " or " crucifixion " is something infinitely more than a mere renouncing of fleshly lusts, or even the severest asceticism. Some little idea of what it involves may be gathered from such works as *Light on the Path* or *The Voice of the Silence*.[3]

Paul's " resurrection from the dead "—however it may be represented in certain passages in his Epistles as being the

---

[1] King, *The Gnostics and Their Remains*, p. 90.   [2] **Koran**, xxvii, 88.
[3] See Bibliography, p. 219.

resurrection of the body at " the last day "—is really the resurrection of the Christ in us from the " tomb " of our carnal nature, the " body of sin " (*Rom.* vi. 6); the " body of death " (*Rom.* vii. 24); in short, our present earthly and mortal nature. For assuredly the Christ, the higher spiritual Self, is " buried " in the " tomb " of this same mortal self, even as it is " crucified " on the " cross " of matter. Herein lies the key to the whole Bible allegory.

But most assuredly as it is now " buried," so also shall it be " resurrected." Why the Divine Man, the Christos, the Logos, should be thus " buried in this our lower nature " is a profound *cosmic* mystery; yet this " grave " will certainly have no power ultimately to hold the Divine Man, who must inevitably " rise from the tomb on the *third day* "—another occult cosmic allusion.

As for the resurrection stories which we have in the Gospels, with their variants and contradictions: these are merely stories which gradually accumulated and gained credence. Let us briefly review them.

Matthew says that it was the two Marys who first saw Jesus, immediately after the apparition of an angel at the empty tomb. Subsequently he appeared to the *eleven* disciples at Galilee.

Luke says that the two women saw " two men in dazzling apparel," but says nothing about the appearance of Jesus; and that when they told this " to the eleven," they were not believed. Peter, however, went to the tomb to verify their story that it was empty, and found it so, but he is not said to have seen any vision. It was " two disciples . . . one of them named Cleophas " who first saw Jesus according to this account. Farther on (verse 34), however, he is said to have already appeared to Simon (Peter); but it was at Jerusalem, not in Galilee, that he first appeared to the *eleven*.

John tells a story of Mary Magdalene first seeing the empty tomb, and then running to tell Peter and " the other disciple whom Jesus loved." These two set out to run to the tomb, and the " other disciple " outran Peter, though it was Peter who first went into the empty tomb. Meanwhile " Mary was standing without at the tomb weeping." But she also looked into the tomb, and saw two angels, who asked her why she was weeping. When she had told them she turned round and saw Jesus, but thought that he was the gardener. When he spoke to her, however, she recognized him. How is it that we are not told that Peter and the other disciple saw the angels and also Jesus? Afterwards we are told that Jesus appeared twice to the other disciples in a room with closed doors; and the " doubting Thomas " incident is described. After this Jesus is said to have manifested himself to some of the disciples at the sea of Tiberius, where he performed the miracle of the draught of fishes.

Mark also records the visit of Mary Magdalene, Mary the Mother of James, and Salome to the tomb, on reaching which they saw that the heavy stone that had closed it had been rolled away, and that there was " a young man sitting on the right side, arrayed in a white robe." He told them to tell the disciples and Peter that Jesus had risen, and was going before them into Galilee, where they would see him. Strange to say, this account, which is supposed to be the earliest, says nothing about any subsequent appearances of Jesus, but ends with the statement that the women " said nothing to anyone; for they were afraid." In the subsequent Appendix, however, it is stated that he appeared first of all to Mary Magdalene; next to " two of them, as they walked, on their way into the country," and subsequently to the eleven " as they sat at meat." We may gather from this that the resurrection stories—with their palpable discrepancies and variation—grew up after Mark's Gospel had been written, and were then added in subsequent manuscripts.

It is not possible here to enter into any discussion as to how these resurrection stories arose, or as to how much credence should be given to them, or in what kind of a body Jesus may be supposed to have appeared. It will suffice to say that modern psychical research fully corroborates the possibility of such appearances; but it by no means follows that we can base thereon the theological dogmas which subsequently became attached thereto. We might note, however, that the tradition in the main as accepted by the early Christians was that of a *physical* resurrection. The empty tomb story confirms this in the first instance. Why, we might ask, should the disciples who had already seen Moses and Elijah in the transformation scene[1] be astonished to hear that Jesus had been seen alive? Why should they be so " terrified and affrighted " as the account in *Luke* represents them to be as " supposing that they beheld a spirit "? It shows them in a very poor light as subsequent expositors of " the mysteries of the kingdom of heaven." And, in fact, these men never were such expositors. Paul is the only one who had any apprehension of the real *esoteric* significance of the Christ Myth in its cosmic aspects, while at the same time he was obliged to base his teachings principally on the *exoteric* beliefs of his hearers which centred round the personal Jesus.

The belief of the early disciples in a *physical* resurrection of Jesus would appear to have been intimately associated with their conception of a physical resurrection at the almost immediate Second Coming of Jesus, when the dead would rise from their sleep in the grave in their physical bodies, while those who were still alive on earth would be " caught up in the clouds to meet the Lord in the air " (1 *Thess.* iv. 17). The Church has perpetuated this carnal doctrine of the resurrection of Jesus, and of the " resurrection day," or day of Judgment. To-day, however, we have every evidence that the individual does not " sleep " in the tomb, but on the contrary is very much alive after the body has been buried; and we doubt not that this was just as well known to the instructed in those earlier days.

We may now turn to the reputed writings in the canon of Scripture of the one Apostle who really understood the *cosmic* principles involved in the Incarnation, and the relation of these principles to the " salvation " of the individual.

[1] *Matt.* xvii. 3.   *Mark* ix. 4.   *Luke* ix. 30.

CHAPTER VI

THE NEW TESTAMENT SCRIPTURES

II. PAUL'S EPISTLES

THE Epistles of Paul have always been a stumbling-block and an enigma for the theologians: so much so that at the one extreme it has been suggested that " Paulinism " should be cut out of Christianity altogether, and the teachings of Jesus made the sole reference for Christian Doctrine, while at the other extreme he is regarded as the great exponent of orthodox Christian theology, and indeed by some writers as the real founder of the Christian religion.

Doubtless there is much in his Epistles *as we have them* to support this latter contention; but then we cannot accept them as we have them. They are too full of contradictions to be credited to one and the same author, let alone what we know to have been the practice of over-writing, interpolating, and revising, in Gospels, Acts, and Epistles alike, in the interests of a gradually hardening and materializing orthodoxy.

But apart from this there is ample evidence that Paul had both an exoteric and an esoteric teaching. Also, as in the Gospels so in his Epistles, we must distinguish between the *man* Jesus and the Christ *principle*, the Logos, from which each individual derives that " spark " of the divine which it is his great task to bring to a flame *here and now*, so that he may himself become as truly a manifestation thereof as those instances which have been put before us in several historically recorded Incarnations or *Avataras*: in Krishna, in Gautama Buddha, and now in Jesus Christ. What these were as *men* they were because of their realization of their inmost divine nature in its *oneness* with " That Subtle Being of which this whole universe is composed," the ONE, the " Father " of the Gospels.

We may regard these *Avataras* under two aspects, either as it were from below, from the *human* side as being the individual *man* who has thus attained to the full consciousness of his divinity, with all the supernormal powers which that brings with it; or we may regard them as it were from above, as being the Supreme Spirit, the Logos, *using* that particular personality to manifest his divine nature to the world, and thereby the potentiality of that nature as existing in every man. Thus Clement, the Gnostic Church " Father," writes:

" The Logos of God became man that from man you might learn how man may become God."[1]

Both of the above views are possibly true, yet it must be pointed out that even in this latter case the *personality* through which the Logos can manifest must be an exceptional one; it must be one which is the resultant of a long series of incarnations devoted to this great achievement of knowledge of the real SELF, and must even have a special physical heredity, though this would follow more or less naturally as the good *Karma* of the individual.

I have already pointed out that in the Gospels Jesus is represented as speaking sometimes as the personal teacher, the Adept, the Initiator, and sometimes as the Logos. What we have to recognize now in Paul's Epistles is that he deals principally with the aspect of the historical Jesus as a manifestation of the Logos, and hardly at all with his history and teachings. Whether he actually wrote all the Epistles ascribed to him or not: or whether he actually wrote all the words therein ascribed to him—which we certainly consider was not the case—there is ample evidence that he was familiar with the Gnostic teachings, and more particularly with this fundamental principle of the " Christ *in* you "; and that he endeavoured to teach it in so far as the level of understanding of those whom he addressed would permit. But this understanding, as a matter of fact, did not go very far. He had to reproach the Galatians for going back from the spiritual truth which set them free from the " Law " (chapter iii).

" O foolish Galatians . . . are ye so foolish? having begun in the Spirit, do ye now make an end in the flesh? . . . How turn ye back

[1] *Strom.* iv. 23.

again to the weak and beggarly rudiments (or *elements*), whereunto ye desire to be in bondage over again? Ye observe days, and months, and seasons, and years. I am afraid of you, lest by any means I have bestowed labour upon you in vain."

" My little children, of whom I am again in travail until Christ be formed *in* you."

Again he says in 1 *Corinthians* iii:

" And I, brethren, could not speak unto you as unto spiritual, but as unto carnal, as unto babes in Christ. I fed you with milk, not with meat; for ye were not yet able to bear it."

And in chapter ii:

" And I, brethren, when I came unto you, came not with excellency of speech or of wisdom, proclaiming to you the mystery of God. . . . Howbeit we speak wisdom among the full-grown; yet a wisdom not of this world (or age)."

What was that " Wisdom " which Paul could not declare openly? We say that it was the ancient Gnosis, and that there is abundant evidence of it for those who know what that Gnosis is. Or let those who think that there is nothing further to disclose turn to the *Pistis Sophia* and try to master the cosmical and anthropological facts which the *symbolism* therein employed covers. And what of those " unspeakable words which it is not lawful for a man to utter" which Paul says that he heard when he was " caught up into paradise "? Nay, is it not the common experience of all mystics, of whatever age or religion, that they *cannot* in the nature of things communicate what they thus experience? Apart from that there is the traditional " mandate " of the Mysteries to which Plotinus refers in the quotation I have already given on pp. 74–5.

It is well known that with the classical Christian mystics, the crucifixion and the resurrection are a continual process. In *Colossians* ii. 20 Paul speaks of dying with Christ and being raised with him as a process that had already taken place in his hearers.

" If ye died with Christ ";

And in iii. 1:

" If then ye *were* raised together with Christ."

In *Colossians* i. 23, Paul speaks of the Gospel as having been " preached in all creation under heaven." What Gospel? Certainly not that which was only just beginning to be preached by Paul and the other Apostles. Jesus is said by Paul to have " abolished death, and brought life and immortality to light through the gospel " (2 *Tim.* i. 10). How can such a claim be made for the historical Jesus? It shows an absolute lack of knowledge of other Scriptures and beliefs—for example, the books of the Vedanta, or the Egyptian *Book of the Dead*. The one thing that the Egyptians most firmly believed in was immortality—as the quotations I have already given show. Was Paul unaware of this? Did he really mean the *historical* " Saviour Christ Jesus "? We can hardly think so, for the passage is certainly not true in that sense. It is only true in the sense that *Christ*—not the historical Jesus—is that indwelling principle which is the " light which lighteth every man coming into the world," pre-Christian as well as post-Christian. Paul hardly refers to any events in the life of the historical Jesus save only the crucifixion, which he uses in the proper allegorical sense as indicating a continual happening. There is no mention in his Epistles of any Virgin Birth, nor does he refer to any of the supposed miracles. He only quotes Jesus twice, one quotation which is not in the Gospels, and another which is differently worded.

" It is more blessed to give than to receive " (*Acts* xx. 25).

" This is my body which is (broken) for you: this do in remembrance of me. . . . This cup is the new covenant in my blood: this do, as oft as ye drink it, in remembrance of me " (1 *Cor.* xi. 24–5).

Apart from these words of Jesus at the Last Supper as here quoted by Paul, we have them in *John* vi. 53:

" Jesus therefore said unto them, Verily, verily, I say unto you, except ye eat of the flesh of the Son of man and drink his blood, ye have not life in yourselves."

Is it not perfectly obvious that " flesh " and " blood " are here used as symbols of *spiritual* sustenance? For verily and indeed, unless we can and do assimilate that *cosmic spiritual*

principle which is the " Christ " of St. Paul, we cannot have
any abiding life in us.   Yet see how this symbolical language
has been degraded and materialized by the Church in the
doctrine of the " real presence."   This carnalization of the
symbolism is clearly derived from the *pagan* rites, and the
concept that by partaking of the flesh and blood of the
sacrificed animal victim offered to the god, the devotee
actually partook of the nature of the god.

And as regards this same " Christ " of St. Paul, what of
the remarkable opening verses of the tenth chapter of
1 *Corinthians*:

> " For I would not, brethren, have you ignorant, how that our fathers
> were all under the cloud, and all passed through sea; and were all
> baptized unto Moses in the cloud and in the sea; and did all eat the
> same spiritual meat; and did all drink the same spiritual drink; for
> they drank of a spiritual rock that followed them; and the rock was
> Christ."

Here we have symbolism, allegory, through and through.
How could the " fathers " partake of " Christ " if the Christ
was only Jesus of Nazareth?   Paul here uses the same
words " eat " and " drink " as in the symbolical eucharistic
rite, which, as I have previously said, was a pre-Christian
rite.   However much Paul may have been made to appear
to have been speaking of the historical Jesus in other passages
in his Epistles, it is quite clear to those who have some
knowledge of the inner teaching of the Gnosis, that it was
this inner *spiritual* truth of our inherent truth of our inherent
divine nature that he was endeavouring to convey in his
teachings, but found the greatest difficulty in doing so to his
" spiritual babes."   Nor is it any easier to-day in a Church
wholly given up to the exoteric materialistic and " carnal "
doctrine.

Paul claimed no enlightenment either from the life of the
man Jesus or from any of his Apostles.   Indeed, as is well
known, he was in opposition to Peter.   In *Galatians* ii. 6, he
says that " They who were of repute (i.e. the Apostles) im-
parted nothing to me."   Also in i. 11: " For I make known
to you, brethren, as touching the gospel which was preached
by me, that it is not after man.   For neither did I receive it

from man (or a man), nor was I taught it, but *it came to me* through revelation of Jesus Christ." He says (i. 16) that it came to him " when it was the good pleasure of God . . . to reveal his Son *in* me." Here, again, we have not the inspiration or doctrine or teachings of the man Jesus of Nazareth, but the direct inspiration of the " Christ *in* you."

Thus it is that we never find Paul referring in any way to the teachings of Jesus as the Master and Guide. His real doctrine—whatever else he may have been made to say—is that our resurrection from our present spiritual deadness by this same power of the indwelling Christ principle which he claims to have enlightened him.

He says, again, in *Ephesians* iii. 3: " How that by revelation was made known unto me the mystery . . . of Christ (*Christos*)." And in 1 *Corinthians* ii. 10–16:

" But unto us God revealed them (the things of the Spirit) through the Spirit; for the Spirit searches all things, yea, the deep things of God. . . . But we received, not the spirit of the world, but the spirit which is of God; that we might know the things that are freely given to us by God. Which things also we speak, not in words which man's wisdom teacheth, but which the Spirit teacheth. . . . But we have the mind of Christ."

This direct spiritual knowledge of " the things of the Spirit " has been the goal and the achievement of the *Initiate* in all ages. It is no prerogative of Christianity in any shape or form.

Apart from the Logos doctrine which Paul preached, but which Christian theology subsequently limited and applied to the man Jesus as being the one and only incarnation of the Logos, it is of course open for the devotees of the Christian religion, and who know no other, to regard the man Jesus as a supreme example of the manifestation of the nature of the Supreme Spirit or " God." In other words, that through the person of the man Jesus " God " was able to manifest in a degree which had never before been possible. Yet even this is quite a different matter from regarding him as the one and only " Saviour " of the world, or as being " very God of very God," an " only-begotten Son." Can we repeat too often that it is the " Christ *in* you " who is the " Saviour," and not the historical man, however valuable his life may be as an example of what each individual may and must become.

" But we all, with unveiled face, beholding as in a mirror the glory of the Lord, are transformed into the same image from glory to glory."[1]

Dr. Dibelius, in his work, *Die Formgeschichte des Evangeliums*, in an illuminating chapter on the Mythological elements in the Scriptures, has some remarks *re* St. Paul's teaching which are confirmatory of the view I am here putting forward.   After saying that:

" What the Churches preserved of the words of their Master (the ' sayings ') as rules and for teaching purposes shows *the sign of a teacher rather than a god*,"

he goes on to say:

" Paul brings a striking confirmation.   He knows this tradition of the sayings and makes use of it when he desires to regulate the life of the Church.   But where he preaches the cult of his God, i.e. of the ' Lord ' Jesus Christ, one looks in vain for a reference to any actual word of Jesus.

" The letters of Paul are un unambiguous proof that there once was a *Christ Mythology*.   At the same time they are a proof that this mythology could not be supported directly from the tradition of the life of Jesus.   For Paul knew this tradition to some extent (1 *Cor.* xi and xv), and if he had needed it he could have made its acquaintance much more closely.   But the Christ-myth through which for his churches he explains the great act of Divine redemption, had no need of the data handed down."[2]

Note here the words " *for his churches*."   In other words, and as we have already contended, Paul used a certain defined teaching *for his churches*, such teaching being adapted to their as yet infantile spiritual understanding and development.   But behind that teaching which centred round the *myth* of Jesus as the incarnated Son of God, Paul had the deeper teaching of the Cosmic Christ, the " Christ in you," which has been that of the Initiates of all ages.   He says (1 *Cor.* ii. 2): " For I determined not to know anything among you save Jesus Christ, and him crucified," obviously

[1] 2 *Cor.* iii. 18.   [2] *From Tradition to Gospel*, p. 267.

implying that there was something else to know.   And moreover, as shown in verses 6 and 7, that it was a superior, deeper
knowledge, a mystery-teaching, a *Theo-Sophia* (θεοῦ σοφίαν
ἐν μυστηρίῳ) which *could* only be disclosed to the " full-
grown," the *spiritual* adult.   Notwithstanding this reserva-
tion, this deeper mystery does appear in the doctrine of the
Cosmic Christ, the " Christ *in* you," but only as applicable
to the growth of the individual to spiritual maturity, to a
full consciousness of his inner divine nature.   There is depth
within depth in the *cosmic* aspect of the *Christos*, some idea
of which may be gleaned from the *Pistis Sophia*, but still
more from Eastern sources of the Gnosis or Ancient Wisdom.
It is hinted at, however, by Paul in *Colossians* i. 16, where
he speaks of " things visible and things invisible, whether
thrones or dominions or principalities or powers."   These are
called *Æons* in the *Pistis Sophia*, but more commonly and
exoterically *gods*, as Paul himself calls them in 1 *Corinthians*
viii. 5, " though there be that are called gods."   The
Initiate does not worship these, much less does he make idols
to represent them.   He commands them.   He goes to the
Root and Source of his own being, the ONE God, the " Father "
exoterically.   We have already seen that though the
Egyptians had a multiplicity of " gods," they recognized
the ONE uncreated God who was the " Father " of the " gods "
of " creation," the Hierarchies of the *manifested* universe.
So also is it in the Hindu and other Pantheons.   Paul
nowhere attempts to teach a cosmogony, but it has to be
learnt by the Initiate who would attain to the highest ranks
of the " Sons of God "; for that, as we have aforesaid, means
knowledge and *conquest* of every condition of existence on all
the planes of the universe.

" Paul," says Dr. Dibelius,[1] " is not the only creator of a
Christ-mythology.   He only makes a greater distinction than
others between the revelation of the humiliation and exaltation
of the Son of God on the one hand and the human tradition
of His earthly life on the other."[2]

Now by a *myth* Dr. Dibelius understands " stories *which
in some fashion tell of many-sided doings of the gods*."[3]   The

---

[1] *From Tradition to Gospel*, p. 268.   [2] Ibid.   [3] Ibid.

following is his statement of the Christ-myth as understood by Paul.

" This myth told the story of the Son of God who abandoned His cosmically intermediate place; in obedience to the Will of God He suffered a human fate, even to death on the Cross; He was finally raised by the power of God from the deepest humiliation to the status of ' Lord ' to whom all the world owed honour till He should come to conquer His enemies and to rule His Kingdom.   The earthly life of this Son of God is only a stage.   That He took this life upon Himself "in the form of a servant " is more important than *how* He lived it in detail. The happenings of His everyday life on earth are unessential as compared with the great Cosmic turning-points of His path, viz. (1) In Divine form. (2) Arrival upon the earth. (3) Raised to a new heavenly glory.   The earthly opponents disappear before the demonic, i.e. before sin, to conquer which He came to earth; before the powers and authorities which bring Jesus to the cross, but which, as risen, He overcomes through His resurrection.   It is of no particular importance to observe in this mythical connection that even the human life of the Son of God is full of blessed power.   When we turn over in our minds the mythical journey of Christ from Heaven back to Heaven we shall not regard it as a miracle that the Son of God is superior to men but rather that He is like them."[1]

But this god-myth is common to many of the " pagan " traditions. I have already referred to it in connection with Krishna; and it is well known that there are a considerable number of " crucified Saviours " in other traditions.   Precisely how this tradition became attached to the historical Jesus we do not know; but there can be no question as to its being a *mystery-teaching*, having a deep cosmological as well as anthropological significance taught only in the inner schools of initiation.   Paul made use, " for his churches," of the *exoteric* doctrine which he found already centred on the historical Jesus; yet, as I have already shown, the *esoteric* doctrine of the *Christ-principle* is clearly to be discerned in many of his phrases.

Over and over again the recovery of his divine nature by " fallen " man by means of this Christ-principle is allegorically and symbolically set forth in the Christian Scriptures. Both the crucifixion and the resurrection is a continual process taking place for the salvation of the whole Race,

[1] *From Tradition in Gospel*, p. 268.

individual ƀy individual; but yet, alas! how very very far
off as regards the Race as a whole.

" The Fall is a present and not a past fact. Man's real fall is that he
is content with the shadow of good. He still eats of the tree of good
and evil, and until the Christ fills the whole consciousness, man will ever
be at war with himself, his brother, and his God."[1]

Paul's teaching that the resurrection is something which
has to be accomplished *here and now*, and not at some future
" Judgment Day," is clearly brought out in *Ephesians* v. 14:

" Awake, thou that sleepest, and arise from the dead, and Christ shall
shine upon thee."

Not Jesus, not Jesus Christ, but the Cosmic *Christ Principle*
which is the inner, real, immortal, and divine SELF of every
individual, and which, as Paul says elsewhere, has to be
" formed," or " brought to birth " *in* you. But this is the
oldest of the old teachings of the Ancient Wisdom, as, indeed,
I hope has already been shown. Neither Jesus nor Paul
could teach anything that was fundamentally new. They
could only put the supreme knowledge of Man's origin,
nature, and destiny which had been taught over and over
again by the ancient Sages and Initiates into a *form* appropriate to their own times and hearers.

Look also at the distinction which Paul makes between
that earthly body which we now possess and the heavenly
body—the " Robe of Glory " of the *Pistis Sophia*—which he
represents in 2 *Corinthians* v. 1 as already existing.

" For we know that if the earthly house of our tabernacle (or bodily
frame) be dissolved, we have a building from God, a house not made
with hands, eternal, in the heavens.

" For verily in this we groan, longing to be clothed upon with our
habitation which is from heaven."

The metaphor here is a little mixed. We can hardly be
" clothed upon " with a " building " or " house." Yet the
meaning is clear enough. It is our Christ or Buddhic body
that we must resume. It is there already, but we have lost
the consciousness of it through our attachment to this our
lower carnal nature.

[1] *Christ in You*, p. 104.

Here again, then, Paul shows himself familiar with the esoteric teaching of the ancient Gnosis; for the existence of this " heavenly body " or " Robe of Glory " is indicated in several ancient Scriptures. The Egyptians called it the *Ba*, or *Bai*. In Buddhism there are three " robes " or " bodies " which the perfected Adept may assume: that of the Nirmānakāya, of the Sambhogakāya, and of the Dharmakāya.[1] In Tibetan Yoga also it is known as the *jai-lüs*, or " rainbow body."

" Triumphing over all Directions, may I be enabled to serve every being with whom I have come into contact. Thus may my divine mission be crowned with success, and may I attain to the Body of Glory."[2]

In a footnote on p. 318 of this work the Editor says:

" The ' Body of Glory ' synonymous with the ' Rainbow Body,' is said to be the highest body attainable by a *yogin* who is still within the *Sangsāra*. It is comparable to the glorified body of the *Christos*, as seen by the disciples on the Mount of Transfiguration. In the Body of Glory the master of *yoga* is said to be able to exist for aeons, possessed with the *siddhi* of appearing and disappearing at will in any of the many mansions of existence throughout the Universe."

Or in other words on any of the *planes* of existence.

One of the latest studies in St. Paul is that of Mr. J. S. Stewart entitled *A Man in Christ*. Mr. Stewart remarks very aptly that " Orthodoxy varies from age to age, and each age has read back its own particular brand of orthodoxy into the Apostle." Yes, but he does not appear to see that it is his own particular brand that he has read into him. Shall we be accused of doing the same? Well, at all events it is not any brand of *orthodoxy* that we are reading into him.

There are many sentences in the work by this author, however, which come very near to the view we are now presenting. For example:

" The secret of all power and gladness, as Paul was later to discover, lies in three words, ' Christ in me.' For while legal religion is a burden bearing a man down from above, Christ is a living power bearing him

---

[1] See *The Voice of the Silence*. Notes on " The Seven Portals."

[2] From the Tibetan Book, *The Path of Mystic Sacrifice*. Cf. *Tibetan Yoga*, edited by Dr. W. Y. Evans-Wentz, p. 318.

along from within.   To be in union with Christ means the joy of possessing interior sources of a supernatural order, and of feeling within you the power of an endless life " (p. 87).

Amen, say we; but this " living power " is the *Cosmic Christ Principle,* not the personal Jesus.   It is a definite *cosmic* power, and has been known and *realized* by Adepts and Initiates ages before it became embodied in the Christian Gnosis.   The difficulty with our author is that although in one or two places he speaks of the *Cosmic Christ,* he identifies the term *Christ* absolutely with the personal Jesus.

" Paul . . . yearned to lead his converts to a fuller understanding of the faith which they themselves professed; and his glorious delineations of the cosmic Christ, the ultimate reality of the universe, were the result " (p. 23).

We may point out, however, that according to the Scriptures themselves Christ is not " the ultimate reality of the universe." That reality is the " Father," the ONE, the ABSOLUTE.

" When Paul declares to the Colossians that all things ' cohere in ' Christ, when he depicts Christ as the unifying principle of life, the form of expression at last is reminiscent of Stoic doctrine, and may have been chosen deliberately to bring home Christ's cosmic significance to those whose minds had already been familiarized by the work of non-Christian preachers with the thought of a world-soul binding all creation together " (p. 59).

Precisely.   It was no new doctrine

" In Paul's cosmic Christ, it is said, the Jesus of the Gospels is barely recognizable " (p. 273).

Of course it is; for it was not the historical Jesus, the *teacher*, who *was* the cosmic Christ absolutely, but only one who had realized to a supreme degree his identity therewith, as innumerable initiates had done before him.   We have already seen that when he speaks *as the Logos* he must be regarded as speaking impersonally, just as Krishna does in the *Bhagavad Gītā.*

Our author admits that " There is certainly less reference in the epistles to the events of Jesus' earthly life than might have been expected " (p. 276).   In chapter vi he endeavours however, to explain this away.   But we must really protest when he attributes to Paul the presentation of God as " a God of endless resource " (p. 114); or as when he says (p. 221):

" Paul speaks always of man, not God, being reconciled? Doubtless when the reconciliation is accepted and the estranging barrier disappears, *a new situation arises for God* as well as for man." (Italics ours.)

Doubtless these two quotations present the orthodox Christian view of God. But are we to think of the ONE, the ABSOLUTE, the CAUSELESS CAUSE—or even of the Logos—as a schemer, a being of " resource," one who has to *change* because a human being has changed his attitude towards—not *Him*, but IT?

The absolute identification of the cosmic Christ with the personal Jesus which our author supposes Paul to have made, is presented in the following paragraph (p. 284):

" We naturally expect him (Paul) to use the name ' Christ ' where the exalted Lord is intended, and ' Jesus ' where he is thinking of the earthly story; and, in point of fact, this is often what we find. But what is important to observe is that sometimes this rule is reversed. Sometimes Paul uses ' Jesus ' of the heavenly One, and ' Christ ' of the human figure. This is another witness to the truth we are maintaining, namely, that for Paul's mind and heart and conscience there was no hiatus between Christ in glory and the Jesus who had ' lived on earth abased.' That the man who knew the former so well deliberately ignored the latter is clearly incredible, alike to psychology and to religion."

For ourselves we should rather regard this indiscriminate use of the terms " Christ," " Jesus Christ," of " Jesus " only as the result of the subsequent editing to which we have referred; and the scanty references to the events of Jesus' earthly life—which our author admits—as proof positive that Paul did *not* identify the personal Jesus with the cosmic Christ.

We might note here that when Paul refers to his vision on the way to Damascus in *Galatians* i. 15, he says: " When it was the good pleasure of God . . . to reveal his Son *in* me." If the reference had been here to a *personal* Saviour, i.e. Jesus, would he not have said " *to* me "?

In 1 *Corinthians* xv. 8, Paul undoubtedly identifies his vision on the road to Damascus with the risen Jesus. " And last of all, as unto one born out of due time, he appeared to me also." But his statement (verse 5) that he " appeared to Cephas (Peter); then to the twelve " is altogether out of line with the accounts given in the Gospels.[1] And how could he appear " to the *twelve* " when Judas had hanged himself? The Gospel narratives all say eleven; but then these narratives are *subsequent* to the Epistles. Was, then, the story of Judas unknown to Paul, or possibly invented subsequently, since the Gospels were not then in existence?

Let us glance for a moment at the accounts given of Paul's conversion. There are three accounts in *Acts*. In the first of these (ix. 3–9) he is said to have been on the road to Damascus in order to persecute the Jewish Christians there. Suddenly there was a great light, which caused him to fall to the ground, and he heard a voice saying: " Saul, Saul, why persecutest thou me?" He replied: " Who art thou, Lord? " The voice then said: " I am Jesus whom thou persecutest; but rise and enter into the city, and it shall be told thee what thou must do." Saul was blind because of the light, but his sight was restored to him three days afterwards by Ananias, who was instructed in a vision to go to Paul. We must note that in verses 19–20 Paul is said to have remained in Damascus, and that he immediately began preaching in the synagogues, and from there he went to Jerusalem, where he was in close touch with the Apostles. This is in flat contradiction with his own statement in *Galatians* that he " conferred not with flesh and blood," but " went away into Arabia," and afterwards returned to Damascus, and that he did not go to Jerusalem until three years later.

The second account (xxii. 6) is represented to be Paul's own statement to the crowd at Jerusalem when he was rescued from the mob of Jews by the " chief captain." This account is almost word for word the same as the first one. It omits, however, any reference to his preaching in the synagogues, but leads us to understand that he returned almost immediately to Jerusalem, where he was warned by the Lord in a trance to go away quickly because the Jews in

[1] See p. 169 *et seq.*

Jerusalem would not " receive of thee testimony concerning me." The Lord also said to him: " I will send thee forth far hence unto the Gentiles."

The third account (xxvi. 12 ff.) is represented to be Paul's own account given to Agrippa. Here we have a greatly extended statement of what the voice said to him. Here also it is said that he " declared both to them of Damascus first, and at Jerusalem, and throughout all the country of Judaea, and also to the Gentiles, that they should repent and turn to God."

In each of these accounts, then, there is a contradiction as to Paul's movements with that which he gives in *Galatians*. The second and third account is, of course, equally with the first that of the author of *Acts*, whether that author was, as is generally supposed, Luke, or some other person. But in any case, the author is, as I have already shown, absolutely discredited as a reliable historian, and we must fall back on Paul's brief references in the Epistles for the real inner meaning of this vital change in his life. As I have already noted, that account falls into line with the whole *esoteric* teaching of Paul of the *Christ in you*, for, as we have seen, he speaks in *Galatians* i. 16 of God's good pleasure " to reveal his Son *in* me."

We may note further that whereas in *Acts* xiii. 1–3 it is stated that Paul had his mission to the Gentiles delivered to him by certain " prophets and teachers " at Antioch who were directly instructed by the Holy Ghost to " Separate me Barnabas and Saul for the work whereunto I have called them," Paul consistently claims—even in the second and third accounts as given in *Acts*—that he had his mission directly revealed to him by the Lord. Also it was by interior revelation that the mystery of Christ was made known to him. " How that by revelation was made known unto me the mystery . . . *to wit*, that the Gentiles are fellow-heirs, and fellow-members of the body, and fellow-partakers of the promise in Christ Jesus through the gospel, whereof I was made a minister, according to the gift of that grace of God which was given me according to the working of his power."[1]

[1] *Eph*. iii. 3, 6, 7.

And again, a little farther on (verse 10), the *cosmic* note appears. " To the intent that now unto the principalities and powers in the heavenly *places* might be made known through the church the manifold wisdom of God, according to the eternal purpose which he purposed in Christ Jesus our Lord."

How can we conceive of the Christian *Church* making known " the manifold wisdom of God " to " principalities and powers in the heavenly places "? In *Ephesians* i. 22 he refers to the Church as being the *body* of Christ. And what a curious reference there is to the Church in chapter v. 23–28 of this Epistle in his comparison between husbands and wives and Christ and the Church. " That he might present the church to himself a glorious *church*, not having spot or wrinkle or any such thing; but that it should be holy and without blemish." Then after speaking of husband and wife as being one flesh, he says: " This mystery is great, but I speak in regard of Christ and of the church." Surely Paul's metaphors are very mixed; or is it his editors who have mixed them in an endeavour to bring his statements into line with the orthodoxy of the times? We can hardly present our *body* to ourselves, though we can and should make it " holy and without blemish " through the power of the *indwelling* Christ principle.

As regards the principalities and powers who are to be instructed by the Church, he refers to some of these principalities, etc., in chapter vi. 12 as " the spiritual hosts of wickedness in the heavenly places." It is hardly in consonance with our ordinary conception of " heavenly places " to think of there being " spiritual hosts of wickedness " there. But here, again, we recognize on Paul's part a deeper knowledge of cosmic facts than that of the crude *exoteric* conceptions which govern the whole range of Christian doctrine. In *Colossians* i. 16, where Paul enunciates the Logos doctrine, the " Son " is said to have created all things, " in the heavens and upon the earth, things visible and things invisible, whether thrones or dominions or principalities or powers." So then we must conclude that the " spiritual hosts of wickedness in heavenly places " were also created by him:

whereby, indeed, lies a *cosmic* mystery hard for the " Christian " to understand, though it was well understood by Eastern philosophers, and was also understood and expounded by that great Christian mystic Jacob Boehme.

In brief: for those who know something of the profound cosmic principles of the Ancient Wisdom or Gnosis, it is not difficult to recognize references to these in many of Paul's sayings, whether his doctrine in general is an accommodation to the Jewish basis on which Christian *exoteric* doctrine has rested from the very first, or whether much of it is the result of editorial efforts and interpolations. Perhaps both aspects are true.

We may, in fact, consider the Gospel narrative to be in the main historical—though we can in no case accept much of it as such—or we may consider it to be wholly mythical and allegorical. In the former case we should consider the historical Jesus to have been one who had realized in a supreme degree his divine nature and oneness with the " Father ": in fact, a *Christos*, an " anointed," an Initiate.

But whether we consider him thus, or merely as a mythical representation of a man " in whom dwelt all the fullness of the Godhead bodily " (*Col.* ii. 9), he stands before us as our example: an example of the work which each one of us has to accomplish *in himself* through repeated reincarnations—for how much of it do we accomplish in any single life? Each of us has to tread the way to Calvary, to crucify the man of flesh, and to rise again from the dead—the spiritual deadness of our present estate—so that at long last we accomplish the great work which Paul represents as:

" The building up of the body of Christ (in us); till we attain unto the unity of the faith, and the knowledge of the Son of God, unto the full-grown man, unto the measure of the stature of the fulness of Christ " (*Eph.* iv. 12).

This, indeed, was taught in the East ages before Paul, and is known as *Raja Yoga*.

But this " building up of the body of Christ " is not a mere individual thing: it has to be done in the whole Race. The first " Adam "—Humanity as a whole—" of the earth, earthy," has to become the second " Adam " who is " of the heaven, heavenly " (1 *Cor.* xv. 47).

Let us ever remember, then, that we do not individually attain for the mere sake of our own individual salvation, but in order that the whole Race may attain; even as we are told that the Buddha of Compassion vowed that he would not desist from his work, or take the great reward of *Nirvana*, till every individual human being was saved from " this ocean of incarnation and death."

And so also we have that magnificent passage in *The Secret Doctrine* which tells us of the " Silent Watcher."

" He is *the* ' Initiator,' called the ' GREAT SACRIFICE.' For, sitting at the threshold of LIGHT, he looks into it from within the circle of Darkness, which he will not cross; nor will he quit his post till the last day of this life-cycle. Why does the solitary Watcher remain at his self-chosen post? Why does he sit by the fountain of primeval Wisdom, of which he drinks no longer, as he has naught to learn which he does not know—aye, neither on this Earth, nor in its heaven? Because the lonely, sore-footed pilgrims on their way back to their *home* are never sure to the last moment of not losing their way in this limitless desert of illusion and matter called Earth-Life. Because he would fain show the way to that region of freedom and light, from which he is a voluntary exile himself, to every prisoner who has succeeded in liberating himself from the bonds of flesh and illusion. Because, in short, he has sacrificed himself for the sake of mankind, though but a few Elect may profit by the GREAT SACRIFICE " (vol. i, p. 208).

Do the Christian Scriptures give us any other doctrine than this—of individual salvation, for example, of certain " elect " of a personal God, and the Devil may take the rest? Then, and in that case, those Scriptures are not for those of us who have apprehended this nobler doctrine. Only—we do not think that in their origin and intention they *did* present any other doctrine, whatever they may do in their present form, or in their literal interpretation, so sadly overlaid with " the precepts and doctrines of man."

Thus, as in our " Adamic " or *human* nature all die, so also in our " Christ " or *spiritual* nature shall all be made alive again.

CHAPTER VII

PRACTICAL RELIGION

WE have seen that the great fundamental *Fact* which lies at the root of all forms of religion, and of man's *instinct* that he possesses a spiritual nature, is the Fact of the oneness of his real inner nature, his real *Self*, with that Supreme Being, or Power, or Principle which is the Universe in its totality. Thus *practical* religion must aim at *the full realization of this oneness*: a realization which necessarily brings with it, degree by degree as it is attained to, the possession of god-like powers over the material world, and over life and death itself. It is the complete conquest of sin, suffering, and death; and—though this is a highly metaphysical teaching, difficult for the ordinary individual to grasp—the *illusion* of a personal self.

" And the last enemy that shall be conquered is death."

The real conquest of death is something vastly different from that which the ordinary Christian understands by the term. It is freedom from necessity for reincarnation, freedom from the weary round of physical birth and death— known in the East as *samsara*—to which, as we have previously shown, the individual must necessarily submit until he has really *attained* " unto a full-grown man, unto the measure of the stature of the fulness of Christ." Thus Jesus says of his life in the body: "I have power to lay it down, and I have power to take it again " (*John* x. 18).

This achievement, this *practical* realization of the nature of the real spiritual man and the acquirement thereby of god-like powers, is the fundamental teaching and sign-manual of the Gnosis, and of all teachers who belong to that Gnosis, and of those who have endeavoured, in one form or another, to communicate that Gnosis to the nation, race, or community of the times in which they lived. Necessarily each teacher had to teach in a form appropriate to the intelligence or ideas of his hearers: hence the difference in form between the teachings of Gautama Buddha and those of Jesus Christ, for example. But in each of these we find this fundamental principle which marks the teacher or hierophant as belonging to the great primary stream of true knowledge, the Ancient Wisdom or Gnosis. Nothing higher than this knowledge could or can possibly be revealed by the divinest teacher, the highest Avatar, or the greatest Initiate who ever undertakes to instruct the world in " the mysteries of the kingdom of heaven "; that kingdom which is *within* each one of us, could we but realize it.

But even so, the greatest teacher can hardly do more than point out the way of attainment, and some *method* by which, according to the stage at which we have arrived, we may achieve this glorious realization of our true nature. The method—in other words, *practical* religion—necessarily varies with the individual.

" The Path is one for all, the means to reach the Goal must vary with the Pilgrim."[1]

Yet here again we may distinguish certain fundamental principles as being those which each and all of these Masters of the Gnosis have taught as the first essentials for any real progress.

We may, and can, and ought to understand intellectually both the one fundamental principle, the ultimate goal of our great quest and endeavour, and also those fundamental principles which we should attempt to *practise*. In other words, it is quite possible to obtain a very clear theoretical knowledge of the fundamental principles of this Ancient Gnosis, and of the Path of attainment; but, nevertheless, in the circumstances in which most of us find ourselves, there is much that we can understand theoretically but which it is not possible for us to put into practice. Yet it is certain that in proportion as we keep these ideas and principles in view, and ever press forward to their realization, we shall find that the disabilities of our circumstances are gradually removed, and opportunities for further advance open out. These opportunities may not possibly come to us in our present lives. It is here that the law of *Karma* operates. We must reap what we have sown in former lives. But we are also sowing for our coming ones. Thus—to quote the words of the Buddha, so beautifully expressed by Sir Edwin Arnold in his *Light of Asia*:

> " The Books say well, my Brothers! each man's life
>   The outcome of his former living is;
>   The bygone wrongs bring forth sorrows and woes,
>   The bygone right breeds bliss.
>
> " That which ye sow ye reap. See yonder fields!
>   The sesamum was sesamum, the corn
>   Was corn. The Silence and the Darkness knew!
>   So is a man's fate born.
>
> " He cometh, reaper of the things he sowed,
>   Sesamum, corn, so much cast in past birth;
>   And so much weed and poison-stuff, which mar
>   Him and the aching earth."

One of the first things, then, which we have to learn in practical religion is how to exhaust our old bad *Karma*, and to see to it that the new *Karma* which we generate contains none of that " poison-stuff " which shall hinder our further progress. How is this to be done?

> " If he who liveth, learning whence woe springs,
>   Endureth patiently, striving to pay
>   His utmost debt for ancient evils done
>   In Love and Truth alway;
>
> " If making none to lack, he thoroughly purge
>   The lie and lust of self forth from his blood;
>   Suffering all meekly, rendering for offence
>   Nothing but grace and good;
>
> " If he shall day by day dwell merciful,
>   Holy and just and kind and true; and rend
>   Desire from where it clings with bleeding roots,
>   Till love of life have end:
>
> " He—dying—leaveth as the sum of him
>   A life-count closed, whose ills are dead and quit
>   Whose good is quick and mighty, far and near,
>   So that fruits follow it."

Looking broadly at the nature of the Path of Attainment as it has been set before us by various teachers, we may distinguish two stages. The first of these we might designate as comprising that which may be practised by the ordinary individual whatever his circumstances; and the lines we have just quoted indicate the nature of that stage. It must be practised " Till love of life have end." Now there is a great deal more in those simple words than appears on the surface; and in its full meaning it applies to the second stage as well as to the first. But as regards the first it simply means *non-attachment* to " the things of this world."

Let me quote again from *The Light of Asia* concerning this first stage which is for those who, having perceived the far-off goal, are still immersed in worldly affairs and duties.

" Spread no wings

" For Sunward flight, thou soul with unplumed vans!
　　Sweet is the lower air, and safe and known
　The homely levels; only strong ones leave
　　The nest each makes his own.

" Dear is the love, I know, of Wife and Child;
　　Pleasant the friends and pastimes of your years;
　Fruitful of good Life's gentle charities;
　　Firm-set, though false, its fears.

" Live—ye who must—such lives as live on these;
　　Make golden stair-ways of your weakness; rise
　By daily sojourn with those phantasies
　　To lovelier verities.

" So shall ye pass to clearer heights and find
　　Easier ascents and lighter loads of sins,
　And larger will to burst the bonds of sense,
　　Entering the Path."

Do we feel that these attachments which we have forged for ourselves are hindrances on the Path of Return? Well, so they undoubtedly are as regards that further stage where all such attachments must be left behind; yet they belong to the stage at which we individually stand; and moreover there is not one of them which may not be made to serve some lesson, some practice which is necessary for us at our present stage; and the great thing that we have to learn from them is this same *non-attachment*. We have to learn to be *in* the world and yet not *of* it. We shall scrupulously fulfil all the duties of our position and circumstances, but we shall do this in such a way that the doing clears the account, and leaves nothing of attachment, either of further desire or of regret.

Let us glance at a few other passages from other Scriptures of the East before we turn to similar teachings in the Christian Scriptures.

In the *Bhagavad Gītā* we read:

" Make pleasure and pain, gain and loss, victory and defeat, the same to thee, and then prepare for battle, for thus and thus alone shalt thou in action be free from sin."[1]

" Therefore perform thou that which thou hast to do, at all times unmindful of the event; for the man who doeth that which he hath to do, without attachment to the result, obtaineth the Supreme."[2]

The Crest Jewel of Wisdom:

" Endurance is the bearing of all pains without rebelling against them, unconcerned and unlamenting."[3]

The Brihad-Aranyaka Upanishad (4, 4, 7):

" When all desires that were hid in the heart are let go, then a mortal becomes immortal, and reaches Brahma."

Hermes, *The Secret Sermon on the Mountain*:[4]

" Throw out of work the body's senses, and thy Divinity shall come to birth."

These are only a very few of the dozens of similar aphorisms and exhortations which might be given. Let us now turn to the Christian Scriptures for a similar teaching. For those who are familiar with those Scriptures it is hardly necessary to quote. All through the Gospels and Epistles renunciation of the world, or non-attachment thereto, is the keynote. Nevertheless, I may refer my readers to the following passages:

[1] Chapter ii.   [2] Chapter iii.   [3] Johnston's translation, p. 4.
[4] Mead, *Thrice Greatest Hermes*, vol. ii, p. 223.

" Love not the world, neither the things that are in the world. If any man love the world, the love of the Father is not in him " (1 *John* ii. 15).

" If thou would be perfect, go sell that thou hast, and give to the poor, and thou shalt have treasure in heaven" (*Matt.* xix. 21).

" How hardly shall they that have riches enter into the kingdom of heaven " (*Mark* x. 23).

" He that loveth father or mother more than me is not worthy of me; and he that loveth son or daughter more than me is not worthy of me " (*Matt.* x. 37).

Let us pause a moment here, and ask whether this latter saying is really intended to be taken literally as applying to the personal Jesus. If so, it is certainly a very *hard* saying; and how many professing Christians to-day could claim to be thus " worthy "?

But this saying is preceded and followed by the eminently mystical sayings:

" A man's foes shall be they of his own household " (verse 36).

" He that findeth his life shall lose it; and he that loseth his life for my sake shall find it " (verse 39).

Surely the assertion of Jesus (verse 35) that he has come " to set a man at violence against his father, and the daughter against her mother," etc., should show us that all this is simply the use of familiar similies for deeper realities, and should put us on our guard against a literal interpretation. " Father," " mother," " daughter," " they of his own household," etc., stand for those active *inner* causes of our attachments to " the things of this world." Who or what are " they of a man's own household " in this sense but those thoughts and desires which bind him to this sense world of incarnation and death, and therefore are the *foes* to that spiritual knowledge and quality of life which would liberate the man therefrom.

In the *Pistis Sophia* (m.p. 131) it is explained that by *parents* is meant the " Rulers of the Fate ": which we might translate in our modern language to be those active agents in the *subconscious* of the individual which were generated in previous incarnations, and which determine that a man shall be such and such a character, and shall meet with such and such events (fate, *Karma*) in this present one. Dr. Jung, in his *Contributions to Analytical Psychology* (p. 264) tells us that these " complexes " " behave just like independent beings." And indeed such, in a certain sense, they are. They are " Rulers of our Fate." See then how the Gnosis anticipates our modern psychological science.

And so it is only as a man cuts himself free from these " rulers " of his desires, actions, and destiny—that complex of Karmic entities which he himself has created in his past incarnations and which drag him back into that physical sense-life which constitutes his present *personality*, the conventional " I "—that he can find the real *Self*, the immortal spiritual Ego which is birthless and deathless.

> " Never the spirit was born; the spirit shall cease to be never;
> Never was time it was not; End and Beginning are dreams!
> Birthless and deathless and changeless remaineth the spirit for ever;
> Death hath not touched it at all, dead though the house of it seems! "[1]

This is the oldest of old teachings in Eastern Scriptures, and the basis of that *Yoga* which has been practised for thousands of years by the great Indian Adepts, Rishis, and Masters. Jesus does but repeat it; and it is one more evidence of the connection of the Christian Scriptures with this ancient Gnosis.

But how are we to reconcile these exhortations in the Christian Scriptures to come out and separate ourselves from the " world " with such a saying as, " Make to yourselves friends out of the mammon of unrighteousness; that, when it shall fail, they may receive you into the eternal tabernacles " (*Luke* xvi. 9)?

This is surely, if taken literally, not merely—as regards the first part of the sentence—a very low-down counsel, but also exceedingly enigmatical in any apparent connection between the first and second halves. Who does the *they* in the second half refer to? Surely not to " the mammon of unrighteousness," for how could *they* " receive you into the eternal tabernacles "? And what is the *it* that shall *fail*? Is it " the mammon of unrighteousness "? But if that *fails*, what will be the use of the *friends* you have made therein?

[1] *The Song Celestial* or *Bhagavad Gītā*, Sir Edwin Arnold.

Now let us see what light the Gnosis throws on such a passage as this, and incidentally recognize the mystical and Gnostic nature of this and similar sayings of Jesus, and therefore the gnostic origin of his teachings.

We turn again to the *Pistis Sophia* (m.pp. 334, 335):

" Mary then answered and said: ' My Lord, this is the word which thou hast spoken unto us aforetime, *in a similitude*, saying: " Make to yourselves a friend out of the Mammon of unrighteousness, so that if ye remain behind, he may receive you into the everlasting tents." Who, then, is the Mammon of unrighteousness, if not the dragon of the outer darkness? This is the word: He who shall understand the mystery of one of the names of the dragon of the outer darkness, if he remaineth behind in the outer darkness or if he hath completed the circuits of the changes (reincarnations), and speaketh the name of the dragon, he will be saved and go up out of the darkness and be received into the Treasury of the Light. This is the word, my Lord.'

" The Saviour answered again and said unto Mary: ' Well said, spiritual and pure (one). This is the solution of the word.' "

Now " the dragon of the outer darkness " is simply a term for that " outer darkness " which is referred to in *Matthew* viii. 12. It might be identified with the lower Astral plane. In *Ephesians* vi. 12, Paul also refers to " the world rulers of this darkness, the spiritual hosts of wickedness in the heavenly places."

At the commencement of the Fourth Book of the *Pistis Sophia*, Jesus says:

" The outer darkness is a great dragon, whose tail is in his mouth, outside the whole world and surrounding the whole world.[1] And there are many regions of chastisement within it. There are twelve mighty chastisement-dungeons and a ruler is in every dungeon."

He then goes on to enumerate these; but this enumeration does not concern us here. What we have to note is that anyone who finds himself at death in one of these twelve regions or " dungeons " of the " outer darkness "; if he know the *mystery* of that region and speaks the word of power

[1] It is the " astral light," " astral place," or *Kamaloka*, as students of occult literature will understand. The symbol of the serpent with the tail in the mouth is found on some of the Gnostic gems; but is probably much older, and was also used as a symbol for eternity.

("the name of the dragon"), he can free himself and rise
out of the "darkness" into "the Treasury of the Light," or
what is referred to in the canonical Gospels as "the kingdom
of heaven."

It will be observed that not merely is the explanation here
of the term "Mammon of unrighteousness" quite different
from what is commonly understood by that term, but the
quotation itself is quite different from that given in the
Gospel, and can hardly have been taken from it.   There were,
in fact, many traditional "sayings" of Jesus current in the
first two centuries before a certain number were selected
and *adapted* to the requirements of the Canonical Gospels.

Incidentally there is in the previous quotation from the
Pistis Sophia a reference to reincarnation, which is an essential part of the teaching all through the work, as it always
has been in the Ancient Wisdom.   This reference is in the
phrase "completed the circuits of the changes," i.e. of
bodies in incarnations.   It is elsewhere referred to as "the
circuits in the changes of the body"; and it is taught that
those who have not learnt the mysteries when in one body, or
incarnation, will—if they are not hopelessly lost—be given
the opportunity of doing so in another body, or incarnation.
Why did the Christian Church ever lose sight of this fundamental teaching?   What an immense difference it would have
made in Christian doctrine and practice if they had retained it.

I give the above somewhat in detail to show (*a*) the connection of the Canonical Scriptures with the Gnosis which
gives their *esoteric* interpretation; and (*b*) that practical
religion is knowledge (Gnosis), not mere belief or "faith"
(*Pistis*).   It is just as necessary to know the laws (*natural*
laws) of our inner nature—our astral, mental, and other
"bodies" or vehicles of the immortal *Self*, and of the corresponding planes of the Cosmos, as it is to know the laws of
the physical plane and of our physical bodies if we would be
masters thereof and not ignorant sufferers.

A man must have *faith*—yes.   He must have faith that
he can achieve this higher knowledge; faith in his own
supreme divine nature in its oneness with the ONE.   But
without knowledge he is powerless.

"But amen, amen, I say unto you: Even if a righteous man hath committed no sins at all, he cannot possibly be brought into the Light-Kingdom, because the sign of the kingdom of the mysteries is not with him. In a word, it is impossible to bring souls into the Light without the mysteries of the Light-kingdom."[1]

Such a *faith* as we see in so many devoted Christians, a faith which doubtless sustains them in many of life's grievous afflictions, can hardly be said to be anything but of the greatest possible value to those who possess it; but it will not *save* them where *knowledge* is required. It will not save them from sickness if they do not know and obey the laws of health —not to speak of that higher knowledge of *yoga* which gives absolute control of the physical body, and also of the inner subtle bodies which each of us possesses. Nature has no excuse for ignorance; and the laws of our deeper nature, psychic and spiritual, are as *natural* as those of the physical.

In Paul Brunton's book, *A Search in Secret India*, he gives examples of the exhibition of this higher knowledge of *yoga*, some of which he himself witnessed. For example, the Yogi Narasingha Swami exhibited before the doctors of the University of Calcutta his ability to swallow corrosive acids— sulphuric acid, carbolic acid, and the deadly poison, potassium cyanide—without injury. In another case the action of the heart was stopped and recommenced at will. It is well known that yogis have been buried for weeks at a time, and resuscitated when dug up.[2]

What says the Christian Scripture?

"If they drink any deadly thing, it shall in no wise hurt them" (*Mark* xvi. 18).

Did the writer of those lines know of yoga? They are ascribed to Jesus, but are a later addition to the Gospel. But why did he so mislead as to say that "these signs shall follow them that *believe* in my name"? Mere *belief* will not accomplish it; yet we see it actually accomplished by those

---

[1] *Pistis Sophia*, m.p. 263.

[2] Madam David-Neel and Dr. Evans-Wentz also testify in their works on Tibet to the power which some of the yogis develop of generating a psychic heat which enables them to exist without clothing in the arctic temperature of the Himalayan heights.

who are not Christian believers. We must either set this down as an absolutely futile saying, or else we must give a significance to the words " my name " which is something totally different from what is understood by " belief in Christ " nowadays. We must, in fact, here again refer back to the Gnosis for this deeper meaning, and turn to the *Pistis Sophia*, where there are several references to the occult power of a *Name*. We have already seen one such reference in connection with one of the *names* of " the dragon of the outer darkness." It will be instructive here to give a considerable quotation from chapter cxliii.

" Thereafter his disciples said unto him: ' Rabbi, reveal unto us the mystery of the Light of thy father, since we heard thee say: " There is still a fire-baptism and there is still a baptism of the holy spirit of the Light, and there is a spiritual chrism; these lead the souls into the Treasury of the Light." Tell us, therefore, their mystery, so that we ourselves may inherit the kingdom of thy father.'

" Jesus said unto them: ' There is no mystery which is more excellent than these mysteries on which ye question, in that it will lead your souls into the Light of the lights, into the regions of Truth and Goodness, into the region of the Holy of all holies, into the region in which there is neither female nor male, nor are there forms in that region, but a perpetual indescribable Light. Nothing more excellent is there, therefore, than these mysteries on which ye question, save only the mystery of the seven Voices and their nine-and-forty powers and their ciphers. And there is no name which is more excellent than them all, the name in which are all names and all lights and all powers.

" Who then knoweth that name, if he cometh out of the body of matter, nor smoke nor darkness nor authority nor ruler of the Fate-sphere nor angel nor archangel nor power can hold down the soul which knoweth that name; but if it cometh out of the world and sayeth that name to the fire, it is quenched and the darkness withdraweth."

And are we not also told of the power of the *Name* in the Canonical Scriptures?

" I am come in my Father's *name* " (*John* v. 43).
" The works that I do in my Father's *name* " (*John* x. 25).
" In my *name* they shall cast out devils," etc. (*Mark* xvi. 17).
" And when they had set them in the midst, they inquired, By what power, or in what *name*, have you done this? " (*Acts* iv. 7).

Dozens of similar passages will doubtless occur to my readers; and when we associate them with their almost universal use as signifying the possession of certain powers, it throws a totally different light on the character of the Scriptures.

" To him that overcometh . . . I will give him a white stone, and upon the stone a new *name* written " (i.e. I will confer upon him a new power) " which no one knoweth but he that receiveth it " (*Rev.* ii. 17).

In the Egyptian *Book of the Dead* it is all important for the individual, the Initiate, who is making his way through the various regions up to that of Osiris, that he should know the *name* of the god who is the keeper of the Portal, or Pylon, or *Arit* to each region.   Thus in chapter cxlv we read:

" The Osiris Auf-ānkh, triumphant, saith:
" ' Homage to thee, saith Horus, O thou first pylon of the Still-Heart.   I have made my way.   I know thee, and I know thy name, and I know the name of the god who guardeth thee.' . . .
" Saith the pylon: ' Pass on, then, thou art pure.'—And similarly for each of the twenty-one pylons."[1]

In chapter cxlvi, from the Papyrus of Nu, the same affirmations are made by the triumphant Osirified Nu:

" The Osiris Nu, the overseer of the house of the overseer of the seal, triumphant, when he cometh to the first pylon of Osiris, saith: ' I have made my way.   I know you, and I know your name, and I know the name of the god who guardeth you.' "[2]

In Eastern Occultism the power of a " name " is very well understood.   It is intimately connected with the occult power of sound, and so everything depends on the correct intonation.   A " sacred " name, such as that of the tetragrammaton IHVH (Jehovah), was credited with enormous power·by the Jewish Kabalists if properly pronounced; while in the East the word AUM is regarded in a similar manner.

We read of frequent baptism " in the *name* of Jesus."   But baptism was originally an *initiation* ceremony conferring *power*—or at all events supposed to confer power—on the candidate; for the " word of power " was communicated at the same time.   At the baptism of Jesus by John he is said to have received the power of the *Spirit*, which he saw descending upon him in the form of a dove.

[1] Budge, *The Book of the Dead*, p. 448.   [2] Ibid., p. 464.

In the baptism by John with *water* and by Jesus with " the Holy Ghost and with *fire*," we have once more an intimation of the derivation of the narrative from the *Mysteries*; for *water* is the symbol of the astral plane, and *fire* of the spiritual plane; and the initiate must learn the laws of the astral regions and obtain their conquest before he can pass on to the higher or more Cosmic plane of " Spirit," that region which is, in the words of the *Pistis Sophia* (m.p. 378):

" The Light of the lights, the region of Truth and Goodness, the region of the Holy of all holies, the region in which there is neither female nor male, nor are there any forms in that region, but a perpetual indescribable Light."

Students of the Ancient Wisdom will readily recognize the correspondence of this brief description with many other statements in other Scriptures.

We can hardly accept the statement that if Jesus did not himself " baptize " into this region by means of any outward ceremony, his disciples were able to do so. As showing that real baptism was an initiation conferring real knowledge and power, we might quote again from the *Pistis Sophia*, where Jesus is recorded as saying (m.p. 363):

" I will give you the baptism of those of the Right, our region, and its ciphers and its seals and the manner of invocation for reaching thither."

In the *Pistis Sophia* Baptism is a mystery rite. Jesus says:

" Now, therefore, he who shall receive the mysteries of the Baptisms, then the mystery of them becometh a great, exceedingly violent, wise fire and it burneth up the sins and entereth into the soul secretly and consumeth all the sins which the counterfeiting spirit hath made fast on it " (m.p. 300).

In the great Temple of Philae there is a bas-relief showing a baptismal ceremony. Two God-Hierophants, one with the head of a hawk representing the Sun, and the other the Ibis-headed Thoth, the god of wisdom and secret learning, are pouring a double stream of " water "—small ansated crosses, the symbol of life, alternating with a sceptre, a symbol of power—over the initiate. Where to-day in the Christian Church is the real Hierophant, the real Master Initiate who can communicate the true " word of power "; the word which gives command over the " spirits," both good and evil, so that it can be said of any using that " name " that " they shall cast out devils "? Our lunatic asylums are filled with cases of obsession, and our so-called " Spiritualists " instead of casting them out are in many cases opening wide the door of "mediumship" for the entry of the lowest denizens of the astral plane.

I am not now saying that this danger has not been perceived by the more intelligent " Spiritualists." Many warnings against promiscuous mediumship have been published but the great majority of the cult are seeking nothing but phenomena, and still more phenomena, whilst the phenomena themselves have no claim whatsoever to be called " spiritual." There is nothing " spiritual " in the mere fact of survival; and in any case proof of survival is not proof of immortality; whilst that which survives and " communicates " is never anything but that bundle of experiences, thoughts, and desires which constitutes the lower self, the *personality*, which all practical religion teaches must be *lost* before the true spiritual Self—the Self eternal and immortal in its own right and inherent nature—can be found.

As regards the necessity for adding knowledge to " faith," it will be useful here to note what the Gnostic " Father " Clement of Alexandria says of this, as it confirms all that I have been here saying as to the early connection of the Gnosis with Christian doctrine, and the transcendental nature of the Gnostic's achievement.

I will quote from the article on Clement in Smith and Wace's *Dictionary*, vol. i, p. 565.

" Faith is the foundation; knowledge the superstructure (*Strom.* vi. 26, p. 660), by knowledge faith is perfected (*id.* vii. 55, p. 864), for to know is more than to believe (*id.* vi. 109, p. 794). Faith is a summary knowledge of urgent truths: knowledge a sure demonstration of what has been received through faith, being itself reared upon faith through the teaching of the Lord (*id.* vii. 57, p. 865). Thus the gnostic grasps the complete truth of all revelation from the beginning of the world to the end, piercing to the depths of Scripture, of which the believer tastes the surface only (*id.* vi. 78, p. 779; 131, p. 806; vii. 95, p. 891). As a consequence of this intelligent sympathy with the Divine Will, the gnostic becomes in perfect unity in himself ($\mu o \nu a \delta \iota \kappa \acute{o} \varsigma$), and as far as possible like God (*id*. iv. 154, p. 633; vii. 13, p. 835). Definite outward observances cease to have any value for one whose whole being is brought into an abiding harmony with that which is eternal; he has no wants, no passions; he rests in the contemplation of God, which is and will be his unfailing blessedness (*id*. vii. 35, p. 851, 84, p. 883; vi. 71, p. 776; vii. 56, p. 865).

" In this outline it is easy to see the noblest traits of later mysticism.[1] And if some of Clement's statements go beyond subjects which lie within the powers of man,[2] still he bears impressive testimony to two essential truths which require continual iteration, that the aim of faith through knowledge perfected by love is the present recovery of the divine likeness; and again, that formulated doctrine is not an end in itself, but a means whereby we rise through fragmentary propositions to knowledge which is immediate and one."

Let us finally look at the most modern evidences of the powers of the real Adept.

There have been many books written dealing with the achievements of the eastern Yogis, and also with the methods of Yoga by means of which these powers are obtained. I have already referred to one of the latest of these, *A Search in Secret India*, by Mr. Paul Brunton. I have Mr. Brunton's kind permission to give two or three extracts from his work. The most instructive Master that Mr. Brunton met is known as The Maharishee. Now I have already shown that the central doctrine of the Gnosis is the power which every individual potentially possesses to realize the *Self* in all its depths as *one* with the universal SELF, whether called God or otherwise. Here is what the Maharishee says of this:

" The sense of ' I ' pertains to the person, the body and brain. When a man knows his true self for the first time, something else arises from the depths of his being and takes possession of him. That something is behind the mind; it is infinite, divine, eternal. Some people call it the kingdom of heaven, others call it the soul, still others name it Nirvana, and we Hindus call it Liberation; you may give it what name you wish. When this happens a man has not really lost himself; rather, he has found himself."

[1] Not *later* mysticism only, but also of that which long antedated the introduction of Christianity.

[2] No doubt the learned but orthodox authors of this work considered them to be so, and would place a limit on human knowledge. But where is the limit?

And again:

" Unless and until a man embarks upon this quest of the true self, doubt and uncertainty will follow his footsteps throughout life. The greatest kings and statesmen try to rule others, when in their heart of hearts they know that they cannot rule themselves. Yet the greatest power is at the command of the man who has penetrated to his inmost depth. There are men of giant intellects who spend their lives gathering knowledge about many things. Ask these men if they have solved the mystery of man, if they have conquered themselves, and they will hang their heads in shame. What is the use of knowing about everything else when you do not yet know who you are? Men avoid this inquiry into the true self, but what else is there so worthy to be undertaken? "

Now let us turn to a little work written by Mme H. P. Blavatsky in 1889, and entitled *The Voice of the Silence.* It is said by her to be derived from *The Book of the Golden Precepts*, one of the works put into the hands of the mystic students in the East. It discloses the difficulties and dangers on that *Path* to self-knowledge and self-conquest which the aspirant must face and overcome if he would achieve that goal which lies so infinitely beyond the ideas of the ordinary religionist, or even those of the devotional mystic. Here is what is said of the *Master* who has accomplished the final liberation.

" He standeth now like a white pillar to the west, upon whose face the rising Sun of thought eternal poureth forth its first most glorious waves. His mind, like a becalmed and boundless ocean, spreadeth out in shoreless space. He holdeth life and death in his strong hand.

" Yea, He is mighty. The living power made free in him, that power which is HIMSELF, can raise the tabernacle of illusion high above the gods, above great Brahm and Indra."

But here we may note that the Master who has thus achieved does not do so for his own individual sake, but that he may now be a strong power to help and save his fellows:

" Now bend thy head and listen well, O Bodihisattwa—compassion speaks and saith: ' Can there be bliss when all that lives must suffer? Shalt thou be saved and hear the whole world cry? ' "

Is not this teaching far, far beyond that miserably inade-

quate teaching of orthodox " Christianity " of one little lifetime for each individual, and then an eternity of bliss for
the little *personal* self, whatever its sins may have been—and
the Devil may take the sinners who have not " believed " ?

Strange that with all the wealth of noble doctrine of the
Ancient Wisdom and Gnosis that has been quite plainly
given to the world from time to time, these paltry ideas of
Man's nature and destiny, the work of ignorant dogma
makers of the 2nd and 3rd centuries, aspirants for *temporal*
power, and totally lacking in any *cosmic* sense—strange, I
say, that these—even though now being widely repudiated—
should still command the adhesion of thousands of otherwise
intelligent people, and should be taught even in high places.
Such, however, is the power of tradition, authority, and—
superstition.

It is interesting to note that the work from which I have
just quoted opens with the statement that:

> " The Mind is the great Slayer of the Real.
> Let the Disciple slay the Slayer."

Now one of our most modern philosophies, that of M. Henri
Bergson, has precisely this idea as its main thesis.

" Intellectuality and materiality have been constituted, in detail,
by reciprocal adaptation. Both are derived from a wider and higher
form of existence. It is there that we must replace them, in order to
see them issue forth."[1]

But it is precisely this *replacing* process which the Yogi
practices, and which gives him the power—as the Maharishee
says—to go into and to come out of " That out of which the
sense of the personal ' I ' arises, and into which it shall have
to disappear " (p. 159).

Another little modern work of the highest value for aspirants
to the deeper knowledge is entitled *Light on the Path*.

" Each man is to himself absolutely the way, the truth, and the life.
But he is only so when he grasps his whole individuality firmly, and,
by the force of his awakened spiritual will (the divine ' spark ' or *Christ*
within), recognizes this individuality as not himself, but that thing which
he has with pain created for his own use, and by means of which he

[1] *Creative Evolution*, p. 197.

purposes, as his growth slowly develops his intelligence, to reach to the life beyond individuality."

" Make the profound obeisance of the soul to the dim star that burns within. Steadily as you watch and worship, its light will grow stronger. Then you may know that you have found the beginning of the way. And when you have found the end its light will suddenly become the infinite light."

One more invaluable source of information I should like to refer to, *The Mahatma Letters to A. P. Sinnett*, written between 1880 and 1884, but only published in 1923, give us precisely the same teachings, but also a wealth of detail in anthropology and cosmology the value of which can hardly be overestimated.

" It is not physical phenomena but universal ideas that we study, as to comprehend the former, we have first to understand the latter. They touch man's true position in the universe in relation to his previous and future births; his origin and ultimate destiny; the relation of the mortal to the immortal; of the temporary to the eternal; of the finite to the infinite; ideas larger, grander, more comprehensive, recognizing the universal reign of Immutable Law, unchanging and unchangeable in regard to which there is only an ETERNAL NOW, while to uninitiated mortals time is past or future as related to their finite existence on this material speck of dirt. This is what we study, and what many have solved " (p. 24).

This is practical religion, a real knowledge (Gnosis) of our spiritual nature and powers.

" What you call religion I call only a reasoning about religion," says H. Fielding in a quotation I have already given.[1] The modern religionist is content to rest in his " faith "; he does not seek—probably does not believe in— this super-sensual knowledge of the Self, which alone can liberate him from " this ocean of incarnation and death."

This is but a brief outline of the great Gnosis, the great Wisdom, the great *knowledge* which has existed in all ages for those who—as Plotinus puts it—" are fortunately able to perceive it."

In its outward expression and formulation it has taken many varying modes of exposition; sometimes by a real Master, but more often by only partially initiated teachers

[1] Page 52.

who more or less rigidified the teachings into a system. And such, indeed, is what is known historically and dogmatically as *Christianity*. In its historical form it was constructed by certain early-century Prelates who had not the capacity to understand the inner mystical truths which Jesus, Paul, and other Gnostics taught: the truth, not of salvation by the act of some historical person, but of the eternal " Christ in you "; the Cosmic Christ *principle*, " eternal in the heavens "; which, indeed, is that " Robe of Glory " referred to in the *Pistis Sophia*, and which, as I have already intimated (pp. 88 and 181) St. Paul says (2 *Cor.* v. 2) " we long to be clothed with."

We cannot accept dogmatic and creedal Christianity other than as a very imperfect presentation of Man's nature and destiny; other than as one of a very large number of such attempts, and indeed very inferior to many of them, and only suitable for minds that can think only in terms of material things and historical happenings, and of God as a magnified human being. Religion itself is altogether independent of history. Man's " salvation," the recovery of his spiritual nature, never did and never can depend on any single historical event. His " fall " and his " redemption " is a continual process.

" Here in time we make holiday because the eternal birth which God the Father bore and bears increasingly in eternity is now born in time, in human nature. St. Augustine says this birth is always happening. But if it happen not in me what does it profit me? What matters is that it shall happen in me " (Meister Eckhart).

" The Fall is a present and not a past fact. Man's real fall is that he is content with the shadow of good. He still eats of the tree of good and evil, and until the Christ fills the whole consciousness, man will ever be at war with himself, his brother, and his God."[1]

History is only the way in which humanity and the individual work out the great Cosmic Process, of Fall and Return.

Christianity is having to-day to re-adapt itself to our modern knowledge; it is having to discard much which we now see so obviously owed its existence to the *ignorance* of its framers. But what it needs more than anything else

[1] *Christ in You*, p. 104.

is to come into line with *ancient* truth; with fundamental principles which were taught ages before it came into existence as a theological *system*, centred round a certain historical teacher.

But it is not merely Christianity as a *system* that we have to reject as the " truth." We cannot accept any one system, whether " Gnostic " or otherwise, as being anything but a very imperfect effort to give some faint idea *in terms of intellect* of those " Universal Ideas," or " Eternal Archetypes " which lie beyond intellect, beyond the phenomenal world of time and space, and of which, indeed, this latter is but the faintest reflection.

What we must endeavour to do is to distil from each and all of these systems some slight understanding of these Eternal Principles operating in our little Cosmos as Immutable Laws. There is no finality in any system. The more rigid it is, and the more we think that here we have some final statement of truth, the more we are killing in ourselves that deeper *intuition* which alone can carry us forward to the super-intellectual region of absolute truth, remembering always that that region is *within*.

Speaking of this attainment of clear knowledge, the Mahatma " K.H." writes to Mr. Sinnett:[1]

" Believe me, there comes a moment in the life of an adept, when the hardships he has passed through are a thousandfold rewarded. In order to acquire further knowledge, he has no more to go through a minute and slow process of investigation and comparison of various objects, but is accorded an instantaneous, implicit insight into every first truth. Having passed that stage of philosophy which maintains that all fundamental truths have sprung from a blind impulse—it is the philosophy of your Sensationalists or Positivists; and left far behind him that other class of thinkers—the Intellectualists or Skeptics—who hold that fundamental truths are derived from the intellect alone, and that we, ourselves, are their only originating causes; the adept sees and feels and lives in the very source of all fundamental truths—the Universal Spiritual Essence of Nature."

In this search for " truth " in exoteric systems we must specially avoid attaching importance to some one particular name. The same thing or the same idea may be expressed

[1] *Mahatma Letters*, p. 241.

exoterically by many different names, but the real *name*, as I have said before, expresses the *nature* of the thing, whether of a god or of a plant or a stone. But who—apart from the high Initiate—knows the real nature or *name* even of the commonest plant or stone? And how, then, can any presume to know the real nature, the "ineffable Name" of that Rootless Root, that Causeless-Cause, that "Subtle Being of which this whole Universe is composed"?

IT has been called by innumerable names in *exoteric* religions, where IT is invariably anthropomorphized. Look, for example, at the character ascribed to Jehovah, Yahweh— the exoteric name for the mystic and Kabalistic Tetragrammaton IHVH or YHVH—in the Old Testament, and so unfortunately "fathered" upon the Christian Church by the early creed-makers. But the Initiate, and even the intuitive mystic, will give no name to THAT which is beyond all names.

"The things which are in part can be apprehended, known, and expressed; but the Perfect cannot be apprehended, known, or expressed by any creature as creature. Therefore we do not give a name to the Perfect, for it is none of these. The creature as creature cannot know or apprehend it, name or conceive it " (*Theologia Germanica*).

"Now mark! God is nameless, for no one can know or say anything of him " (Eckhart).

"This is the Father, Ineffable, Unspeakable, Beyond Knowledge, Invisible, Immeasurable, Infinite. He has produced those that are in Him, within Himself. The Thought of His Greatness has He brought forth from non-being that He might make them to be " (*The Gnosis of the Light*).

It is precisely because, as St. Paul says, " *In* him we live, and move, and have our being," that this *Gnosis* of our inherent divine nature is recoverable. The traditional theological " Christianity " has set aside this fundamental teaching of its own Scriptures, and for ever separates God and Man as Creator and " created." And see the familiarity with which " God " is spoken of and addressed in our churches and pulpits to-day, as if the priest or the preacher knew exactly what " God " might or could or would do if he were only petitioned sufficiently strenuously—even to sending rain! Thus there is an ungraven image worshipped which is only one remove from the graven image of still lesser minds.

But the mystic, the initiate, the gnostic, the yogi, has ever sought *within* for the knowledge of the root and source of his being.

" The wise man recognizes the idea of God within him. This he develops by withdrawing into the Holy Place of his own soul " (Plotinus).

" For thou art I, and I am thou. Whate'er I speak, may it for ever be; for that I have thy *Name* to guard me in my heart " (Greek Invocation to Hermes).

" Every one hath the key to God in himself, let him but seek it in the right place " (Jacob Boehme).

(Man) " is the likeness (or similitude) of God; the great *Arcanum* lieth *in* him " (Jacob Boehme).

Innumerable other quotations could be given. This seeking for the God *within* is the beginning and the end of the Gnosis; as also it is the beginning and end of the Christian Scriptures when stripped of those accretions of a lesser knowledge which have overlaid and gathered round it, and it is interpreted in the light of this Ancient Wisdom.

Clement of Alexandria in many of his sayings confirms the interpretation we are here placing upon the teaching of Jesus and of Paul as to man's inherent divine nature and the possibility and method of its recovery by the lower personality. Thus, for example:

" If anyone knows himself he shall know God, and by knowing God he shall be made like unto him " (*Pacd.*, i. 3).

" That man with whom the Logos dwells . . . is made like God . . . that man becomes God " (Ibid., i. 5).

And just as in the first centuries of our era it was the Christian Gnostics—Basilides, Valentinus, and others—who could and did claim to be the real Christians, so also we would say that to-day it is not those who rely upon a personal historical Jesus for their salvation by " belief," but the real Christians are those who have recognized that the Cosmic Christ *principle* is verily and truly their own higher Self, and who strive to have that " brought to birth " *in* them, so that even here and now they may act in the *power* of that supreme divine nature, even as the historical man Jesus is reputed to have done. It is these alone who can truly say that their " life is hid with Christ in God " (*Col.* iii. 3).

" The discovery of the Mystic Christ in you is being ' born from above.' This knowledge is of the utmost importance to human victory over the lower self. The imperishable secret of human life is the Mystic Christ in all men, their hope of glory."[1]

Yet verily this is a *mystery*. We can but dimly apprehend the heights and depths of it. We can but follow, each in his own manner and circumstances, that Road, that

" Path by which to Deity we climb,"

which has been pointed out to us by the great teachers of the past, *and of the present.*

" There is a road, steep and thorny, beset with perils of every kind— but yet a road; and it leads to the Heart of the Universe. I can tell you how to find those who will show you the secret gateway that leads inward only, and closes fast behind the neophyte for evermore. There is no danger that dauntless courage cannot conquer. There is no trial that spotless purity cannot pass through. There is no difficulty that strong intellect cannot surmount. For those who win, onwards there is reward past all telling—the power to bless and save humanity. For those who fail, there are other lives in which success may come."[2]

Yes, to-day, in the present Cycle of Man's evolutionary progress, and in the present state of the world, the aspirant who would press on to the farthest heights of Adeptship will find that the road is certainly " steep and thorny, beset with perils of every kind."

Even of the first initial step, of the very entrance Gate to that road which " leads to the Heart of the Universe "; is it not written in the Christian Scriptures that:

" Narrow is the gate, and straight is the way, that leadeth unto life, and few be they that find it " (*Matt.* vii. 14).

Why few? And what of the rest?

Few because at the present stage of Man's recovery of his lost spiritual estate, there *are* only a comparative few capable of appreciating what really has to be done to recover that

---

[1] Archdeacon Wilberforce, *Mystic Immanence*, p. 5.
[2] H. P. Blavatsky.

estate. Humanity as a whole has barely commenced the return journey of the Prodigal Son, notwithstanding all the teachings of Sages and Initiates. So-called " Christianity," the Christianity of the theologians, has from the very commencement grossly misled the Western world into thinking that " salvation " is only a matter of *belief* in certain *dogmas* which to-day are largely unbelievable—whereas belief—belief in one's own divine nature, in the Christ *Within*—is only the commencement of the way. For the rest—they must reincarnate until through bitter experience they have learnt the worthlessness of " the things of this world," and so turn their steps again to their " Father's home."

Thus one by one shall the Race as a whole return to its original Paradise, even as Jacob Boehme wrote in a quotation I have already given (p. 72):

" Such a man as Adam (Humanity) was before his Eve, shall arise, and again enter into, and eternally possess, Paradise."

But here we may note what we might call a law of acceleration. Each one who attains raises the Race as a whole, and that not, so to speak, in arithmetical progression as being merely one more unit added to the sum total, but let us say, in geometrical progression. He makes it so much easier for all the rest. Nay, it is his reward and his privilege to do this. His " reward past all telling " is " the power to bless and save humanity." Thus there is a *cumulative* effect.

But no one can attain to the final conquest, the final goal, in that incarnation in which he first realizes the great task which lies before him in the recovery of his spiritual nature and powers. All depends now on the fixity of his purpose, and he will doubtless have some, if not many, backslidings.

" Be of good cheer, Disciple; bear in mind the golden rule. Once thou hast passed the gate Srotapatti, ' he who the stream hath entered '; once thy foot hath pressed the bed of the Nirvanic stream in this or any future life, thou hast but seven other births before thee, O thou of adamantine Will."[1]

And since it is thus only *the few* who can or will in this

[1] *The Voice of the Silence.*

present cycle of Man's evolution " enter in at the straight gate " which leads to the life eternal; it will only be *a few* who will accept that underlying teaching of the Christian Scriptures which I have here endeavoured to elucidate as being in line with what the Sages and Initiates of the Ancient Wisdom have taught in all ages, i.e. the great *fact* of Man's inherent divine nature, and the potentiality which every individual possesses of realizing that divine nature in all its potency to overcome every human disability—sin, sickness, death— and thereby to attain, even here and now, " the peace which passeth all understanding."

* * *

Let me summarize.

If unhappily we have formerly endeavoured to arrive at some conclusions as to the truth of the Bible narratives and the Christian doctrines from the learned expositions of scholars and theologians, for ever in dispute with each other, we now at last find ourselves altogether outside of these: not as being " rationalists " or " agnostics "—for these are simply fighting on the same ground as the theologians—but as having apprehended a teaching as to Man's nature and destiny which is to be found in ancient Scriptures long antedating those commonly called Christian, and which we now recognize as embodied in the Christian Scriptures in allegory and symbol, and is clearly to be discovered therein, notwithstanding that those Scriptures are but mutilated fragments sadly overlaid with the " precepts and doctrines of men."

What, then, is this ancient teaching as to Man's nature and destiny, and how is it embodied in the Christian Scriptures?

(1) Man (Humanity as whole) commenced his existence " in the beginning " (the beginning of this present manifested or objective Universe)[1] as a divine spiritual Being.

(2) But he had to play his part in the great Cosmic process; he had to " descend into matter," to become a physical Race,

---

[1] The cosmological aspect of the teaching is that the *Manifested* Universe comes into and goes out of existence periodically, whilst its ever unknowable Root and Source, THAT, or the ABSOLUTE, *remains*.

to be clothed in his " coats of skin," and to submit to physical generation in a separation of the sexes. This is his *Fall*, and the result of it is for Humanity in its present " fallen " state sin, suffering, and death.

(3) But as Man thus *had* to " go out " as a pilgrim of the Universe, so also he *must* in due course return to his original estate. It is with this return that the New Testament principally deals.

" For the creation was subjected to vanity, not of its own will, but by reason of him (the Logos) who subjected it " (*Rom.* viii. 20).

(4) Although Man has " fallen," and has lost the consciousness of his real spiritual nature, and the powers which he should possess as a " god," or as a " Son of God ": he still retains that spiritual nature as the inmost part of his being, and this spiritual man is symbolized in the New Testament as the *Christ* or *Christos*. It is by belief in or recognition of this great fact of the indwelling " Christ " (not the historical Jesus) that the individual may start on his return journey to his " Father's home," and step by step may attain at last, *here and now*, to the conquest of sin, suffering, and death, even as the man Jesus is represented as having attained.

* * *

So much for the fundamental teaching of the Ancient Wisdom or Gnosis, clearly seen to be embodied in the Christian Scriptures in *allegory*.

It remains only to take the principal events narrated of the man Jesus, and to show how " history " is used here, as in the Old Testament, to cover the " wisdom in a mystery."

" The narratives of the doctrine are its cloak. The simple look only on the garment that is upon the narrative of the doctrine; more they know not. The instructed, however, see not merely the cloak, but what the cloak covers."

The three great events of the Gospel history (or allegory) are (*a*) the Virgin birth; (*b*) the Crucifixion; (*c*) the Resurrection. Round each of these controversy has raged from the very earliest centuries, and still rages to-day; the main

question being as to whether they were historical as regards
the man Jesus. Let us take each of them in turn; merely
observing that each of them is a pre-Christian allegory or
mythos. (a) Whether the man Jesus was or was not born
of a Virgin, the " birth " of the *Christ*, the Divine Man, the
Logos, was necessarily an immaculate conception. For how
can that which is divine and spiritual be born of flesh and
blood? But here we must note what is perhaps the greatest
mystery of the relation of the divine to the human. We have
seen that *Man* has " fallen into matter," but that he still
retains within him the " divine spark." In other words,
spiritual man still *remains*, " eternal in the heavens," although
in some way it is at the same time He who, as *Humanity*, is
crucified on the Cross of Matter. This is simply a repetition
in connection with Man (one of innumerable Cosmic Hierarchies) of the whole Cosmic Process whereby the ONE, the
ABSOLUTE, *becomes* the Manifested Universe, and yet remains,
and is thus both Being and Becoming—a metaphysical
difficulty which the *intellect* never has solved and never can
solve. But as regards the individual, we may here simply
quote the words of Angelus Silesius:

> " Though Christ our Lord a thousand times
>   in Bethlehem be born,
> And not in thee, thy soul remains
>   eternally forlorn."

or Ruysbroeck:

" At each moment of time in the fullest meaning of the word *now*
Christ is born in us and the Holy Ghost proceeds, bearing all Its gifts."

This *mystical* aspect is well stated by Evelyn Underhill in
her work *Mysticism* (p. 141):

" The Incarnation, which is for popular Christianity synonymous
with the historical birth and earthly life of Christ, is for the mystic not
only this but also a perpetual Cosmic and personal process. It is an
everlasting bringing forth, in the universe and also in the individual
ascending soul, of the divine and perfect Life, the pure character of
God, of which the one historical life dramatized the essential con-
stituents. Hence the soul, like the physical embryo, resumes in its
upward progress the spiritual life-history of the race. ' The one
secret, the greatest of all,' says Patmore, ' is the doctrine of the Incarna-

tion, regarded not as an historical event which occurred two thousand years ago, but as an event which is renewed in the body of every one who is in the way to the fulfilment of his original destiny.' "

(b) Here, again, whether the man Jesus was or was not crucified by the Jews as narrated in the Gospel, the *Christ*, the Divine Man, the Logos *is* crucified in physical *Humanity*, and thus becomes the sacrificial victim.

As concerns the individual, however, it is he who has to crucify his lower nature; for only as he does this can he attain to the glorious resurrection from the deadness of his spiritual nature, and the " tomb " in which the Christ principle within him is buried.

(c) The resurrection is not a physical but a spiritual matter. Whether the man Jesus did or did not " rise from the dead " in his physical body; or whether he did or did not appear to his disciples and others in that physical body, or in his " astral " body: what concerns us is that that resurrection of the *Christ* (not of Jesus) shall happen in *us*.

> " But if it happens not in me what does it profit me?
> What matters is that it shall happen in me."[1]

And does not Paul plainly state it in the following words?

" For if we have become united with him (Christ) by the likeness of his death, we shall be also by the likeness of his resurrection; knowing this, that our old man was crucified with him."[2]

The whole of the opening verses of this chapter down to verse 11 embodies this *esoteric* doctrine of the Christos as the type of man " fallen " and regenerated. The theological doctrine of atonement and redemption cannot in any way be read into it. And if the man Jesus, or Jesus Christ, was " very God of very God," how can Paul say that:

" The death that he died, he died unto sin once (or once for all); but the life that he liveth, he liveth unto God."

* * *

I do not think that I can more fittingly conclude this work than in the words of a living Master of the Ancient Wisdom:

[1] See p. 208 *supra*.   [2] *Rom.* vi. 5.

" Behold the truth before you: a clean life, an open mind, a pure heart, an eager intellect, an unveiled spiritual perception, a brotherliness for one's co-disciple, a readiness to give and receive advice and instruction, a loyal sense of duty to the teacher, a willing obedience to the behests of TRUTH, once we have placed our confidence in, and believe that teacher to be in possession of it; a courageous endurance of personal injustice, a brave declaration of principles, a valiant defence of these who are unjustly attacked, and a constant eye to the ideal of human progression and perfection which the Secret Science (Gupta Vidya) depicts—these are the golden stairs up the steps of which the learner may climb to the Temple of Divine Wisdom."

* * *

What I have now set forth in this work is but an outline of a vast subject, many aspects of which I have not been able even to mention.   But may I not at least hope that what I have now said will lead many of my readers to turn their attention to the existence of this Ancient Wisdom and Path of attainment, so that step by step they may achieve, even to the final conquest.

" He that overcometh, I will make him a pillar (a cosmic power) in the temple of my God, and he shall go out thence (into incarnation) no more " (*Rev.* iii. 12).

BIBLIOGRAPHY

ANGUS, DR. S.: *The Mystery Religions and Christianity*. London, John Murray, 1925.

ANONYMOUS: *Christ in You*. London, John M. Watkins, 1910.

ARNOLD, SIR EDWIN: *The Light of Asia*. London, Trubner & Co., 1884. (A very large number of editions.)
   The Song Celestial, or *Bhagavad Gītā*. London, Trubner & Co, 1888. (Many editions.)

AUGUSTINE, SAINT: *Confessions*. Library of Devotion, London, Methuen & Co., Ltd., Tenth Edition, 1919.

BACON, BENJAMIN W.: *The Making of the New Testament*. The Home Universities Library. London, Thornton Butterworth, Ltd., 1912.

BECK, L. ADAMS (E. Barrington): *The Story of Oriental Philosophy*. New York, Farrar & Reinhart, 1928.

BLAVATSKY, HELENA PETROVNA: *The Secret Doctrine*. 2 vols. in one. An exact reproduction of the First Edition. Los Angeles, The Theosophy Company. 1925. *Isis Unveiled*. 2 vols. in one. Theosophy Company. 1931. *The Voice of the Silence*. London, The Theosophical Publishing Society, 1889. Also the Peking Edition, with Notes and an endorsement by the Tashi Lama. Peking, The Chinese Buddhist Research Society, 1927. *The Esoteric Character of the Gospels*. Toronto, The Blavatsky Institute, 1927.

BRADLEY, F. H.: *Appearance and Reality*. London, Oxford University Press, Ltd., Eighth Impression, 1925.

BRUNTON, PAUL: *A Search in Secret India*. London, Rider & Co., 1934.

BUDGE, SIR A. E. WALLIS: *The Book of the Dead*. London, Kegan Paul, Trench, Trubner & Co., Ltd., 1928.

BUNSEN, CHRISTIAN C. J.: *Egypt's Place in Universal History*. 5 vols. Translated from the German by Chas. H. Cottorell. London, Longman, Brown, Green & Longmans, 1848.

CARPENTER, EDWARD: *Pagan and Christian Creeds*. London, George Allen & Unwin, Ltd., 1920.

CHUANG TZU: *Musings of a Chinese Mystic*. London, John Murray, 1906. (Wisdom of the East Series.)

CLEMEN, CARL: *Primitive Christianity and its Non-Jewish Sources*. (Trans. R. G. Nisbet.) Edinburgh, T. & T. Clark, 1912.

COLLINS, MABEL: *Light on the Path*.   London, The Theosophical Publishing House.   Reprint, 1925.

CONYBEARE, F. C.: *Myth, Magic, and Morals*.   London, Watts & Co., 1910.

COSTER, GERALDINE: *Yoga and Western Psychology*.   London, Humphrey Milford, 1934.

DEUSSEN, PAUL: *The System of the Vedanta*.   Translation by Charles Johnston.   Chicago, The Open Court Publishing Company, 1912.

DIBELIUS, MARTIN: *Die Formgeschichte des Evangeliums*.   2nd Edition, translated by Dr. Bertram Lee Woolf under the title *From Tradition to Gospel*.   London, Ivor Nicholson & Watson, Ltd., 1934.

DICTIONARY OF CHRISTIAN BIOGRAPHY, ETC.: (Wm. Smith and Henry Wace, D.D.).   London, John Murray, 1877–87.

DOANE, T. W.: *Bible Myths*.   New York, The Truth Seeker Company, 1882.

DOVE, C. CLAYTON: *Paul of Tarsus, His Life and Teaching*.   London, Watts & Co., 1927.

DURVILLE, HENRI: *Mystères Initiatiques*.   Second Edition.   Paris, Henri Durville, 1925.

EINSTEIN, ALBERT: *The World as I See It*, translated by Alan Harris.   London, John Lane, The Bodley Head, Ltd., 1935.

EISLER, ROBERT: *The Messiah Jesus and John the Baptist*.   London, Methuen & Co., Ltd., 1931.

ENCYCLOPAEDIA BIBLICA (Rev. T. K. Cheyne and J. S. Black).   London, Adam & Charles Black, 1899–1903.

EVANS-WENTZ, W. Y.: *The Tibetan Book of the Dead*.   London, Humphrey Milford.   1927.

   Tibetan Yoga and Secret Doctrine.   London, Humphrey Milford, 1935.

FABRE-D'OLIVET: *La Langue Hébraïque Restituee*.   2 vols.   Paris, 1815–16.

FAIRWEATHER, WILLIAM: *The Background of the Gospels*.   (Third Edition.)   Edinburgh, T. & T. Clark, 1920.

GIBBON, EDWARD: *The Decline and Fall of the Roman Empire*.   Published 1776.   Many Editions.

HATCH, EDWIN: *The Influence of Greek Ideas and Usages upon the Christian Church*.   The Hibbert Lectures, 1888.   London, Williams & Norgate, 1914.

HOLMES, EDMOND: *Self Realisation*.   London, Constable & Co., Ltd., 1927.

HUME, R. E.: *The Thirteen Principal Upanishads*.   London, Humphrey Milford, 1921.

INGE, W. R. (Dean): *Christian Mysticism*. London, Methuen & Co., Ltd., 1899.

JAMES, WILLIAM: *The Varieties of Religious Experience*. The Gifford Lectures, 1901–2. Thirty-third Impression. London, Longmans, Green & Co., 1922.

JOHNSTON, CHARLES: *The Bhagavad Gītā*. New York, The Quarterly Book Department, 1908.

    The Yoga Sutras of Patanjali. New York, The Quarterly Book Department, 1912.

    The Crest Jewel of Wisdom. New York, The Quarterly Book Department, 1925.

KING, C. W.: *The Gnostics and Their Remains*. Second Edition. London, David Nutt, 1887.

KINGSLAND, WILLIAM: *An Anthology of Mysticism and Mystical Philosophy*. London, Methuen & Co., Ltd., 1927.

LAMPLUGH, REV. F.: *The Gnosis of the Light (Codex Brucianus)*. London, John M. Watkins, 1918.

MAHATMAS: *Letters to A. P. Sinnett*. Second Edition, revised. London, T. Fisher Unwin, Ltd., 1926.

MANSEL, HENRY LONGUEVILLE (Dean): *The Gnostic Heresies of the First and Second Centuries*. London, John Murray, 1875.

MEAD, G. R. S.: *Fragments of a Faith Forgotten*. London and Benares, The Theosophical Publishing Society, 1900.

    Thrice Greatest Hermes. Three vols. London and Benares, The Theosophical Publishing Society, 1906.

    Echoes of the Gnosis. Ten small works. London and Benares, The Theosophical Publishing Society, 1907.

    Pistis Sophia. Revised Edition. London, John M. Watkins, 1921.

    The Subtle Body. London, John M. Watkins, 1919.

MÜLLER, F. MAX: *Theosophy or Psychological Religion*. The Gifford Lectures, 1892. London, Longmans, Green & Co., 1893.

OESTERLEY AND ROBINSON: *An Introduction to the Books of the Old Testament*. London, Society for Promoting Christian Knowledge, 1934.

PEEL, ALBERT: *Q, The Earliest Gospel?* London, Independent Press, Ltd., 1923.

PHELIPS, VIVIAN (Philip Vivian): *The Churches and Modern Thought*. The Thinker's Library. London, Watts & Co., 1931.

RICHARDSON, ALAN: *Creeds in the Making*. London, Student Christian Movement Press, 1935.

SMITH, BENJAMIN WILLIAM: *Ecce Deus*. London, Watts & Co., 1912.

STEWART, JAMES S.: *A Christ. The Vital Elements of St. Paul's Man in Religion*. London, Hodder & Stoughton, Ltd., 1935.

UNDERHILL, EVELYN: *Mysticism*. London, Methuen & Co., Ltd., 1911.

VIVEKANANDA, SWAMI: *Raja Yoga*. London, Kegan Paul, Trench, Trubner & Co., Ltd., 1896.

WEIGALL, ARTHUR: *The Paganism in Our Christianity*. London, Hutchinson & Co., Ltd., 1928.

WILBERFORCE, BASIL (Archdeacon): *Mystic Immanence*. London, Elliot Stock, 1914.

WILDER, ALEXANDER: *Theurgia, or the Egyptian Mysteries*. New York The Metaphysical Publishing Company, 1911.

INDEX

Abraham, 46, 124

Absolute, The, 19, 43, 62, 65, 79, 115, 119, 124, 183, 184

Acts of the Apostles, quoted, 55, 68, 185, 186

Adam, 72, 111, 122, 123, 128, 132, 188

Adepts, *see Initiates* and *Mahatmas*

Aelohim, 123, 124

Aeons, 104, 179

Akhmim Codex, 76

Alchemy, 86

Allegories, 12, 26, 40, 143
  Scriptural, 40, 81 *et seq.*, 94, 111, 121, 122, 167, 215

Anaxagoras, 97

Ancient Wisdom, The, 20 *et seq.*, 74, 94 *et seq.*

Angels and Archangels, 104

Angelus Silesius, quoted, 216

Angus, Dr. S., quoted, 18, 56, 75, 103, 109

Anthropology, 43, 51, 66, 207

Appearance and Reality, 16 *et seq.*, 43, 101, 114

Apostles, The, 31, 38, 46, 84, 142, 166, 171, 176

Apostolic Succession, 100, 163

Apollo, Oracle of, quoted, 106

Apocrypha, 73 *et seq.*

Apollonius of Tyana, 37

Archetypes, Eternal, 115, 119

Aristotle, 97

Arius, 136

Arjuna, 156

Arnold, Sir Edwin, quoted, 19, 22, 45, 61, 68, 70, 138

Aryans, The Early, 19, 68, 158

Asceticism, 53, 168

Askew Codex, 76

Astral Body, 29, 198, 217

Astral Plane, 108, 197

Astrology, 102, 105

Athanasius, 12, 136, 137

Atlantis, 146

Atom, The Physical, 27, 63, 123, 147

Atonement, Doctrine of, 12, 86, 98, 111, 148, 167

At-one-ment, 57, 70

Attainment, 45, 46, 71, 72, 154, 161, 191, 193, 205, 218

Atwood, Mary Ann, quoted, 106

Avataras, 31, 96, 97, 139, 143, 148, 149, 156, 172, 190

Ba or Bai, 182

Bacon, B. W., quoted, 41

Baptism, 99, 148, 201, 202

Basilides, 97, 211

Beck, Mrs. Adams, quoted, 76

Being—
  The Supreme, 124, 141, 162, 190
  and Becoming, 147
  and Non-Being, 116 *et seq.*

Beings, Celestial, 94, 122

Belief, supposed power of, 137, 140, 199 *et seq.*

Beraeshith, 123, 127

Bergson, M. Henri, quoted, 63, 64, 206

Bhagavad Gītā, quoted, 12, 135, 136, 144, 145, 155, 161, 194

Bible, The, 73 *et seq.*
  Allegories, 40, 81, 82, 84, 121, 122, 167, 215

Blavatsky, Mme. H. P., 107, 109, 120, 128
  quoted, 60, 61, 121, 191, 205–6, 212–13

Blood Sacrifice, 148, 167
  Symbolism, 175, 176

Boehme, Jacob, quoted, 66, 72, 75, 90, 129, 134, 211, 213

Book of the Dead, Egyptian, 29, 66
  quoted, 24, 29, 30, 67, 74, 90, 97, 119, 120, 201

Book of the Dead, Tibetan, 220

Bradley, F. H., quoted, 114
Brahma, 29, 118
  Days and Nights of, 20, 115,
  123, 141
Browning, Robert, quoted, 20
Bruce Codex, 76, 100
Brunton, Paul, quoted, 204-5
Buddhi, 147
Budge, Sir A. E. Wallis, quoted,
  30, 59, 75, 119, 120
Buddha, Gautama, 46, 97, 150,
  172
  teachings of, 22, 45, 62, 138,
  161, 192, 193
Buddhism, 61, 62
Bunsen, C., quoted, 39

Carpenter, Edward, quoted, 92
Christ—
  Principle, 21, 80, 81, 139, 140,
  154 et seq., 172, 181
  The Cosmic, 123, 140, 183, 184
Christians, 13, 26, 31, 32, 139,
  160, 195
Christian Scriptures, 73 et seq.,
  161 et seq.
Christian Creeds, 11 et seq., 41
  et seq., 80, 84, 102, 103, 159
Christian Church, see Church-
Christian Doctrine, 104, 144
Christian Origins, 40, 73 et seq., 84
Christian Mystics, 174
Christianity, 12 et seq., 23, 30, 31,
  46
  Ecclesiastical, 17, 41, 47, 55,
  75, 163
  Esoteric, 44 et seq., 57, 70, 82,
  92, 156, 159 et seq., 161, 171,
  180
  Origins of, 12, 17, 84
Christ in You, quoted, 28, 181, 208
Christos, 21, 24, 83, 140, 150,
  153, 179
Chuang Tzu, quoted, 89
Church, 11 et seq.
  Anglican, 78
  Councils, 84, 138

Church—*continued*
  Dogmas of the, 11, 16, 17, 35,
  47, 51, 64, 137, 163
  Fathers, 15, 31, 38, 48, 73, 84,
  99, 100, 102
  Persecutions, 35, 48, 83, 163
  Roman Catholic, 41, 42, 46,
  58, 78, 100, 102, 160, 163
Civilization, 53, 76, 144
Clement of Alexandria, 48, 73,
  97, 173, 203
Clemen, C., quoted, 32
Confucius, 97
Cosmic Process, The, 20, 94,
  105 et seq., 128, 130, 132, 162,
  168
  Sense, 55, 103
Cosmology, 43, 66, 102, 104 et seq.,
  111 et seq., 122 et seq., 207
Creation, 111 et seq.
Creeds, 12, 41, 64, 80, 102, 103,
  159, 165
Crest Jewel of Wisdom, quoted,
  194
Crucifixion, The, 148, 167, 217
  Symbolism of the, 167, 168
  A continual process, 174, 180

Dark Ages, 48, 57, 74, 76, 100, 146
Dark Night of the Soul, 109
Death, 25, 175, 197
  Conquest of, 69, 190
  Second, 44
Demiurgos, The, 104, 119, 125
Demons, 102, 152
Devil, The, 36, 64, 99, 206
Devils, Casting out, 200, 203
Devaki, 156
Dharmakaya Body, 182
Dhyan Chohans, 47
Dibelius, Dr. Martin, quoted, 34,
  37, 40, 178, 179, 180
Dionysius, 17, 19, 79
Disciples, The, 25, 26, 82, 140, 170
Divine Instructors, 97, 121, 143,
  145
Divine, Hierarchy of, 94

Doane, *Bible Myths*, 143
Dogmas, *see under* Church
Dove, C. Clayton, quoted, 37
Dualism, 19, 64 *et seq.*, 119
Dzyan, Book of, quoted, 121, 130, 131

Ebionites, The, 101
Eckhart, Meister, quoted, 79, 80, 90, 125, 208, 210
Eddington, Professor, quoted, 27
Egyptian Priests, 127
Egyptian Mysteries, 66, 68, 77
Egyptian Religion, 24, 58, 98
Einstein, Professor, 53
Eisler, Dr., quoted, 34
Elect, The, 105
Elementals, 108
Elijah, 171
Emanation, 85, 94, 102, 118, 122, 135
Empedocles, 139
Essenes, The, 15, 24, 101, 150 *et seq.*
Eternity, 115, 116
Ether, The, 63, 108, 112, 125, 126
Eucharist, The, 12, 99
Eusebius, 39, 100
Evans-Wentz, Dr. 182
Eve, 128
Evil, Origin of, 66
Evolution, 71, 105, 128, 145 and Involution, 20
Exodus, quoted, 19

Fabre-d'Olivet, quoted, 77, 98, 122 *et seq.*, 127
Fairweather, Wm., quoted, 151
Faith, 13, 21, 32, 44, 89, 137, 138, 143, 161, 198 *et seq.*
Fall of Man, *see* Man
Fate, 195
Fatherhood of God, 58, 158
Father of the Gods, 58
Father-Mother-Son, 20, 127
Fielding, H., quoted, 52
Forged Documents, 34, 38, 39

Fraser, J. G., quoted, 62
Freemasonry, 92

Garden of Eden, 26, 47, 82, 99, 111, 122, 131, 132
Genesis, 111 *et seq.*
quoted, 59, 117
Geology, 99
Gibbon, E., quoted, 38–9, 41
Gnosis, The Ancient, 14, 18, 57, 83, 93 *et seq.*, 142 *et seq.*
Christian, 16, 21, 76, 91, 100
Coptic, 83
Destruction of Documents, 12, 34, 40, 76, 98, 160
Greek, 83
Spurious, 83, 84, 102
Gnosis of the Light, quoted, 100, 155, 210
Gnostic Sects, The, 14 *et seq.*, 83, 101, 102
God, 19 *et seq.*, 58, 62, 78 *et seq.*, 114, 128 *et seq.*, 134, 141 and Godhead, 125
Gods, 20, 90, 126, 179 *et seq.*
Egyptian, 58
Golden Bough, The, quoted, 62
Good and Evil, 36, 66, 129
Gospel, The—
of Christ, 47, 153 *et seq.*
of Paul, 175 *et seq.*
Gospels, The, 39, 40, 140 *et seq.*
Apocryphal, 26, 38
Canonical, 25, 26, 39 *et seq.*, 148, 198
Esoteric Interpretation of, 25, 44, 46, 70, 83, 143, 156, 161, 171, 180, 182
Greek Philosophy, 135

Harnac, Prof., quoted, 38
Hatch, Edwin, quoted, 97
Heathen, 46
Heaven, 87
Hell, 87, 147
Heresy, 17, 96, 98 *et seq.*, 138, 165
Heretics, 84, 163

Hermes, 77, 96
  quoted, 90, 194
Herutataf, Prince, 97
Hierarchies, Celestial, 47, 104, 122, 128, 179
Higher Criticism, The, 91
Hilary, Bishop, quoted, 41
Hippolytus, 101, 168
Holmes, Edmond, quoted, 43
Holy Ghost, 186
Homoousion, 41
Horus, 143
Humanity, *see* Man
Human Nature, 42, 146
Hyle, 28

Iamblichus, 97
Ideas, Archetypal, 115, 119, 209
Ihoah Aelohim, 123
Ignorance, 22, 208
Illusion or *Māyā*, 19, 86, 112, 113
Immortality, 23 *et seq.*, 175, 203
India, Ancient, 97
Inge, Dean, quoted, 17, 162
Initiates, 14, 22, 28, 33, 57, 58, 69, 74, 76, 107, 108, 142, 152, 177
  Hierarchy of, 67 *et seq.*, 91, 94, 105 *et seq.*, 137, 163
Initiation, 27, 77, 149 *et seq.*
Inspiration, 77
Intellect, 11, 18, 23, 42, 50 *et seq.*, 63 *et seq.*, 127, 209, 146
Intuition, 63
Invisible Helpers, 104
Irenaeus, quoted, 46
Isaiah, quoted, 66
Isha Upanishad, 132
Isis and Horus, 143
Isis Unveiled, quoted, 86

Jacks, Prof. L. P., quoted 37
Jalalu'd-Din Rumi, quoted, 19, 168
James, Prof. William, quoted, 56, 65, 79
Jehovah, 58, 78, 201

Jesus, 30 *et seq.*, 80, 142 *et seq.*, 155 *et seq.*, 172
  quoted from the Gospels, 26, 80, 144, 145
  quoted from the *Pistis Sophia*, 85, 87, 125, 131, 138, 148, 197
  An Initiate, 14, 149, 153, 159
  Sayings of, 143, 147, 155–6, 198
Jews, 57, 58, 78, 162, 185
John the Baptist, 34
John, Gospel of St., quoted, *see Saint John's Gospel*
Josephus, 34, 151
  quoted, 151
Judas, 185
Jung, Dr. C. G., quoted, 196
Justin Martyr, 99, 100, 139

Ka, The, 29
Kabala, The, 82, 122, 128
Kant, Emanuel, 19
Karma, 25, 62, 74, 104, 173, 192, 195
Khepera, 58, 119, 120
Khnemu, 58
Khufu, 97
King, C. W., quoted, 46
Kings, Divine, 68, 77, 96 *et seq.*
Kingdom of Heaven, 131, 132
Knowledge, 14, 16, 22, 28, 58, 66, 69, 86, 93 *et seq.*, 95, 101, 107 *et seq.*, 147, 203
  Supreme, 93 *et seq.*, 211
Koran, The, 24
Krishna, 97, 139, 144, 145, 147, 155 *et seq.*, 172

Lamplugh, Rev. F., quoted, 100
Lao-Tse, 89, 97
Law, Natural, 36, 61, 86, 87, 147, 198, 199
  Immutable, 61, 62, 209
Life, the ONE, 47, 54, 89, 90, 126
Light of Asia, quoted, 19, 22, 25, 45, 61, 68, 70, 138, 192, 193
Light on the Path, quoted, 206
Logia, The, *see* Jesus, Sayings of

Logos, The, 16, 19, 20, 66, 81, 115, 116, 124, 125, 135, 136, 155 *et seq.*, 173
Solar, 105
Lord's Prayer, The, 57
Luke, Gospel of St., quoted, *see Saint Luke's Gospel*
Loisy, M., quoted, 37

Mahatmas, 22, 69
Mahatma Letters, quoted, 107, 207, 209
Mahābārata, 156, 158
Mahomedanism, 49
Man—
Archetypal, 123, 124
Creation of, 94, 122 *et seq.*
Divine Nature of, 21, 52 *et seq.*, 130, 162
Evolution of, 71, 94 *et seq.*, 105, 128, 145 *et seq.*
Fall of, 71, 94, 128, 130, 132, 141, 142, 181, 208
Future of, 71, 72, 133
Hermaphrodite, 128
His return to his Source, 71, 94, 129, 132, 136 *et seq.*, 162
Nature and Destiny of, 82, 132 *et seq.*
Oneness with God, 29
Origin and Nature of, 92, 94, 122 *et seq.*
Present day state of, 42, 133, 136, 146, 149, 212, 213
Mammon of Unrighteousness, 198
Manichaeism, 163
Manu, Laws of, quoted, 75, 126
Manvantara, 115, 121, 141
Marcionites, 101
Mark, Gospel of St., quoted, *see Saint Mark's Gospel*
Martyrdom, 39, 53
Matter, 26, 28, 63
Materialism, 47, 51, 59, 60, 164
Matthew, Gospel of St., quoted, *see Saint Matthew's Gospel*
Maxwell, Clerk, quoted, 27

Māyā, 19, 112
Mead, G. R. S., 85, 194
Mediumship, 152, 203
Messiah, The, 165, 166
Mind, 11, 23, 64, 69
Cosmic, 52, 63, 66, 115, 116, 147
Stuff, 125
Mithra, 12, 56, 99
Modernism, 30, 78, 51
Moses, 68, 77, 127, 171
Motion, Eternal, 127
Müller, Prof. Max, quoted, 16, 65, 135
Mysteries—
The Ancient, 12, 14, 25, 26, 74, 81, 91, 93, 147 *et seq.*, 162
The Christian, 79, 174 *et seq.*, 180
The Egyptian, 66, 68, 77
The Gnostic, 97
The Greek, 83, 97
Final Object of, 86, 93
Schools of, 29, 97
Secrecy of, 25, 26, 75, 82, 88, 109, 148, 179
Mysticism, Christian, 21, 66, 108, 124
Mystics, 65, 108, 174
Mystical Experience, 65, 108
Myth, The Christ, 149, 171, 178 *et seq.*

Naassenes, The, 101
Name, Power of a, 200, 201
Natural Law, *see* Law
New Testament Scriptures, 141 *et seq.*
Newman, F. W. (Cardinal), 42
Nicea, Creed of, 138
Nirmanakaya, 182
Nirvana, 70, 71, 113, 189
Non-Attachment, 193 *et seq.*
Nu, The Egyptian, 58, 119, 201

Occultism, 36, 60, 102, 112, 146
Old Testament Scriptures, 73 *et seq.*, 82, 111 *et seq.*

One, The, 85, 87, 94, 118, 119, 122, 126, 153, 154, 158, 172, 179
Oneness, Consciousness of, 81, 107, 154
Origen, 48, 97
    quoted, 82, 138
Oracle of Apollo, quoted, 106
Orpheus, 12
Orphites, The, 46, 101, 168
Osiris, 29, 66. 90
Osirification, 29, 90
Outer Darkness, 197
Orthodoxy, 37, 38

Pantheism, 66, 179
Paul, see Saint Paul
Pauliciani, 35, 142
Pharaohs, 97
Pharisees, 150, 152
Phelips, Vivian, 12
Philae, Temple of, 202
Philosophy, 19, 44, 113, 114, 135
Philo Judaeus, 15, 97, 124
    quoted, 16, 105, 151
Pistis Sophia, 76, 88
    quoted, 85, 87, 125, 131, 138, 148, 197, 199, 200, 202
Planets, 105
Plato, 97, 115, 119, 139
Plotinus, 97
    quoted, 75, 79, 127, 211
Poison, drinking, 199
Prayer, Christian, 104
    for rain, 104
Priestcraft, 15, 29, 55, 103, 160, 165
Primordial Substance, see Substance
Principalities and Powers, 187
Prodigal Son, 136, 138
Protestantism, 35
Psychical Research, 108
Psychology, 11, 53, 95, 104, 112, 113, 154, 196
Ptah, 58
Purification, 23
Pythagoras, 77, 97, 139

"Q" Source, 40

Rā, 30, 59, 119, 120
Race, The Human, see Man
Rain, Prayer for, 104
Raja Yoga, 57, 164, 188
Rationalism, 59 *et seq.*
Reality, 18, 93 *et seq.*, 113 *et seq.*, 126, 183
Reason, 42, 53
Redemption, 162
Reincarnation, 23, 45, 69, 70, 76, 85, 87, 96, 133, 138, 144, 148, 198
Religion—
    and Religions, 49 *et seq.*
    Comparative study of, 51, 69, 78
    Consolations of, 23, 44
    Definition of, 49, 53, 61 *et seq.*, 68
    Nature of, 28, 49, 52 *et seq.*, 61, 63, 68, 70, 190 *et seq.*
    Transcends intellect, 51, 64, 146
Religious instinct, 49, 53, 59 *et seq.*, 190
Resurrection, 12, 45, 129, 137, 148, 168 *et seq.*, 174, 180, 217
Revelation, Book of, quoted, 131, 201, 218
Rig Veda, quoted, 117
Rishis, 97, 196
Ritual, 55, 56, 92
"Robe of Glory," 88 *et seq.*, 131, 181, 182, 208
Roman Catholicism, see Church
Russia, 51
Ruysbroeck, quoted, 216

Sacraments, 56, 99, 176
Saint Athanasius, Creed of, quoted, 136, 137
Saint Augustus, quoted, 163, 164
Saint John's Gospel, quoted, 26, 29, 69, 134, 139, 144, 145, 155, 157, 195, 200
Saint Luke's Gospel, 146, 148, 165
Saint Mark's Gospel, quoted, 157, 165, 195, 200

Saint-Martin, quoted, 106
Saint Matthew's Gospel, quoted, 14, 25, 56, 157, 165, 195, 199, 212
Saint Paul—
    quoted, 19, 28, 29, 45, 54, 82, 83, 88, 129, 130, 134, 154, 160, 165, 167, 173, 174, 175, 176, 177, 178, 181, 188, 200, 217
    conversion of, 185 *et seq.*
Saint Peter, 73
Salvation, 13, 14, 86, 137, 142, 144 *et seq.*, 155, 158, 161, 189, 208
Sambhogakaya, 182
Sankaracharya, 97
Saviours—
    Crucified, 148
    World, 144, 158, 177
Scholarship, Modern, 31 *et seq.*, 47, 91, 143, 144, 149, 159
Schrödinger, Erwin, 27
Scriptures—
    Ancient, 81, 110, 113, 145, 194
    Canonical, 39, 73 *et seq.*, 148, 198, 200
    Christian, 28 *et seq.*, 44 *et seq.*, 92, 161
    Jewish, 80, 149, 162, 165
Second Birth, 148
Second Coming, The, 12, 33, 140, 143, 165 *et seq.*, 171
Secret Doctrine, The, 109, 128
    quoted, 61, 121, 130, 131, 189
Self—
    The Higher, 53, 68, 71, 80, 86, 88 *et seq.*, 113, 114, 136, 149, 153, 156, 173 *et seq.*, 203
    the Lower, 11, 29, 57, 86, 89, 153 *et seq.*, 167, 203
    Sub-conscious, 36, 53
Septuagint, 73
Silent Watcher, The, 189
Sin, 12, 69, 142, 190, 206
Smith and Wace, *Dictionary of Christian Biography*, 15, 35, 38, 100, 139, 150, 203

Smith, Dr. W. B., *Ecce Deus*, 34
Society for Promoting the Study of Religions, Journal of, quoted, 52
Socrates, 97, 139
Solar System, 43, 105
"Sons of God," 28, 29, 129 *et seq.*, 137, 179
Sophia or Wisdom, 179
Soul, The, 26, 28, 138
Sound, Occult Power of, 134
Space, 115 *et seq.*, 121, 122
Spark, The Divine, 172
Spirit, 11, 52, 53
    and Matter, 64, 102
Spiritualism, 102, 108, 203
Stewart, Basil, quoted, 83
Stewart, James S., quoted, 182, 183, 184
Subconscious, The, 53, 154, 195
Subject and Object, 112, 126
Substance—
    Primordial, 27, 66, 109, 112, 118, 122, 125 *et seq.*
    Planes of, 107 *et seq.*, 112, 126
Sun, The, 43
Supraconscious, The, 53, 154
Swedenborg, quoted, 128
Symbolism, 26, 66, 85, 109, 120, 174 *et seq.*

Tacitus, 34
Tem, 58
Temptation, in the wilderness, 148, 150
Tertullian, quoted, 99, 100
Testament—
    The New, *see New Testament*
    The Old, *see Old Testament*
Tetragrammaton, 201, 210
Theologia Germanica, 79, 210
Theologians, 28, 133, 145, 213, 214
Theology, 16, 50, 64, 132, 142, 158, 172, 177
Theosophy, 91, 101, 104, 107, 179
Therapeuts, The, 101
Thoth, 66, 96, 202

Tibetan Yoga, 182, 199
Time, 115 *et seq.*
Tomb, The Empty, 169 *et seq.*
Transfiguration, 148
Trinity and Trinities, 20, 127
Truth, 43 *et seq.*

Underhill, Evelyn, quoted, 216
Union, Mystical, 108
Universe—
    The Manifested, 110 *et seq.*, 125
    The Unmanifested, 110
Upanishads, The, quoted, 19, 65, 80, 89, 93, 118, 194

Valentinians, 101
Valentinus, 97, 100, 211
Vedanta, The, 62, 175
Virgin Birth, 12, 127, 143, 175, 215

Voice of the Silence, quoted, 60, 191, 205, 206, 213

War, Prayers, 61
Water, Symbolism of, 109, 118
Weigall, Arthur, 92
Wilberforce, Archdeacon, quoted, 21, 212
Word, Power of, 203
World-Egg, 109
World Process, 109, 116
World, This, 105
Worship, 56

Yoga, 57, 69, 95, 113, 147, 163, 164, 188, 196, 199, 204
Yoga, Tibetan, 182, 199
Yogi Narasingha Swami, 199

Zohar, The, 82
Zoroaster, 97

QUEST BOOKS

are published by The Theosophical
Society in America, a branch of
a world organization dedicated to the
promotion of brotherhood and the
encouragement of the study of religion,
philosophy, and science, to the end
that man may better understand
himself and his place in the universe.
The Society stands for complete
freedom of individual search and belief.
Quest Books are offered as a
contribution to man's search for truth.

THE THEOSOPHICAL PUBLISHING HOUSE

Wheaton, Ill., U.S.A.

Madras, India   London, England

Publishers of a wide range of titles on many subjects including:

Mysticism

Yoga

Meditation

Extrasensory Perception

Religions of the World

Asian Classics

Reincarnation

The Human Situation

Theosophy

Distributors for the Adyar Library Series of Sanskrit Texts, Translations and Studies

---

The Theosophical Publishing House, Wheaton, Illinois, is also the publisher of

QUEST BOOKS

Many titles from our regular clothbound list in attractive paperbound editions

For a complete list of all Quest Books write to:

QUEST BOOKS
P.O. Box 270, Wheaton, Ill. 60187